# Market Society

History, theory, practice

*Market Society: History, theory, practice* explores the social basis of economic life, from the emergence of market society in feudal England to the complex and interwoven markets of modern capitalist society. This lively and accessible book draws upon a variety of theories to examine the social structures at the heart of capitalist economies. It considers how capitalism is constituted, the institutions that regulate economic processes in market society and the experience of living in contemporary market societies.

*Market Society: History, theory, practice* provides students of both political economy and economic sociology with a more nuanced understanding of how markets and people interact, and how this relationship has influenced the nature and structure of modern economies.

**Ben Spies-Butcher** is Senior Lecturer in Economy and Society in the Department of Sociology, and Director of the Masters in Policy and Applied Social Research, at Macquarie University.

**Joy Paton** is Lecturer in the Department of Political Economy at the University of Sydney. She is the author of *Seeking Sustainability: On the Prospect of an Ecological Liberalism*.

**Damien Cahill** is Senior Lecturer in the Department of Political Economy at the University of Sydney. He is the co-founder of the Markets and Society Research Network at the University of Sydney.

# Market Society
History, theory, practice

Ben Spies-Butcher, Joy Paton and
Damien Cahill

# CAMBRIDGE
## UNIVERSITY PRESS

University Printing House, Cambridge CB2 8BS, United Kingdom
One Liberty Plaza, 20th Floor, New York, NY 10006, USA
477 Williamstown Road, Port Melbourne, VIC 3207, Australia
314-321, 3rd Floor, Plot 3, Splendor Forum, Jasola District Centre, New Delhi - 110025, India
79 Anson Road, #06-04/06, Singapore 079906

Cambridge University Press is part of the University of Cambridge.

It furthers the University's mission by disseminating knowledge in the pursuit of education, learning and research at the highest international levels of excellence.

www.cambridge.org
Information on this title: www.cambridge.org/9780521184908

© Ben Spies-Butcher, Joy Paton, Damien Cahill 2012

This publication is in copyright. Subject to statutory exception and to the provisions of relevant collective licensing agreements, no reproduction of any part may take place without the written permission of Cambridge University Press.

First published 2012
Reprinted 2012

Cover design by Adrian Saunders
Typeset by Aptara Corp

*A catalogue record for this publication is available from the British Library*

National Library of Australia Cataloguing in Publication data
Spies-Butcher, Ben.
Market society : history, theory, practice /
Ben Spies-Butcher, Joy Paton, Damien Cahill.
9780521184908 (pbk.)
Includes bibliographical references and index.
Economic history.
Markets – History.
Markets – Social aspects.
Paton, Joy.
Cahill, Damien.
306.3

ISBN 978-0-521-18490-8 Paperback

**Reproduction and communication for educational purposes**
The Australian *Copyright Act 1968* (the Act) allows a maximum of one chapter or 10% of the pages of this work, whichever is the greater, to be reproduced and/or communicated by any educational institution for its educational purposes provided that the educational institution (or the body that administers it) has given a remuneration notice to Copyright Agency Limited (CAL) under the Act.

For details of the CAL licence for educational institutions contact:

Copyright Agency Limited
Level 15, 233 Castlereagh Street
Sydney NSW 2000
Telephone: (02) 9394 7600
Facsimile: (02) 9394 7601
E-mail: info@copyright.com.au

Cambridge University Press has no responsibility for the persistence or accuracy of URLs for external or third-party internet websites referred to in this publication, and does not guarantee that any content on such websites is, or will remain, accurate or appropriate.

NOTICE TO TEACHERS
The photocopy masters in this publication may be photocopied or distributed [electronically] free of charge for classroom use within the school or institution that purchased the publication. Worksheets and copies of them remain in the copyright of Cambridge University Press, and such copies may not be distributed or used in any way outside the purchasing institution.

# Contents

Acknowledgements   *page* ix

**Chapter 1 Introducing market society**   1
Market society in historical perspective   4
Theories of market society   8
Structure of the book   12

**Part 1 Constituting market society**

**Chapter 2 Production, value and commodification**   19
The commodity production system   19
  From use value to exchange value   20
  The regulatory force of the 'price mechanism'   26
Beyond consumer sovereignty   28
  Institutional and sociological critiques   28
  The Marxian critique   31
The process of commodification   34
  Fictitious commodities   34
  Making markets   37
  Conclusion   41

**Chapter 3 Growth, accumulation and crisis**   43
Economic growth in market societies   43

| | |
|---|---|
| What is economic growth? | 44 |
| How does growth occur? | 47 |
| The politics of modelling growth | 49 |
|     Surplus or efficiency? | 50 |
|     Other contributions to understanding growth | 54 |
| Crises and economic growth | 57 |
|     Theorising crisis | 58 |
|     The politics of crisis, growth and legitimacy | 64 |
|     Conclusion | 65 |

## Chapter 4 Inequality, distribution and conflict — 67

| | |
|---|---|
| The distribution of economic resources | 68 |
|     Inequality in market societies | 68 |
|     How capitalism changed inequality | 71 |
| Class and inequality | 75 |
|     Theorising class | 76 |
|     Class, politics and inequality | 79 |
| Struggles beyond class | 81 |
|     Inequalities and gender justice | 82 |
|     Race, colonialism and empire | 84 |
|     Conclusion | 89 |

## Part 2 Regulating market society

## Chapter 5 States, politics and welfare — 93

| | |
|---|---|
| States, legitimacy and the economic process | 93 |
|     Establishing the capitalist state | 94 |
|     Questioning the state's legitimacy | 97 |
| The political economy of the welfare state | 101 |
|     The growing role of the state | 101 |
|     Welfare state regimes | 105 |
| Diversity, change and continuity | 108 |
|     Varieties of capitalism | 109 |
|     Winding back the state? | 110 |
|     Conclusion | 114 |

## Chapter 6 Markets, risk and globalisation — 116
The regulatory force of markets — 116
   Markets and the governance of conduct — 117
   Markets and globalisation — 120
The new global market — 124
   Money and trust — 124
   Trade and industry — 130
Marketising the state — 133
   Social protection and the market — 133
   Market logic in the state — 135
   Conclusion — 137

## Chapter 7 Firms, corporations and competition — 139
The rise of the corporation — 140
   The history of the capitalist firm — 140
   Theoretical perspectives on the firm — 145
Corporations and the workplace — 152
   Conflict, cooperation and control in the workplace — 152
   The rise of management — 154
Corporations and the global economy — 155
   The race to the bottom? — 156
   The challenge for democracy — 159
   Conclusion — 160

## Part 3 Living market society

## Chapter 8 Work, consumption and quality of life — 165
Work and society — 165
   The importance of work — 165
   The work society — 167
Changes in the work society — 171
   Post-Fordism — 171
   A post-industrial society? — 177
Consumption and beyond — 179
   Approaches to consumption — 179

| | |
|---|---:|
| Quality of life | 184 |
| Conclusion | 188 |

**Chapter 9 Family, environment and sustainability** — **189**

| | |
|---|---:|
| The family and the household | 190 |
|    Economising the family | 190 |
|    The family and social reproduction | 192 |
| The environment and market society | 197 |
|    Perspectives on environmental degradation | 197 |
|    Economic responses to environmental challenges | 201 |
| The question of sustainability | 205 |
|    Alternative approaches to the environment | 205 |
|    Addressing environmental damage | 209 |
|    Conclusion | 212 |

**Chapter 10 Civil society, community and participation** — **214**

| | |
|---|---:|
| Understanding civil society | 214 |
|    Three conceptions of civil society | 216 |
| Civil society in practice | 225 |
|    Activism, social movements and economic change | 225 |
|    Social capital, community and participation | 230 |
| Civil society and the welfare state | 234 |
|    Who rules? | 235 |
|    Conclusion | 236 |

**Concluding remarks** — **238**

| | |
|---|---:|
| References | 240 |
| Index | 257 |

# Acknowledgements

THIS BOOK IS dedicated to our colleagues and students who seek diversity rather than simplicity in their analysis of economic phenomena. We would like to thank a number of people for their valuable support during the writing of the book, including Frank Stilwell, Michael Gilding, James Goodman, Georgina Murray, Bill Dunn and Michael Scott. We would also like to acknowledge the influence of Frank Stilwell and Evan Jones who have pioneered the teaching of political economy in Australia. We would also like to thank the staff at Cambridge University Press, in particular Lachlan McMahon for having faith in the project to begin with and Bridget Ell for ensuring it was brought to fruition. Finally, our thanks must also be extended to our families who have been very patient through this process.

# 1 | Introducing market society

MUCH OF OUR everyday life revolves around markets. This is because markets are central to the way contemporary society organises the production and distribution of goods and services. Our work comes through a labour market. We find our accommodation through a housing market. Our food, clothes and entertainment are largely purchased in markets. Even markets we have little direct knowledge or experience of can have a profound impact, as became evident in 2007 when the subprime mortgage market collapsed. Although many people had never heard of the complex financial markets and instruments associated with the 'global financial crisis', its implications were immense. People lost jobs and homes, and rumours emerged that whole national economies might collapse because of the severe disruption to the market processes at the heart of the economy.

Markets are clearly important to the economy, but they are only part of what is in fact a complex institutional system. Governments also play a central role in the economy. Despite decades of economic restructuring purportedly aimed at reducing state activity in the economy, governments continue to establish and regulate markets. They provide services, redistribute income and are directly involved in production. Other institutions are also central. Much trade and most production do not take place directly in markets but within and between firms, particularly large corporations. While corporations operate within markets, their size and structure give them considerable power to shape both their internal production process and their external environment.

However, the economy is not confined to these institutions of markets, states and corporations. Making goods and providing services for sale in markets is only one part of total production. Production also takes place in households and in communities. Furthermore, the system of market production itself is supported and shaped by social, biological and ecological processes. These reproduce the very conditions needed for production to occur. Families and communities raise, socialise and support the workers who undertake production. They are also important sites of consumption. Environmental resources provide the raw materials for production as well as the support systems that absorb waste and enable life.

Across the social sciences, including within the study of economics, there is a growing recognition that the economy is not a separate system independent of the social, cultural and political forces that shape our lives. Instead, the economy is increasingly understood as part of a bigger picture and intimately linked to other aspects of society.

This connection works both ways. Not only is the system of market production and consumption shaped by social and political forces, but the organisation of our economy profoundly shapes our lives. The centrality of markets in modern economies is historically unique. Developing over a number of centuries, the rise of an integrated market system brought enormous growth and prosperity. But in the early case of England, as elsewhere, such a system also required the complete reorganisation of social and political relations. It was part of a set of developments that changed where people lived and worked, what they consumed, how they saw themselves and how they related to others. A 'market economy', in the words of Karl Polanyi, 'can exist only in a market society' (1944, p.71).

This book attempts to understand the complex connections between society and economy. It draws on several different theoretical traditions which, we argue, are increasingly producing common ground. This commonality is not a conceptual synthesis. There are important theoretical divisions that are unlikely to be resolved. Rather, the commonality is expressed by changes in a number of disciplines, such as the growing interest in the role of institutions, rationality and social networks within neoclassical economics and the renewed interest in similar themes within sociology and political economy. We suggest that engaging more substantively with developments across the social sciences is likely to produce a better intellectual toolkit for the analysis of economic phenomena.

A particular focus of this book is on the role of institutions. This reflects not only the rise of New Institutional Economics within the neoclassical tradition, but also the renewed importance of institutions to political economy. Examples of this orientation in political economy are evident in the developing regulation school, the growing interest in the work of Karl Polanyi, and the relevance of institutional political economy in policy studies. Importantly, these various trends suggest that we focus greater attention on how current institutions and practices came to be the way they are. History matters, and the operation of economic and social systems cannot be understood without understanding how they developed. History shapes how such systems operate in the present and how they will continue to develop.

The focus on institutions also suggests the need to consider the detail of how socio-economic systems actually operate in practice; going beyond abstract or theoretical understandings of how they might ideally operate. This too has been a theme of recent analytical work. The 'transaction cost' tradition within neoclassical economics, along with behavioural and experimental economics, has begun to pay closer attention to how real markets, firms and individuals actually behave. Likewise, we see a focus on understanding the operation of networks and institutions within economic sociology. In political economy there is renewed interest in mapping the operation of particular markets through approaches that acknowledge the diversity in scale and character of capitalist economies. These themes have inspired this book's multi-dimensional approach.

In taking up the concerns of history, theory and practice in relation to economic institutions, we focus on the economic aspects of everyday life. We agree with Polanyi that our current society is best understood as a 'market society' – one in which society has become an adjunct to the operation of markets. Likewise, we draw on the insights of Marx's analysis of capitalism as a system of economic production and distribution that is constituted by particular social relations. Indeed, throughout this book we use the terms 'market society' and 'capitalism' somewhat interchangeably. This is because we suggest that such labels reflect different theoretical understandings of similar phenomena.

Consistent with the pluralist approach we take to our subject matter, market society and capitalism refer to two conceptions of the type of society we now live in. This is one where markets are central not only to economic production but also to the organisation of social, political and cultural life in ways that are historically unique. Throughout the book, we connect the various theoretical approaches discussed to the historical events that both inspired the theorists and which shaped the developments and practices we examine. Some broader historical context is also useful here, particularly in exploring what we consider to be distinct about market society. We turn to this now, and then briefly introduce some of the main theoretical approaches featured in the book, before giving an overview of its structure and content.

## MARKET SOCIETY IN HISTORICAL PERSPECTIVE

Markets have been present in human societies for thousands of years, at least as far back as the ancient Greeks. However, 'market society' is a much more recent development with unique features that make it distinct from earlier forms of social and economic organisation. Before the rise of capitalism, markets were merely an 'accessory feature' of life (Polanyi 2001 [1944], p. 70). They did not have the same importance to people's everyday lives because people themselves directly produced most of what they needed for survival. The nature of economic processes in traditional feudal life underwent gradual but very significant transformations leading to a capitalist system of production. The economic changes constituting capitalism were not independent of broader cultural and political changes such as the rise of new modes of intellectual inquiry and forms of governance that underpinned the social context in which the new capitalist economy evolved.

We begin our discussion by considering the nature and character of pre-capitalist society in England, the birthplace of capitalism and the first modern 'market society'. Feudal life was organised and reproduced through distinct arrangements for producing, distributing and consuming the material things that people needed. Markets were marginal to this process for most people who engaged primarily in agricultural production. They were materially poor, living a subsistence lifestyle in households that were the central economic and social unit of society. In feudalism, the household may have varied in size according to the wealth and standing of its occupants, but it was where people produced and consumed the necessities of life as well as raising and socialising their children.

Production, consumption, reproduction and socialisation were largely integrated within the household itself and were not dependent upon markets in the ways they are today in capitalist economies. But markets themselves were also constituted differently under feudalism. To the extent that exchange occurred, it took place predominantly in local or regional marketplaces, usually close to people's residences where they could easily take their surplus or unneeded items. Most importantly, the market operated according to well-defined and understood rules, all designed to protect against speculation. Goods were sold on the basis of a 'just price'. Within the marketplace, it was prohibited to buy in order to sell at a profit.

These arrangements persisted in some markets during the early phase of capitalism and have been referred to by EP Thompson (1971), as a 'moral economy'. This means that transactions were regulated according to moral concerns rather than according to commercial needs – for example, a concern to ensure the affordability of foodstuffs for buyers rather than profitability of sellers. The shift to capitalism was marked by important changes to these traditions and to the material conditions of everyday life. New economic institutions emerged and the role of existing ones was transformed. Significant changes to customary property relations and the laws governing people's access to land were critical steps in this process.

Under feudalism, peasants had rights to farm land. The access to 'common' lands for subsistence was sanctioned by law and custom. Peasants used these 'commons' to supplement their other productive activities such as through the grazing of cattle or the scavenging of firewood or foodstuffs. The breakdown of feudalism involved a process of 'enclosing' lands as private property with exclusive use rights. This occurred through the erection of fences and through the passing of laws, generating significant conflict over customary rights. The first major efforts to enclose land occurred in the 16th century and they gathered momentum through the 18th century as the demand for commercial property deepened with the onset of industrialisation (Wood 1999).

The breakdown of customary access rights reflected a breakdown of the traditional structures that underpinned feudal society. It disrupted people's way of life. Enclosure created competition for access to land and encouraged landowners to rent parts of their property to farmers. In turn, tenant farmers hired some of the people who were no longer allowed access to land for their subsistence. Instead, they were paid wages to work the land and help produce agricultural commodities for sale in markets. Wages provided the means of purchasing their subsistence needs. A new form of economic relationship – the wage labour relationship – was emerging.

Competition encouraged landowners to improve their farms (Wood 1999). This involved the application of scientific principles to farming practices to increase productivity. Producing more crops gave farmers more to sell. Improvement also encouraged specialisation as people moved from producing most of their needs for direct consumption in households to specialising in the production of just a few crops. This also reduced the proportion of people who earned an income from the land, encouraging many to drift toward emerging urban centres in the hope of finding work in factories or mines.

Producing for the market, rather than directly for needs, the organisation of England's competitive agricultural sector was based on 'landlords, capitalist tenant farmers and wage labourers' (Brenner 1989, p. 294). This arrangement supported England's 'take off' to economic growth. Expanding production in the agricultural sector underpinned expansion of other cottage and manufacturing industries and, eventually, the process of industrialisation.

Driven by competition, the industrial revolution gained momentum with the development and rapid improvement of the steam engine. The government system of granting monopolies to inventors under a patent system was an important institutional element in this process. Steam power promoted changes in other industries, especially iron production which underpinned further large-scale industrial developments in manufacturing and transport. It also fostered development of railways and infrastructure, facilitating the growth of cities away from coastal areas. Large industrial cities soon emerged and, by the 19th century, factories using machine technologies developed in mining and manufacturing, employing large organised labour forces.

The factory system, producing commodities for sale in markets, brought about the final separation of the household from production. Capitalists with their own materials, money and space bought machines and located them in factories. They hired people to work long days producing goods. This early mass production, governed by time rather than the seasons, increased the supply of goods making items less expensive and therefore more easily affordable. These arrangements provided the basis of a new market-centred way of organising the production and distribution of people's material needs.

However, the demand for labour was not consistent, nor was it sufficient to provide work for all who needed it. The peaks and troughs of production for profit created pressures for new institutions to organise the supply of labour and to regulate the conditions of factory work. Following a long period of debate and contest, the determination of wages by tradition and custom – the 'moral economy' – was eventually replaced by removing forms of traditional 'poor relief' and establishing a national labour market. These changes provided a strong form of compulsion to ensure people's participation in the labour market. However, they also meant that people's incomes – the sole means of their survival – were precarious, being determined by market supply and demand. This integration of labour into a market system and its regulation by economic rather than moral forces was a critical step in creating a market society.

It was not only England and Europe that felt the effects of the rise of capitalism. Other regions too were pulled into the capitalist economy, which increasingly took on a global character. However, this process was experienced unevenly between regions, with differences between European and non-European economies. The role of colonialism is particularly important. European nations colonised other countries in Asia, Africa, the Pacific and the Americas, enabling them to import crucial raw materials on favourable terms. Colonisation also gave them a ready outlet for their exports, enabling some relief from international competition. Britain, for example, after helping to destroy the existing cotton industry in India, exported a large proportion of its manufactured cotton textiles to India in the last decades of the nineteenth century (Hobsbawm 1987).

This example highlights the importance of political power, including coercion and violence, in shaping market societies. It is a very different picture from the ideal of free trade and comparative advantage painted by the economists of the time. Indeed, colonialism significantly shaped the development of capitalism outside of Europe, as well as inside. 'Settler' capitalist economies, such as Australia and the US, industrialised fairly quickly because of the large-scale importation of capital equipment, workers, and the brutal suppression of the indigenous population and their economies. Others, such as India, were stuck in a relationship of economic dependence for over a century as the British colonists levied heavy taxes, demanded high interest repayments and suppressed economic independence.

Historically, the ascent of market society can be seen as part of a complex process of intellectual, cultural, social, economic, political and demographic change spanning the 16th to 19th centuries. Sociologists often refer to this broader set of processes as the rise of 'modernity'. During this time, England was transformed from a traditional religious culture based on feudal peasant farming and small-scale self-sufficient communities into an industrialised market society and world capitalist power dominating international trade and colonial expansion.

These economic transformations occurred alongside other important intellectual and political developments. The rise of the nation state and new forms of law and political organisation gave rise to a shift from the divine right of kings to popular sovereignty. Together, the growing integration of economic processes and the centralisation of political authority reorganised social relationships and broke the bonds of traditional 'community', which gave way to the advent of 'civil society'.

Central, too, were transformations in the realm of ideas and culture, especially the decline of religion and the rise of reason and science. These were crucial in fostering the advancements in technology that underpinned economic developments. They were also important to the political transformations of the time. Traditional structures and ideas which underpinned the old feudal economic order were broken down. In their place, new social institutions, ideologies, cultures and ideas developed which underpinned and complemented the emerging capitalist economy.

The rise of capitalism entailed radical transformations in social and economic life which gave markets a new importance, ultimately leading to the creation of market society. We examine the nature and dynamics of market society in this book through its history and practice, as well as different theoretical perspectives that seek to understand economic phenomena in such societies.

## THEORIES OF MARKET SOCIETY

This book draws on various theoretical traditions within the social sciences. However, instead of structuring the book around these different theories, it is organised around aspects of market society, with each chapter drawing on a range of theories. Here we briefly discuss some of these theories. It is not an exhaustive list, but aims to help readers contextualise what is to come.

### Classical political economy

One of the first traditions to examine the rise of capitalist markets was called 'political economy'. Beginning in the 1700s, it integrated the study of politics, economics and history. The school is now called 'classical' political economy to distinguish it from more recent schools of political economic thought.

The classical political economists included Adam Smith, commonly seen as the 'founding father' of modern economics, David Ricardo, Thomas Malthus and John Stuart Mill. All developed important ideas that continue to inform modern economics, and some, like Smith and Mill, also made substantial contributions to other disciplines.

These theorists were largely supportive of the economic growth generated by the emerging market society. They identified the importance of competition and trade to promoting growth, and were often also supportive of trade on ethical and political grounds, seeing it as promoting individual responsibility and liberty.

Classical theorists recognised that different social groups engaged in the economy in different ways, had different interests and received different rewards. They also focused attention on the role of labour in producing value. Their work laid a basis for much of what followed across different theoretical traditions, including both Marxian and neoclassical economics.

### Neoclassical economics

From the late 1800s economic study became more specialised and mathematical. This approach differed from classical political economy by focusing on economics as a separate realm from other social sciences and social behaviour. It remains the dominant approach within the study of economics today.

Neoclassical economics employs a more abstract form of analysis, making assumptions about both human behaviour and market conditions which are then used to develop mathematical models. It is methodologically individualist, meaning it starts with assumptions about individuals and then derives conclusions about the economy as a whole. Thus, the behaviour of the economy is seen to be an outcome of individual choices and actions, with each individual acting independently.

The assumptions used in neoclassical economics are based on rational choice theory. This assumes people are rational and self-interested, meaning they try to maximise their own wellbeing by using the most efficient means possible. Most neoclassical economists also assume competitive markets in which rational agents interact.

These assumptions are controversial, and some argue they predispose neoclassical theory to promoting market competition. Because of this, neoclassical economics is often associated with what has become known as 'neoliberalism'. Neoliberalism refers to a set of policy recommendations that support market competition and are hostile to state regulation. Neoliberalism has been one of the most important forces reshaping economic policy since the 1970s.

### Marxian political economy

Marxian political economy is based on the work of Karl Marx, a critic of classical political economy from the late 1800s. Marx's ideas influenced reform movements and even revolutions, changing real world capitalism in the process. His work continues to inform much contemporary economic and social analysis. Although Marx was critical of classical political economy, he drew on many of its concepts, including the labour theory of value, to focus attention on social relations. This refers to the relationship different groups of people (or classes) have to the means of production: waged workers (proleteriat) and as business owners (bourgeoisie).

Marx examined how these social relations evolved in real time and space and in relation to historical developments. This method has been referred to as 'historical materialism'. It is materialist because it focuses on how material conditions of production and consumption changed over time, in turn influencing the world of culture and ideas. This contrasts with the neoclassical approach which abstracts away from historical detail.

Marx's approach has been very influential in sociology, partly because it connects the economy to broader social processes. But some argue this approach is too materialist, not giving enough weight to cultural processes, while others see it as too deterministic, meaning it sees outcomes as determined by economic structures, rather than allowing for the agency of individuals. Neoclassical economists are also critical of Marx's focus on social groups rather than individuals.

## Weberian sociology

Weber is another of the founding fathers of sociology and one of the most influential figures in economic sociology. Writing later than Marx, Weber was critical of both Marx and neoclassical economics.

Weber's analysis partly inspired modern methodological individualism, as he focused attention on how individuals interacted. His notion of interaction, however, differed from the neoclassical tradition. 'Social interaction', a key sociological concept, is the relationships between individuals and how they engage with each other. It goes beyond the more limited exchange relationships that are the focus of most neoclassical theory.

Weber also argued that sociology required a subjective understanding of people's motivations. This is sometimes called 'interpretative sociology', meaning that we should understand why people act as they do, and how the person views and understands their own actions. This has become an important principle in sociology.

One of Weber's other key concepts is 'rationalisation'. This is the tendency in modern societies to use science and reason to reduce social and economic processes to their constituent parts, making it easier to calculate, measure and predict aspects of economic and social life. Both markets and states promote rationalisation.

More broadly, Weber's analysis was also critical of Marxian class analysis. Weber's focus on subjectivity meant he tended to see economic class as less important than other social divides (such as nationality, religion and profession) in the formation of individual identity and group activity. Much recent work on the importance of education in economic sociology echoes Weber's ideas.

### Institutional analysis

Institutional theory focuses on the importance of history and the way the economy is structured through institutions. It was dominant in the early 1900s within economics. Weber, who saw himself as an economist, was part of one element of this tradition – the historical school of German economists. But it was also very popular in the United States where institutional theorists helped develop the statistical measures and tools used to monitor and regulate the economy.

While many institutionalists viewed themselves as economists, many neoclassical economists viewed them as too sociological, reflecting the interdisciplinary nature of this approach. Institutionalists drew attention to the influence of culture on consumer behaviour and the importance of corporations on the structure of competition. They also examined the role of the state, of unions and of the media. All of these 'institutions' were seen to have a significant impact on the nature of economic life.

More recently, some neoclassical theorists have also focused on institutions. Their work emerges from problems with the assumptions underpinning neoclassical theory. For example, behavioural economics responds to criticisms of the rational economic actor by exploring how people actually make economic decisions. Others responded to criticisms of the 'perfectly competitive market' by exploring the implications of 'transaction costs' (the cost of doing business).

These approaches have inspired New Institutional Economics (NIE). Unlike the older forms of institutional theory, NIE is based firmly in the tradition of methodological individualism. But unlike neoclassical economics, it pays more attention to the context in which individuals act, highlighting the role of past decisions and institutions on current behaviour.

Institutional analysis has enjoyed a resurgence across the social sciences. In political economy, for example, approaches based on the French *regulation* school focus on the social structures that regularise economic activity. In policy studies, institutional analysis examines how policy changes over time, emphasising how past policy decisions continue to influence future directions even when policies are wound back.

### Keynesian economics

British economist John Maynard Keynes is also one of the most significant economists of the twentieth century. His work on uncertainty, macro economics and unemployment provided the foundation of post-war economic policy around the globe. His macro economics has been incorporated into neoclassical orthodoxy, but has also inspired more critical post-Keynesian research on the instability of financial markets and underemployment.

While a tradition in its own right, Keynesian analysis fits well with the resurgence of institutionalism, focusing on how regulation of labour and financial markets can be used to manage instability, and how large institutional entities, such as states and banks, underpin economic activity in a modern capitalist economy.

## Economic sociology

Weberian, institutional and Marxian analysis can all be seen as 'economic sociology'. However, recent economic sociology refers to a more discrete sub-discipline. Its work has focused on understanding what influences individual economic action, and how to reconcile individual agency with the evidence of social structure. New concepts, such as Mark Granovetter's (1985) 'embeddedness' and Pierre Bourdieu's (1990) 'field' theory build on previous work in sociology and economics.

Economic sociology has been particularly influential in the US and Europe where network analysis has had a significant impact, focusing on the web of connections that exist between different economic agents and how this influences behaviour and outcomes. Game theory, a tool developed within the rational choice tradition, has also been applied by sociologists. Both network and game theories focus on the context of individual behaviour, the relationships between people and the 'rules of the game'. They lend themselves to multidisciplinary approaches.

## STRUCTURE OF THE BOOK

Following this introductory chapter, the book is divided into three parts, each focusing on a different aspect of market society, while some concluding remarks draw the book to a close. In Part 1, we examine how capitalism is constituted – what makes this system of economic organisation distinct. This section focuses attention on traditional economic ideas. It also engages with institutional analysis and with economic sociology, the subject matter of which is increasingly being incorporated into more traditional economic accounts. The section 'Constituting market society' is made up of three chapters exploring the system of commodity production, economic growth and crisis and the distribution of economic resources.

Chapter 2 focuses on the importance of production for sale rather than use, and on the corresponding centrality of markets to organising production and distribution. Here we examine commodity production and how prices are determined. We contrast classical theories of value, particularly the labour theory of value, with neoclassical subjective preference theories. But we also explore the broader process of commodification and how the capitalist system changes the process of production and our system of social relationships to produce a 'market society'.

Chapter 3 examines economic growth. The capacity to expand production on an ongoing basis is both a unique feature of capitalist production and is central to how market societies function. We explore several theoretical perspectives that seek to explain what generates growth. Likewise, we examine why economies sometimes fail to grow, giving rise to the problems of economic stagnation and crisis.

Lastly, Chapter 4 examines the distribution of economic resources in market societies. Inequality, in both the distribution of incomes and the ownership of assets is an essential feature of capitalist economies. Without it, the incentives that drive market competition and the social relations that constitute capitalism would not exist. We explore how some social groups systematically receive more than others and how this is related to the dynamics of markets and to the overall distribution of income.

Part 2 of the book considers how different institutions structure our economic lives. The three chapters in this section focus on what we consider to be three of the most significant regulatory institutions of market society: states, markets and corporations.

Chapter 5 analyses elements of the modern nation-state which developed alongside the growing importance of markets. We explore the state as an economic institution which is directly involved in production and distribution, and where governments continue to regulate markets (indeed, continue to create new markets through regulation). We also consider the forces that have shaped the state as well as the way the state has shaped market society and how this varies over time and between countries.

Chapter 6 examines the regulatory aspect of markets. The first part of the book has already laid an important platform for understanding the key elements in market regulation such as the price mechanism and the market distribution of income. Here we examine these themes in a more concrete way, exploring how markets have expanded since the 1970s and how this has restructured economic life. We explore the rise of finance, the introduction of markets within the state sector through marketisation and privatisation, and the impact of the global integration of trade and investment.

The corporation is the subject of Chapter 7. This economic institution now accounts for a significant proportion of global production and trade. In employing millions of people and producing most traded goods and services, corporations exert significant regulatory force. Although they operate within markets and are governed by state laws, their size, market dominance and command of resources give corporations enormous power. We explore the evolution of corporations and the ways they regulate their internal environment through bureaucracies and management structures and through contracts with other firms. We also consider how corporations influence their external environment through shaping consumer preferences and influencing government decision-making.

In addition to understanding the structural dynamics of capitalism, it is important to understand how these structures shape our everyday lives. Part 3 of the book focuses on the experience of living in contemporary market societies. There are elements of this throughout the book, but here we focus more systematically on understanding this lived experience. The section's three chapters explore the experience of the world of work and consumption, the family and the environment and civil society.

For many social scientists, modern capitalist societies are (or at least were) work societies. Chapter 8 considers this very direct experience of the economy and how it shapes people's identities and the way they live. The organisation of work is fundamental to the whole organisation of society, both in the economy and in the home. Changes to work organisation substantially change people's lives. We explore this process of change in market societies through the onset of mass production and the shifts to post-Fordism, examining arguments about the impact of 'flexibility' and individualisation accompanying such changes. We also explore the rise of consumer culture, and consider what drives this trend and the ways in which it affects the quality of life.

Chapter 9 examines ways the economy itself is underpinned by non-market support systems that help reproduce the social and environmental conditions necessary for capitalist production. Both families and the natural environment are important parts of market society and are deeply shaped by their relationship to the economy. We examine how these relationships are understood and how households and ecological resources are integrated into economic life. We analyse the commodification of care and how this reshapes the social relations of the family. We also examine how problems of environmental degradation and depletion are related to economic activity and how these issues might be addressed.

Finally, Chapter 10 turns to civil society where the systems that regulate market society are made and remade. Throughout this book we explore how social forces shape production, particularly the role of social movements and of politics. Here we focus on civil society more directly, examining different accounts of civil society and how they relate to different understandings of market society. While there are important differences, each approach links the development of a distinct and separate realm of civil society to the rise of market society. We consider civil society as an agent of change, as the basis of identity, and as a potential replacement for the welfare state. We examine these debates and explore how the different conceptions shape efforts to remake market society.

# Part 1
# Constituting market society

# 2 | Production, value and commodification

IN THE INTRODUCTORY chapter we discussed how the rise of markets was associated with significant social transformations affecting the way people lived and worked. Workers increasingly left the fields and subsistence production to enter into cities where production was organised in factories and wage labour provided a different form of livelihood. This was a gradual but monumental shift creating the conditions for some to acquire immense material wealth. Subsistence production, in which items were generally produced by households for their own use, was transformed into a system of commodity production.

Commodity production is distinct from subsistence production in feudal economies because items are produced for the specific purpose of selling them for profit. Goods or services produced for sale are commodities. In this chapter we explore the concept of the commodity and its implications for how we understand market society. We introduce key ideas addressed in economic theory including economic value, consumer sovereignty and the price mechanism. We also consider how some commodities are created beyond production through the process of commodification.

### THE COMMODITY PRODUCTION SYSTEM

Commodities are a unique form of output and the unit upon which the broader capitalist system is built. Hence, Karl Marx called them the 'cell-form' of capitalism (1976 [1867]). However, it is important to distinguish this notion of 'commodity' from an alternative use common in business theory and some economic theory. In these contexts 'commodity' refers to undifferentiated or homogenous products, especially raw materials like wheat, iron ore or wool, which are sold in 'commodity markets'. This understanding of 'commodity' contains an important idea, referring to products that are unbranded with many producers making essentially the same thing. But it is not the sense in which we use the term here.

Rather, we use the term 'commodity' to describe all goods and services produced for profit and exchanged at a market price. Using the concept of the commodity in this way helps us to understand how production is organised for markets in capitalism. The onset of commodity production involved the creation of workplaces distinct from the household. This process created a spatial separation between the sphere of production and the sphere of consumption. These changes had profound implications for the organisation of the economy, including our understanding of economic value.

## FROM USE VALUE TO EXCHANGE VALUE

In the subsistence world value is both concrete and specific. This is a local and immediate world where work, production and consumption all take place amongst the same people in approximately the same space. Individuals, families and communities work to make food, clothing and other items that they themselves will use. As a result, value is specific to use. The value of corn is that it can be eaten, the value of a bed that it can be slept in and the value of a well that it provides water for drinking.

These are 'use values', meaning the value of the good is directly related to its use. Such values cannot be easily compared. No matter how big or how soft one's bed might be, it is difficult to eat or drink it. It also makes little sense to say the value of a bed is the same as ten kilograms of corn because they have different uses and those uses cannot be converted. Having ten kilograms of corn does not provide anyone with a good night's sleep.

Such a situation changes in a system of commodity production, where corn, beds and wells may be goods with particular uses, but they are also commodities that can be sold. In capitalism, production is reorganised so that the primary goal is to sell products for a profit, not to produce goods that the producers themselves can use. Markets aid this shift by providing a mechanism for easy trade.

While commodities retain a specific use value, which is realised in the act of consumption, they also have an exchange value. This is the price commodities attract in a market. Exchange value is quite different to use value because it is measurable in a single metric – money – that allows us to equate the values of different goods. We can say, for example, that a $100 bed is worth 10 kilograms of corn at $10 a kilogram. Markets allow us to realise this equivalence by selling the bed and then buying the corn. By reducing value to price, markets allow measurement and comparison and thus promote rationalisation (see Chapter 1).

A crucial question for economic theory is how to explain the exchange values of different commodities. Exchange values are not clearly related to use values. As Adam Smith (1904 [1776]) noted, for example, diamonds are mere luxuries yet attract a high price, while water is essential for life itself but has a low price. Initially, many classical political economists focused attention on the process of production, arguing that the price of a good reflected the time and skill involved in making it.

### The labour theory of value

Classical political economists, particularly David Ricardo, suggested a labour theory of value to explain long-run price and this was later developed by Marx (who also used it to explain the expanding character of wealth in capitalism, see Chapter 3). The labour theory of value focuses attention on the determinants of value in the sphere of production. Value here is an objective property of commodities that is separate from their market price. Marx argued that the value of commodities reflected a common property. The one feature all commodities shared, he claimed, was that they were produced by human labour (Marx 1976 [1867], ch 1). The labour time taken to produce a commodity varies according to the type of machinery used, the intensity of the work performed and the way that the labour process is organised.

Today, the most influential theory of value comes from neoclassical economics. Neoclassical economists focused on exchange processes and consumer preferences to develop a subjective preference theory of value. Where Marx and the classical political economists focused on labour in production as the source of value, neoclassical economics claim the value of a commodity is fully reflected in its market price.

For neoclassical economists, value, and therefore price, is not an objective feature of the production process. Rather, it stems from the interaction of people's subjective desires and the availability of commodities to satisfy them. On this view, water is inexpensive because it is plentiful and diamonds costly because they are rare. With the consumer at its centre, neoclassical economist Lionel Robbins (1945) took up the idea of scarcity and used it to define the central 'problem' of economics.

### Consumer sovereignty

Robbins (1945) claimed economics was focused on explaining how people make tradeoffs in using scarce means among alternative uses. Economics began to focus on allocation – choosing what to do with the resources available. This focused attention on markets as the main allocation institutions of capitalism. For neoclassical economics the concept of value was closely linked to how markets regulate prices in response to consumer preferences.

It was in the marketplace that neoclassical economists argued the consumer was the ultimate authority in the economy. Coined by economist William Hutt (1940) the phrase 'consumer sovereignty' summed up a key element of the emerging neoclassical approach. Hutt meant that in a market society it was consumers and their 'willingness to pay' that ultimately determined what was produced. This process takes place through the price mechanism, which also determines the relative values of different commodities.

The theory of consumer sovereignty is elaborated in the neoclassical theory of supply and demand. This analysis is based on methodological individualism, which means that neoclassical economists start with the individual and then build theories of the economy by deducing how individuals interact with each other. To do this, they make a number of assumptions.

One of the most important assumptions is that individuals are self-interested and seek to maximise their own interests. In the context of markets, this means sellers will always act to maximise the profit they can make, while consumers will always act to maximise their utility (or enjoyment). Thus, sellers will seek the highest possible price for their commodities while also seeking to reduce their production costs. At the same time, consumers will seek the lowest price in order to purchase more of the commodities they desire. This gives the essential logic behind the supply and demand graph common in economic textbooks (see Box 2.1).

## Box 2.1 The supply and demand curve

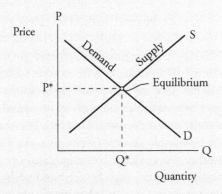

*Figure 2.1 Supply and demand curve*

In this diagram, the price of a commodity is a function of the interaction between buyers (consumers) and sellers (producers) seeking to maximise their utility. The demand curve represents the quantity of a good (or service) that consumers will buy at a given price. It slopes down to the right, suggesting consumers will buy more the lower the price charged. The supply curve represents the quantity of a good (or service) that producers will supply at a given price. It slopes up to the right, suggesting producers will supply more the higher the price charged.

The point at which the two lines intersect is the 'equilibrium' or market-clearing price where supply equals demand. If the price increases above this point, producers will increase production, lured by the potential for higher profits. But the increased output will be greater than consumers are willing to purchase, creating a glut and downward pressure on prices, encouraging a return to market equilibrium. Likewise, if prices are lower than the equilibrium, consumers will demand more than is supplied, causing a shortage, and this will put upward pressure on prices.

### Marginalism

A more complicated pricing story comes from the neoclassical use of marginal analysis and its associated theory of diminishing marginal utility. Marginal analysis emerged as a distinct tradition of economic analysis in the late nineteenth century and it is the foundation of modern neoclassical economics. Its pioneers Stanley Jevons (1871), Carl Menger (1951 [1871]) and Leon Walras (1954 [1874]) developed the method's key elements in different countries at almost exactly the same time. Marginalism signalled the shift away from the concerns and methods of classical political economy toward the more mathematical accounts of neoclassical economics.

The marginal theory of demand is also based on consumer desires, but it recognises limits to a consumer's demand for a commodity. While consumers are rational and self-interested, their wants are also diverse. Different things give us pleasure and as we have more and more of the same thing, we tend to enjoy each new part a little less. For example, you might like apples and the first apple you eat might give you a lot of satisfaction (or utility, as economists would say). You might also enjoy a second apple, but probably not as much as the first. By the hundredth apple you are not gaining much, if any, satisfaction. In other words, the satisfaction gained from buying and consuming an apple changes depending on how many have already been consumed.

For this reason, marginal analysis focuses on the value of the last apple, not the average apple. This focus on changes at the margins, rather than the aggregate, explains why the supply and demand curves refer to the price *per unit*. The theory of diminishing marginal utility means that consumers are willing to pay less for each additional item of a good they consume. We can imagine that for each good each individual has a willingness to pay that looks a little like the demand curve: they are willing to pay a high price for the first unit and then a progressively lower price for each additional unit (see Box 2.2).

### Box 2.2 The marginal utility curve

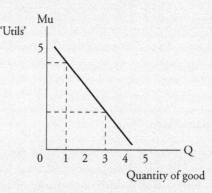

*Figure 2.2 Marginal utility curve*

If utility could be measured in absolute amounts (for example, by the number of 'utils' of satisfaction or pleasure) the demand curve would have the same properties as the marginal utility curve, assuming that each consumer's willingness to pay depends on the utility they derive from the product. The demand curve shows how much the consumer is willing to pay for successive amounts of the product. If each consumer receives less satisfaction from each additional unit of the product consumed, the demand curve would slope downward to the right, as shown in Box 2.1, showing an inverse relationship between the product's price and the quantity of it that is purchased in the market.

If we add the demand curve of each individual together we get the aggregate demand curve, which is the line in the supply and demand graph. At a high price there would be enough people willing to pay for enough units to only sell a small quantity. However, as the price per unit falls, the number sold would increase.

A similar analysis applies to production. Producers are assumed to maximise profit, and one way of doing this is to employ the most productive resources possible while minimising costs. Producers start by purchasing the most productive inputs at their disposal. These 'factors of production' include the most skilled workers, the most fertile land and the most efficient technologies. Initially production uses the most efficient resources, but as production increases, these run out, forcing producers to use less efficient resources and increasing production costs.

Supply and demand analysis can also be used to explain the effect of price changes on a specific industry. For some commodities, the effects of a change in price on the quantity demanded can be quite significant. For other commodities, however, the impact of price changes may be barely noticeable. For example, even if the price of energy (such as oil or electricity) were to rise, we are so dependent on it that it is unlikely the demand would fall very much. Alternatively, the cost of an overseas holiday might make a big difference to how many people travel.

Economists explain these outcomes through what they call the 'elasticity' of demand. Elastic demand means that a change in price makes a big difference to the quantity sold. By contrast, inelastic demand would see little change in the quantity demanded as a result of changes in the level of price. Understanding what lies behind demand (how urgent the demand is, for example) helps us to understand the effects of price changes in any particular industry.

## THE REGULATORY FORCE OF THE 'PRICE MECHANISM'

Markets do not only set prices. Economists see markets playing a key role in regulating production decisions through the ability of the 'price mechanism' to communicate information and coordinate economic activity. This ensures that producers produce what consumers (and other producers) want. At the centre of this process is the concept of competition.

### The role of competition

Competition is the market force that disciplines producers and regulates their behaviour to ensure they meet the demands of consumers. It brings the expectations of producers and consumers into alignment through pressures to eliminate gluts and shortages. This explains why producers, who want to maximise profits, do not simply increase their prices to do so. Competition means that if a firm raises prices above the cost of producing an item, other businesses will undercut their price to gain more customers.

For example, if an efficient business can produce corn for sale at five dollars a kilogram and the going price is seven dollars, the lure of profit will induce more producers to enter the market. This will increase supply, eventually forcing down the price, until the price hits five dollars a kilogram (the new equilibrium price). Economists call this effect the 'self-correcting' or 'self-regulating' nature of markets.

Austrian economist Friedrich von Hayek (1991) takes this idea further, arguing that the pressures of market competition can explain social order in market society. He claims a stable system emerges spontaneously from the interactions of individuals without the need for any centralised control. Such arguments seem to provide a powerful ethical justification for markets. However, the logic of consumer sovereignty is underpinned by assumptions which may not hold in practice. Indeed, the competition that is assumed is an 'idealised' form of competition called 'perfect competition' where there are many small firms, none of which exercise market power. We discuss other conceptions of competition and some critiques of the neoclassical model in Chapter 7.

### Markets and economic welfare

Neoclassical economics claims to be a positive theory, meaning it describes how the world *is*, rather than a normative theory, which would describe what *ought to be*. Neoclassical price theory claims to explain how prices are set in markets, not how they should be set. But clearly, neoclassical analysis also has normative implications because the analysis suggests market outcomes are also good outcomes.

There are several different arguments in favour of markets as the main institution for organising the economy. The Austrian school, including theorists like Hayek, emphasises that markets promote individual freedom and enterprise. But neoclassical economics has a more mathematical justification. The sub-discipline of welfare economics seeks to evaluate different outcomes against the criterion of economic welfare. Here, welfare has a specific meaning. It is a reflection of 'optimal allocation' rather than wellbeing, as such.

Welfare economics, as developed by AC Pigou (1938 [1920]), emerged to guide public policy at a time when economic theory was becoming more mathematical and therefore less accessible to policy makers. Pigou and others thought there was a need to outline the circumstances under which it might be appropriate for governments to 'intervene' in market distributions.

However, because neoclassical economists prefer positive theory to normative theory, they argue that welfare economics should only make weak value judgments that most people would accept. On this basis welfare economists have adopted an approach developed by the Italian economist Vilfredo Pareto. At a social level, Pareto (1972 [1906]) argued that the subjective nature of 'welfare' means we cannot properly compare the welfare of different people. However, we can judge that if a change makes some people better off and no one worse off, then the situation has improved.

An important claim of welfare economics is that under particular conditions of individual rationality and perfect competition, free markets produce the best possible outcomes. Advocates claim that freedom in trade and exchange means that people only ever engage in transactions if they see a benefit. If you value an item more highly than its owner, you can offer to trade an item you value less but they potentially value more. Through such exchanges, the welfare of all would be improved until a situation where no more exchange takes place because no one could be made better off by further trade. This essentially reflects an 'equilibrium' condition.

However, the end result would still depend on the initial distribution of resources. Those with little to trade would be unlikely to make large gains. But improving their lot would also require redistribution, by taking something from wealthier neighbours, and Pareto thought such changes to require strong value judgments. Instead, he simply said markets gave the best results given the distribution of income and was silent on what that initial distribution should be.

Neoclassical theory has since developed this idea, suggesting that free markets deliver the optimal outcome through efficient allocation. Any 'intervention' in the market – whether it is a subsidy to some producers, a tax on trade or a regulation restricting some forms of production – is said to distort prices and thereby reduce aggregate welfare.

This element of neoclassical economics is controversial. Some criticism of this approach rejects Pareto's value judgments. But more commonly, other social scientists have disputed the methodology of neoclassical economics, arguing that its assumptions bias its conclusions. In other words, they argue the theory is not really positive at all. Rather, its individualist methodology leads to a pro-market bias by focusing on some features of the economy, but ignoring others.

## BEYOND CONSUMER SOVEREIGNTY

Neoclassical economics takes the approach of methodological individualism, arguing that theory should start analysis with the individual consumer. It uses a model of the individual sometimes called *homo economicus* or 'economic man'. This model assumes that people are rational, autonomous and self-interested. They are rational in that they find the best means to pursue their ends. They are autonomous in the sense that their actions, beliefs, values and desires originate within them and are not dependent on anyone else. They are self-interested in the sense that they pursue their own goals, not somebody else's. This is not necessarily selfish, although in some economic models (Adam Smith 1904 [1776]) it can become so, but it means consumers maximise their satisfaction and producers maximise their profits.

Making these sorts of assumptions allows neoclassical economists to abstract away from the great diversity of real people to build mathematical models of how *homo economicus* would behave in different circumstances. This simplification and abstraction makes it easier to develop theory. However, these assumptions have, unsurprisingly, been criticised as extreme and unrealistic.

## INSTITUTIONAL AND SOCIOLOGICAL CRITIQUES

One important criticism of the neoclassical approach comes from institutional economics. This approach emphasises the importance of social and economic institutions – such as the state, the corporation and the family. In doing this, it tends to be closer to sociology than neoclassical economics. Indeed, some key sociological thinkers, such as Max Weber and Thorstein Veblen, were also institutional economists. This tradition critiques the model of *homo economicus* embedded in neoclassical theory.

Weber (2002 [1905]), for example, argues that the neoclassical notion of individual rationality is not a universal human trait but a specific historical development associated with the reformation and the rise of protestant religions in Europe. Weber also emphasised the importance of the work ethic and a culture of savings to the commodity production system rather than the role of the consumer that is emphasised by neoclassical theory. Polanyi (1944) argued that the 'rational self interest' apparent in the pursuit of profit or wages stemmed from the institutional organisation of market society rather than universal human tendencies.

Veblen (1899, ch 7) argued that consumption itself was an expression of social forces rather than innate 'rationality'. He argued that for many people consumption expressed their social identity, such as by displaying their status through forms of 'conspicuous consumption'. One example he gives – from the late 19th century when he was writing – is the elaborate gloves worn by the wives of very rich men. The woman herself was an 'object' of display, the property of her husband. But the gloves also signalled social status. Because the gloves made it difficult to do manual work they demonstrated the person was a member of the leisure class who had servants to do household tasks for them. Veblen's approach is reflected in a much broader sociological literature on consumption, which we explore in Chapter 8.

In the second half of the twentieth century institutional economist John Kenneth Galbraith built upon Veblen's focus on affluence. He argued that while the neoclassical picture of many small-scale competitive firms may have been relatively useful in understanding early capitalist economies this approach was far less relevant to modern (or 'postmodern') industrial capitalism.

In much of the modern economy, Galbraith claimed, consumer sovereignty was compromised by producer power, sometimes referred to as 'producer sovereignty'. As incomes increased and production costs fell, people increasingly came to satisfy most of their basic wants such as the need for housing, food and clothing, meaning extra consumption became less urgent. However, continued expansion in markets and rising commodity sales are required for businesses to succeed (see Galbraith 1967).

Galbraith argued that large corporations solved this problem through advertising and marketing. Advertising creates new wants by encouraging people to consume commodities they previously had no desire to consume. He called this the 'dependence effect' (1976 [1958]), because what consumers demanded was dependent on what producers were already planning to produce.

Herbert Gintis (1972) contrasts a more radical Marxian critique of consumer sovereignty with Galbraith's theories. Gintis claims that consumer sovereignty fails not because producers have too much power *per se*, but rather because the political and economic system only offers people a limited range of options. All these options are based on increased commodity consumption, and this effectively removes alternatives from being considered.

## Beyond *homo economicus*?

Some currents within conventional economics have developed a more complex understanding of individual rationality and behaviour. One of the most important is game theory, which developed during World War II alongside the emerging computer sciences. It built on the rational choice approach of neoclassical economics, examining how rational individuals make choices.

It constructs situations as if they were games. The people in the situation are 'players', the game follows 'rules' that dictate what options are open to the players and the game has a 'payoff' for each player associated with what they receive at the end (see Varoufakis 2001). It develops tools that explain how rational players would play particular games and thus how people are likely to respond to particular kinds of economic (or social) situations.

Game theory has two distinct advantages over neoclassical theory in understanding individual behaviour. First, it focuses attention on the 'rules of the game' – the situation in which decisions are made. This makes it easier to integrate into other social sciences by changing the structure of games to reflect different assumptions about economic or social conditions. Second, it is interactive and strategic. Strategic action is where we act on the understanding that our actions might influence the actions of others.

Conventional economics, based on 'perfect competition' assumes individual producers or consumers have little impact on overall outcomes, such as the price of a commodity. As a result, consumers are assumed to buy the cheapest goods while firms produce what consumers demand at the lowest cost. This neglects how their actions shape those of others. Game theory instead assumes that players can influence the actions of other players and that they will take this into account when making decisions.

Game theory also made it easier to test economic assumptions. Its structure is well suited to conducting experiments. Economists could design games that represent particular economic situations and then test their results by getting people to play the game and observing the outcome (Roth 1993).

'Experimental economics' raises interesting findings. Results vary, but in many situations people do not act according to neoclassical theory. People are more likely to cooperate. They also make systematic errors, for example, responding differently to large losses than large gains. Along with developments in behavioural psychology this has led to modified versions of *homo economicus*.

The best-known is Herbert Simon's model of bounded rationality (1957). Simon worked across the social sciences, in economics, politics, sociology and psychology. He argued people usually have only limited information and limited time to gather information. People also find it difficult to evaluate complex situations. Instead of calculating the best approach to each new situation, people develop 'rules of thumb' that appear to deliver reasonable results most of the time. Simon called this 'satisficing' rather than 'maximising' – looking for a satisfactory outcome rather than the best outcome. Some evolutionary economists use this approach to explain the development of social norms. Here norms are seen as the 'rules of thumb' developed by a society over time as a response to a particular type of situation.

These developments are yet to be properly integrated into most neoclassical economic analysis. However, they have been very influential in some new approaches, such as the New Institutional Economics (NIE), which combines traditional neoclassical analysis with elements of game theory, bounded rationality and a focus on institutions. In doing this NIE tends to offer a more historical and social account of economic life; closer to sociology and political economy. Network theory, another approach popular in economic sociology, also attempts to combine elements of individual action and social structure (see Chapters 4 and 10).

## THE MARXIAN CRITIQUE

Like many sociologists, Marx examines individual action in the context of broader social forces. However, he emphasises how the structure of the economy creates different groups of people with distinct, and often contradictory, interests. For Marx, while people are able to make choices, these choices are constrained by circumstances that give some people more power than others. This requires a theory of group interest, rather than the individual interest that characterises neoclassical theory.

## Commodity fetishism

For Marx, examining the interactions of individuals engaging in exchange, and the prices produced by markets, obscures the social and economic structures underlying such activities. Marx describes this neglect as 'commodity fetishism' whereby attention falls upon the object – the commodity – rather than the people and groups in the economy that underpin the production of such commodities (1976 [1867], ch 1). This analysis leads to a different understanding of markets and commodities.

Marx's use of 'fetish' refers to inanimate objects given religious significance; a religious idol in tribal societies, for example. For such a tribal group, the inanimate object takes on a life of its own. However, in reality the significance of that object has nothing to do with its inherent physical properties. Rather, its significance derives from the society out of which the religious practices emerge and that give meaning to that object.

Marx argues that a similar process occurs with commodities in capitalist societies. Commodities and their prices are the products of a market economic system, capitalism. Capitalism is underpinned by specific social relations. These constitute the way that production, distribution and exchange are organised among the different economic classes. Therefore, one can only understand the production of commodities, their prices and the laws that regulate them in relation to these deeper socio-economic structures.

Yet, for Marx, the structure and role of markets in capitalism obscures these relationships. Instead of seeing the people who produce the goods and services we use (as was commonly the case in pre-capitalist society), we only see the commodities and their prices. This creates commodity fetishism where 'relations between people [producers and consumers] become relations between things [commodities and prices]' (Marx 1976 [1867], ch 1). Thus, while market society makes us more dependent on people we do not know – for our food, clothing and shelter – we experience this as becoming more 'independent' from others.

This reinforces the assumption of neoclassical economics that we are autonomous individuals and it helps explain popular understandings of ourselves as 'self-reliant'. However, Marx would argue that capitalism makes us more *inter*dependent than at any other point in history. Hence, commodities, according to Marx, simultaneously express and conceal the social relations at the heart of the capitalist economy.

Marx's theory of commodity fetishism draws our attention back to the world of production and the social relationships underpinning it. These relationships can be exploitative and highly oppressive yet remain invisible (see Box 2.3).

### Box 2.3 Who made your (Nike) shoes?

One of the best-known consumer campaigns of recent years is the anti-Nike sweatshop campaign. It highlights the exploitative conditions under which some Nike shoe manufacturers work. In this sense, the campaign can be understood as an attempt to overcome the problem of commodity fetishism.

Nike is one of the largest sport clothing firms in the global economy. Its logo, the 'swoosh', and its slogan, 'Just Do It', are very recognisable. Nike uses high profile sporting identities such as Roger Federer, Christiano Ronaldo and Serena Williams to promote its products. It encourages consumers to identify Nike products with the attributes of those sportspeople: with winning, with wealth and success and with having healthy, appealing physiques. As the Nike website states: 'Consumers today are smart, sophisticated and demanding. They have more choices and more access to those choices than ever before. They value authentic brands that interact with them on an intensely personal level' (Nike n.d.).

However, the advertising does not mention the conditions under which Nike products are made. Much of the manufacture of Nike shoes, for example, is contracted to factories in which workers labour under poor conditions, they are sometimes not allowed to form unions and receive rates of pay below a living wage, in countries such as Indonesia, Vietnam and Thailand. This does not appear in Nike commercials. Nor can the workers who make the shoes easily tell their stories to consumers.

Here, then, is a potential example of the usefulness of Marx's concept of commodity fetishism. Relations between people (the worker and the factory owner, the producer and the consumer) become relations between people and things (the consumer and the Nike shoe). In this way the conditions under which the commodity is made are hidden from the consumer, while the shoes themselves come to take on a 'mystical character' through advertising.

> The Nike sweatshop campaign attempted to break through this process of commodity fetishism by highlighting the working conditions of those who make Nike shoes. By publicising these conditions the campaign hoped to put pressure on Nike to improve the rights and entitlements of its workers.

## THE PROCESS OF COMMODIFICATION

The discussion of commodity fetishism has identified some of the ways that commodities come to occupy such an important part of people's everyday lives in market society, but there is another important explanation for the proliferation of commodities under capitalism. Commodities are not only made in the production process – such as in factories – they are also created when things that already exist are transformed into goods and services that are sold in markets for a price. Water, for example, exists naturally in the environment, but when it is bottled and sold in a market, it becomes a commodity. There are two other important ways in which this process of commodification occurs and these are of particular interest to economic sociologists and anthropologists.

The first is what Karl Polanyi (1944, p. 73) called the creation of 'fictitious commodities'. This is where the elements needed for production, like land and labour, are incorporated into a capitalist system. Historically, this process was central to creating market society but a similar process occurs today wherever markets are created for items that are not originally produced for sale within the economic system. The second method of commodification takes place when goods or services once provided outside the market system are privatised or marketised. These 'special' commodities show that capitalist economic processes are necessarily embedded in social institutions beyond markets.

## FICTITIOUS COMMODITIES

In *The Great Transformation* (1944), Polanyi wrote about the transition from feudalism to capitalism and the period when Western Europe became a market society. He was interested in the processes that enabled this transformation, especially the creation of 'fictitious commodities' and the 'protective' institutions that accompanied this.

For Polanyi, fictitious commodities are things that are not produced for sale in markets, and yet in a capitalist economy, they have prices and are traded. Thus, they have some of the characteristics of commodities (they are sold in markets for a price), but unlike regular commodities they are not produced for sale.

The most important of these, according to Polanyi, are land, labour and money, none of which exist originally as commodities. Land exists naturally, outside of markets. Labour is the human capacity to work, embedded in people and produced through the family and the education system. Money is a medium of exchange and a store of value embedded in trust and created through social institutions (as discussed in Chapter 6).

Where land and the labour attached to it were once 'transferred' (through marriage or conquest in the feudal system, for example), the rise of capitalism saw the transformation of these already existing natural and social phenomena into commodities. This is because the inputs into a commodity production system must also be commodities, if markets are to regulate the economy as a whole. According to Polanyi, because 'labor, land and money are essential production inputs of industry; they also must be organised in markets' (Polanyi 1944, p. 75).

By creating markets for land, labour and money, the forces of competition could be used to regulate these important inputs. However, Polanyi (1944, p. 60) argues that the development of a market economy in this way also goes hand in hand with the development of a 'market society'. A raft of laws and institutions is necessary to secure the supply and integrity of the fictitious commodities with the result that society itself is shaped to meet the demands of markets. An important example is the English Factory Acts (see Box 2.4).

## Box 2.4 The English Factory Acts

During the nineteenth century, industrial production grew in Britain and dependence on market income became the norm for more and more people. Factories became a much more noticeable feature of the landscape. They were famously described by English poet William Blake as 'dark satanic mills', both because of their appearance and because large numbers of workers laboured in them for long hours under harsh conditions. The early *Factory Acts* were laws that regulated work in the textiles industry, which was the largest industry in Britain and one of the first to industrialise.

The *Factory Act* of 1833 limited the number of hours that could be worked in a day to fifteen. Children were further limited to twelve hours, for those aged thirteen to eighteen, and eight hours, for those aged nine to twelve. In 1844, the *Factory Act* was broadened so that women were treated as equal with children in terms of hours worked, thus limiting their opportunities for waged labour in the textiles industry, and in 1847, both women and children had their working day limited to ten hours. Gradually, over the next four decades, more industries were brought under the Factory Acts, until the 1878 *Factory Act*, which applied limitations on working hours to all industries.

Examining the *Factory Acts* illuminates how the rise of a market society went hand in hand with the rise of new forms of social and economic regulation, and the ways such regulation was shaped by conflict and contestation. New forms of factory work disrupted traditional patterns of production and family. Increasingly, production occurred outside of the household, often in difficult conditions. The movement for the limitation of working hours was supported by the workers directly affected, as well as by reformers, concerned with the destructive effects of wage labour upon workers and the traditional family. They were opposed by most factory owners and their parliamentary allies, although a minority of factory owners, such as the socialist Robert Owen, supported shorter hours.

The outcomes of the Acts were to both regulate and incorporate labour into the economy, thereby underpinning the expansion of market society. By limiting the hours women could work the *Factory Acts* simultaneously protected women from some of the harsher aspects of the wage labour system, and subordinated women in the labour market, constraining their ability to have economic rights equal to those of men. This satisfied many within the reform movement as it was in keeping with its ideal that the proper role of women was in the domestic sphere, looking after children and attending to household duties.

Arguably, the *Factory Acts* also helped to ensure the long-term sustainability of the wage labour system, as it limited the time workers had to spend in punishing and unhealthy manual labour, giving them more time for rest, recovery and leisure. They are also seen by many as marking the beginning of the process of intensive accumulation (increasing output by making workers work more intensively, or with more efficient machines), rather than extensive accumulation (increasing output by making workers labour for longer). Thus, although opposed by most factory owners, the Factory Acts may have contributed to the long-term viability of capitalism by protecting workers and promoting productivity.

## MAKING MARKETS

Some scholars have suggested applying the fictitious commodity concept to other areas not considered by Polanyi, such as the creation of markets in intellectual property (Jessop 2007). In this case it is 'knowledge' that exists prior to commodification. It might be scientific knowledge about the genetic code of an animal, or traditional knowledge of an indigenous community about the medicinal properties of certain plants. New laws, supported by the World Trade Organisation's Trade-Related Intellectual Property Rights (TRIPS), grant individuals or corporations the sole rights to use certain knowledge for commercial purposes. They are granted intellectual property rights over this knowledge, which becomes a commodity, with a price, that can be traded.

We can see a similar logic in the use of markets to provide other goods and services once produced very differently. For example, paid childcare moves an activity once provided in the home according to social norms into the market where it can be regulated by competition. This example highlights the second way in which commodification occurs. Activities already in the economy but which were organised according to non-market principles, such as public health or education, can be moved into the market.

This occurs either through privatisation, which is the sale of public assets, or marketisation, where prices are introduced for using services. These privatised and marketised services are not fictitious commodities as described by Polanyi. However, they do entail the transformation of things that are primarily produced outside of the market for direct use, into things that are produced for an exchange value and distributed through markets.

Sociologists and political economists note that the process of commodification is neither natural, nor purely economic. Social institutions are necessary for it to occur because unlike regular commodities, such as cars, computers or cans of Coca-Cola, fictitious commodities and non-market activities are not produced for sale in markets. They do not exist as ready-made commodities; therefore, something extra is required to convert them into commodities that can be traded in markets. Typically that 'something extra' is the state.

Indeed, most neoclassical economists broadly acknowledge this. They see the state playing a crucial role in establishing and enforcing property rights, without which markets cannot operate. If land, for example, is to become a commodity, state laws are necessary to grant private property rights so it can be owned and traded. The same process can be seen historically with labour. The state was central to creating national labour markets (Polanyi 1944, p. 139), confining access to social assistance to those unable to work, ensuring others continued to stay in the labour market.

The state's role is not limited to creating markets in fictitious commodities. It also has an ongoing role in regulating them. Polanyi argued that the process of commodifying land, labour and money threatened to undermine its foundations, arguing markets for land and labour '*are* essential to a market economy. But no society could stand the effects of such a system of crude fictions... unless its human and natural substance... was protected' (1944, p. 73). The case of 'labour' provides a salient example of this argument.

The existence of a market for labour involves workers (sellers) seeking a job that pays a wage (price) from employers (buyers). However, treating labour simply as a commodity can damage both the 'human capacity to work' and the person whose labour is used in production. This is because the capacity to work, or 'labour power' – the commodity being bought and sold – is inseparable from the human body. Hence, many argue there must be a 'floor' below which wages will not fall because they are the income that serves to 'reproduce' workers and must be sufficient to purchase basic subsistence needs.

This explains the development of minimum wages and forms of social assistance for the unemployed. Similar regulation exists for access to land, such as rent controls and public housing. Such 'protective' regulations were, for Polanyi, the necessary counterpart to market liberalisation in the nineteenth century, a dual process that he called the 'double movement' (1944, p. 143). This term captures the extension of the reach of markets on the one hand, and on the other, the 'socially protective counter-movement', which quarantines fictitious commodities from the full force of commodification. (We explore this further in Chapter 5.)

The double movement is also related to Polanyi's (1944) idea of 'embeddedness' which suggests that all economies are embedded in institutions that regulate the economic process in any given society. Mark Granovetter (1985) popularised the concept of 'embeddedness' in economic sociology. He argues market transactions are embedded in networks of social agents rather than the 'impersonal' market mechanism put forward in neoclassical economic theory. This more micro approach focuses on tracing networks of production and consumption in the economy, as distinct from Polanyi's macro approach to social regulation. (See also Chapters 4 and 10.)

## In and out of commodification

The process of commodification is not a linear movement; rather, it develops unevenly, subject to the interplay of political, social and economic factors. During the last two centuries, social services have been provided, at various times, by both public authorities and private firms. Prisons for example, were mostly operated by private firms in Britain until 1877 when they were nationalised (Mehigan & Rowe 2007, p. 356). Prisons were then 'decommodified', meaning that the service was provided directly by the state, rather than being sold through markets (see also Box 2.5). However, in 1998 the British government moved back toward commodification by contracting private providers to operate new prisons (Mehigan & Rowe 2007, p. 361).

Similarly, when the first majority Labour government came to power in Britain in 1945 it nationalised key industries, such as coal, aviation, electricity, gas and the Bank of England (Parker 2009, pp. 6–7). During the 1980s and 1990s under the Conservative Governments of Margaret Thatcher and John Major, many of these were privatised, and effectively commodified. However, in 2008 there was a partial move back towards nationalisation and decommodification with the 'Northern Rock' bank being nationalised by the British government in the wake of the global financial crisis.

### Box 2.5 Decommodification or recommodification?

The history of capitalism is, in part, the history of the incorporation of ever-greater aspects of social life into the market. Yet, many social services do not neatly fit into the definition of a commodity because people are not dependent upon markets for their use. Consider, for example, healthcare. In many countries, the state guarantees access to healthcare for its citizens. While some healthcare may be provided privately through markets, citizens are not dependent upon markets for the provision of health services. Some scholars use the term 'decommodification' to describe this process.

Gosta Esping-Andersen, one of the most influential theorists of the welfare state, argues that '[d]ecommodification occurs when a service is rendered as a matter of right, and when a person can maintain a livelihood without reliance on the market' (1990, pp. 21–2). Esping-Andersen argues that some forms of sick leave and maternity leave are examples of labour decommodification because the state requires employers to ensure that workers can 'freely, and without potential loss of job, income, or general welfare, opt out of work when they themselves consider it necessary' (1990, p. 23). If labour were a pure commodity then such absences would result in a loss of income because the worker was not involved in production.

However, other scholars contest this conception of decommodification. Claus Offe, for example, argues that part of the state's regulation of labour entails a process of 'administrative recommodification' (1984). Rather than quarantining labour from markets, the state integrates labour into markets. It does this, for example, by providing education and training, thereby ensuring a supply of workers with appropriate skills for the labour market.

Following Offe, it has been argued that programs requiring people to do training or manual labour in order to receive unemployment assistance, are examples of 'administrative recommodification'. This is because the state is acting to ensure that people participate in the labour market, rather than simply allowing them to exist outside of it (Holden 2003). Thus, the state has a contradictory role with respect to commodificiation. On the one hand decommodifying, on the other recommodifying, much like Polanyi's 'double movement'.

One implication is that it is not always easy to determine whether something is commodified or decommodified. Consider public transport, for example. Train and bus services are often provided by the state not to make a profit, but for the broader social objective of enabling people's mobility. However, public transportation is rarely provided for free, and sometimes the state contracts private, for-profit, companies to operate public transport services. This means that public transport does not always conform neatly to Esping-Anderson's definition of decommodification because services are not offered as a matter of right.

One useful way through this conceptual problem is to view commodification and decommodification as 'ideal types' or extreme poles on a spectrum. Few things will conform to the ideal case of either commodification or decommodification. Rather, it is useful to examine the extent to which services and labour are simultaneously commodified and decommodified and how each aspect is shaped by these contradictory processes.

Often the extent of commodification and the nature of regulation is the outcome of periods of economic crisis and conflict between different groups. For example, according to historian EP Thompson, the spread of 'bread riots' in Britain during the eighteenth and nineteenth centuries reflected protests against the price of bread fluctuating according to the market, rather than being set according to the customary 'just price'. He argued the protestors were posing the values of an older moral economy (based on social values, needs or customs) against the profit-oriented logic of the emerging commodity-based market society (Thompson 1980).

Similar principles may be applied to more contemporary struggles against commodification. For example, protest movements opposed to privatisation object to essential goods and services being provided by markets because this limits access to those able to pay. The movement against water privatisation in Bolivia is an example of this. In effect, protesters are appealing to a moral economy of needs that they view as superior to, and more humane than, the profit imperatives of the capitalist market system.

Clearly, the process of commodification is a highly contested, but central, aspect of market society. This is especially the case at times of economic crisis when growth in the production of ordinary commodities falters. Commodification provides new opportunities for profit making – and according to neoclassical economics, for greater efficiency. But it can also challenge social values and equity.

## CONCLUSION

Commodities are clearly central to the capitalist economy. They are objects of consumption produced in a market society, and therefore at the centre of economic life. But the commodity system also reflects a particular form of economic and social regulation – one where market forces are an important, but not the only, aspect of economic organisation. While commodity production promotes the price mechanism in regulating everyday life, this is not independent of the state. The state brings markets into being and continues to influence the operation of markets and the boundaries of commodification. These factors remain important as we now turn to consider the expansionary character of the commodity production system at the centre of market societies.

### Questions

1 What are the major understandings of economic value and how do they relate to the rise of market society?

2 In what sense can prices be understood as regulating people's actions in market societies?
3 How useful is Marx's concept of commodity fetishism for understanding the structure and dynamics of capitalist economies?
4 Why does Polanyi argue that fictitious commodities are central to understanding market societies and their evolution?
5 What are the major forces shaping the processes of commodification?

# 3 | Growth, accumulation and crisis

IN THE PREVIOUS chapter we discussed the character of the commodity-based production system that underpins market societies. The ability of such societies to generate substantial and long-term economic growth is one of their most striking and impressive features. Economic growth has transformed our way of life, leading in many countries to a material standard of living unprecedented in history. When growth is high the economy seems to work well, delivering profits, higher incomes and jobs. However, economic growth sometimes falters. Periods of low growth, or 'recession', can lead to wider economic crises giving rise to unemployment, hardship and social misery which can also generate more serious society-wide crises.

Managing the cycles of economic growth and decline has therefore become a central preoccupation of governments. In this chapter we consider the nature of economic growth and how it is measured and potential problems generated by growth in affluent societies. We also examine some of the different understandings of growth and the political implications of such analyses. Finally, we address the periodic crises that are a feature of capitalist economies as well as the relationships between economic growth and political legitimacy.

## ECONOMIC GROWTH IN MARKET SOCIETIES

Increasing economic growth is generally thought to contribute to rising material living standards. The more an economy grows the more commodities are available for use by consumers and producers. Potentially this means the availability of more goods and services – to meet basic needs and additional 'wants' – as well as more machines to produce these commodities. The ability to produce more goods and services may also lead to the creation of more jobs. However, what we measure and the way we measure it has significant implications for understanding the wellbeing of society.

## WHAT IS ECONOMIC GROWTH?

A common definition of economic growth is the increase in a country's 'national income'. The level of growth is taken to reflect a country's economic performance and is commonly measured by Gross Domestic Product (GDP). GDP measures the market value of all final goods and services produced within the borders of a country over a given period, usually one year or quarter of a year. This indicates that as more commodities are produced, a nation's income grows. However, GDP does not capture all economic activity.

The 'market value' recorded in GDP refers to the price people pay for commodities in markets. This means goods and services that are useful but are not bought and sold do not count. GDP therefore excludes, for example, the 'service' provided in cooking a meal for one's family. Also, the commodities included are 'final' because intermediate goods such as components in a computer are excluded as their value is assumed to be reflected in the price of the final good (the computer).

GDP is described as 'gross', rather than 'net' because, although the figures exclude intermediate goods, no deductions are made for the purchase of capital goods that replace existing machinery. Such replacement means productive capacity is unchanged, yet GDP has increased. Similarly, the loss of 'natural capital' like forests or rivers is also unaccounted for in GDP.

Sometimes GDP is described as 'real' GDP. This means the data has been adjusted to account for inflation, by adjusting the value of production by the inflation rate. This is considered a more accurate indicator of actual production because in high inflationary periods, unadjusted data might give a misleading picture. GDP can also be used to compare one country's economic growth to another. GDP *per capita* takes into account population differences between countries, giving a better indication of the resources available per person.

Growth creates more commodities for use and also leads to new and more efficient ways of producing them. This means increased productivity in the economy, or an increase in output per unit of input. Productivity improvements may also enable higher real wages. Economic growth is also linked to the production of completely new types of goods and services, which lead to the formation of new industries and new types of work.

The idea that economic growth advances human welfare is not new. Adam Smith, for example, noted that the emerging market society was one where 'a general plenty diffuses through all the different ranks of the society' (Smith 1904 [1776]). For Smith, the availability of commodities to the 'poorer classes' was evidence of progress, and sustained economic growth has indeed led to broader prosperity. For example, the long boom after World War II witnessed an impressive 'golden age' of growth which supported low unemployment, high levels of investment and trade (at least in wealthy countries).

There is also a strong empirical link between economic growth and unemployment, with low or negative rates of economic growth usually resulting in large increases in unemployment. Unemployment occurs when people who are actively looking for work are unable to find paid employment. As most working age people derive their income from employment, low growth has devastating consequences through income losses. Alongside this, some people may also be *under*employed, where they have some paid work, but would like, or need, more. And there is often hidden unemployment, where people give up looking for work, but are likely to return to the labour market if employment conditions improve.

All of these forms of unemployment have costs to the individuals and families involved, and also to the economy through lost production. However, while growth has been very important to the development of market societies, expanding commodity production and rising GDP does not always provide additional jobs. Even those involved in developing measures of growth have cautioned against equating growth with economic wellbeing (see Kuznets 1934). As the definition of GDP suggests, it does not include all aspects of economic welfare (see Box 3.1).

### Problems of growth

Economic growth has been challenged as an indicator of economic health and social progress. This is because the focus on expanding the production of commodities in GDP leaves out many reasonable measurements of wellbeing. These include happiness, life expectancy, mental health, the level of equality in the distribution of economic resources and access to basic services such as education and healthcare. Clearly, economic growth is only a partial measure of general wellbeing.

## Box 3.1 GDP and HDI selected country rankings

Table 3.1 Growth v Development, 2010

|  | GDP per capita[1] | HDI[2] |
|---|---|---|
| Qatar | 1 | 38 |
| Luxembourg | 2 | 24 |
| Singapore | 3 | 27 |
| Norway | 4 | 1 |
| United States | 7 | 4 |
| Netherlands | 9 | 7 |
| Australia | 10 | 2 |
| Canada | 12 | 8 |
| Ireland | 13 | 5 |
| Sweden | 14 | 9 |
| United Kingdom | 21 | 26 |
| Japan | 24 | 11 |
| Poland | 44 | 41 |
| Russia | 52 | 65 |
| Botswana | 53 | 98 |
| Mexico | 59 | 56 |
| Brazil | 71 | 73 |
| China | 94 | 89 |
| India | 129 | 119 |

*Notes:* [1] GDP (Gross Domestic Production) figures are Purchasing Power Parity (PPP) *per capita*, (International Monetary Fund 2011); [2] Human Development Index, United Nations (2010).

There is some relationship between GDP and HDI. But there is also considerable variation. For example, Qatar has the highest GDP per capita but ranks 38th on the HDI.

Economic growth also has social and environmental costs that are not in national account figures. GDP measures only those commodities that are priced and traded in official markets. Yet, in the process of creating goods and services for sale other costs arise that are unpriced, and hence not counted towards GDP. These unpriced social and environmental costs are called 'externalities' (see Chapters 5 and 9).

Examples of externalities include climate change resulting from carbon pollution, damage to health resulting from the inhalation of car exhaust fumes, or even the stresses placed upon families due to long or unsociable working hours. GDP figures do not reflect the full social and environmental costs of achieving economic growth. If they did, the figure would likely be much lower.

Perversely, the negative social and environmental impacts of economic activity can actually *add* to GDP! For instance, the clean up and repairs associated with oil spills or toxic dumping actually increase the overall level of economic activity, as do medical services and car repairs after a motor vehicle accident. All of these 'defensive expenditures' increase GDP even as our 'wellbeing' is reduced (Jacobs 1991).

This has led some to search for alternative measures. Nova Scotia introduced a Genuine Progress Index in 1997 and the Australia Institute has developed a similar Genuine Progress Indicator (Hamilton 1997). The Canadian Index of Wellbeing provides another approach (Michalos et al 2010). These different 'measures' consistently show that broader social progress has been considerably slower than the growth in GDP.

At an international level several alternative measures exist, most notably the United Nation's Human Development Index (HDI). This ranks the 'development' of countries based on three key indicators: life expectancy, education and purchasing power. It was developed by the United Nations to put people back in the centre of development policy and is used annually in the United Nations Human Development Reports (United Nations Development Programme 1990–2011) (see Box 3.1).

A recent innovation is the Organisation for Economic Co-operation and Development's (OECD) 'Better Life Initiative'. It ranks countries on several indicators, creating an index that allows people to choose their own priorities. For example, while the US has the second highest income per capita, it ranks 13th in opportunities for individual advancement and 29th on safety (OECD 2011).

## HOW DOES GROWTH OCCUR?

Classical political economists investigated the unique ability of the new industrial market economy to produce great wealth. Thinkers such as Adam Smith, David Ricardo and Karl Marx all explored how production worked and how it contributed to growth. Although they might disagree about the nature of the production process, or the fairness of economic distribution, most agreed growth itself was a good thing. Their ideas have since been incorporated into contemporary theories.

## The division of labour

Adam Smith explored how changes in the organisation of production created a division of labour that aided economic growth. At one level, there is division of labour between different firms. Markets facilitate trade, allowing firms to focus on production for sale. In turn, the proceeds are used to pay wages and profits that are then used by workers and employers to buy the goods and services they each need.

However, Smith also identified a division of labour within each firm (Smith 1904 [1776], ch 1–3). His famous example of the pin factory shows how tasks are divided up between workers. One will draw the wire, another will cut the wire and another will attach the pinheads, and so on. Instead of each worker performing all the tasks and producing a whole pin, an individual worker only ever produces a component of a pin.

Smith argues this specialisation of tasks increases productivity enormously. Workers become expert in their task and perform it more quickly. They do not need to waste time moving between tasks. Workers also become very familiar with the process they are engaged in and can therefore propose new and better ways of working. These ideas were later taken up by Henry Ford, founder of Ford motors, in his use of the assembly line, which divided the production process into a number of simple and repetitive tasks (see Chapters 7 and 8).

Smith's model of specialisation went hand in hand with the expansion of markets and trade. After all, without a growing market, who would buy all the new products? And without a growing pool of urban workers, who would work in the factories and mines? Using improved techniques to produce and supply greater quantities of goods only made sense if there was sufficient demand for such goods. Smith recognised this link when he claimed that 'the division of labour was limited by the extent of the market' (1904 [1776], chapter 3). As people left the land and entered the labour market, so the division of labour and the economy would expand.

## Theories of trade

Extending the idea of the division of labour and building on the theme of market expansion, Smith and other classical theorists argued in favour of greater trade between nations. Just as the expansion of national markets encouraged the division of labour and growth, so the expansion of international markets also fuelled growth. Smith and Ricardo developed theories of international trade to show that if nations specialised (just like firms or workers), then total production would increase. Thus, one country might specialise in producing food, another in producing manufactured goods, and international trade would allow each to trade with the other.

Taking up Smith's earlier work, David Ricardo (1949 [1817]) developed the theory of 'comparative advantage', which has become the foundation of modern neoclassical trade theory. Ricardo argued that even when one country was more efficient at producing all types of goods than another, both could still benefit from trade. In these cases, a country should specialise in what it is relatively (or comparatively) best at producing.

The theory of comparative advantage suggests that what countries are good at producing is related to what economic resources – or 'factors of production' – are most abundant within their borders. Those with large numbers of workers will specialise in labour-intensive production while those with advanced machinery will specialise in capital-intensive production. However, this remains controversial. Nobel Prize laureate Wassily Leontief (1954), for example, demonstrated that the advanced capital-intensive economy of the US imported capital-intensive products and exported labour-intensive products. In this way, it moved in the opposite direction to the prediction of comparative advantage theory.

Michael Porter (1990) developed an alternative trade theory known as competitive advantage. This is where states deliberately develop particular industries. Underlying this theory is a presumption that some industries, such as high-tech manufacturing, are better than others. Strategic decisions made by governments, not market forces or resource abundance, determines a country's industry structure.

The more radical World Systems Theory argues the division of industries and trade between countries reflects the relative power of different nations. On this reading, international trade is not necessarily mutually beneficial, but can be exploitative (see Chapter 4).

## THE POLITICS OF MODELLING GROWTH

Early political economists recognised that economic growth requires investment and an increasing stock of capital. Thus, the benefits of specialisation could either be consumed now or could be used to expand future production, further increasing growth. A number of economists have attempted to model this process of growth through accumulation.

Ricardo assumed workers were a class destined to live at substinence level and that business owners were justified in keeping wages low to facilitate the availability of funds for reinvestment. Hence Ricardo was active in arguing against protective laws that benefited landowners by increasing the cost of basic foodstuffs like corn. Such policies retarded 'progress' because they increased costs in the form of wages and rent, reducing the profits available for reinvestment. Ricardo in particular thought that the 'parasitical' landowning class would be responsible for falling rates of profit.

Taking up Ricardo's ideas, Marx later developed a systematic account of the investment-production cycle but it was also one that challenged the political status quo. He provided an insightful economic analysis of growth which also supported the workers' movements seeking more appropriate rewards for their contribution to the production of economic surplus. In turn, the threat raised by Marx's analysis of capitalism generated counter developments. The emergent neoclassical school emphasised exchange, rather than production, and the 'efficiency', rather than injustice, of market allocation.

## SURPLUS OR EFFICIENCY?

Marx is the most influential theorist of the accumulation model of capitalism. His 'circuit of capital' explains how production generates a surplus. The notion of a surplus focuses attention on how the system of production generates more value as output than it requires as input; this 'surplus' can then be re-invested to further expand production. The focus on the production process in the workplace (within factories, fields and offices) contrasts to the neoclassical model we discuss below which centres on exchange in the marketplace.

### The process of capital accumulation

Marx was one of the first theorists to systematically analyse the growth capacities of capitalism. He described the capitalist 'mode of production' as a system of 'expanded reproduction' whereby in any given period the system's capacity for production expands beyond the previous period. Marx (1992 [1884], pp. 109–43) modelled this expansion through the 'circuit of capital', where capital accumulation can be followed step by step through three phases or 'movements' that start with money (M) and end with more money (M'): $M - C \ldots P \ldots C' - M'$.

While the circuit of capital accumulation may look like a mathematical formula, it is just a shorthand way of explaining a process that is common to all capitalist enterprise (see Box 3.2). Money (M) is advanced to purchase the inputs (C) needed for the production (P) of commodities

## Box 3.2 Movements in the circuit of capital

M − C (L, mp) ... P ... C′ − M′

Stage 1 M − C (L, mp): In the first movement capitalists start with money (M) and they invest in commodities (C). These commodities take two forms – the means of production (mp), which includes the factory, machinery and the raw materials needed to produce the end product, and the labour power (L) embodied in workers. For this movement to be successful, businesses need to be able to buy the commodities they need at a competitive price.

Stage 2 C...P...C′: The second movement is where production actually takes place. Here one set of commodities (C) is transformed into another set of final goods (C′) through a production process (P) – such as when a juicer, oranges and the labour of a cafe worker combine to produce orange juice. Marx argues that new value is only created in the process of production. The value of the final goods is greater than all the inputs combined. This new value is 'surplus value', and Marx argues it comes from the ability of labour to add new value. The more value created compared to the costs of production, the higher the potential for accumulation. This movement will only be successful if production can run smoothly, and disruptions, such as those caused by strikes or the breakdown of machinery, are avoided.

Stage 3 C′ − M′: The third movement involves selling the final goods in the market. This allows the capitalist to realise the surplus value that has been created as profit. This means the business is able to sell the final commodities (C′) for more money (M′) than they started with. This can only happen if production has gone smoothly *and* there is a market in which to sell goods. If consumers are not willing or are not able to spend (as sometimes happens in a recession), then the circuit of capital will breakdown, even if new value and commodities have already been created.

(C') for sale (M'). At the completion of the circuit, accumulation occurs if the business reinvests the money into new production, starting the process again. This highlights the ongoing and constantly expanding nature of capitalist production. However, some of the surplus might not be reinvested. For example some might be used to increase the consumption of business owners now or might be taken by the government in taxes. The more of the surplus that is reinvested, and the quicker it is reinvested, the faster the process of accumulation and economic growth.

There are several important preconditions for the successful completion of the circuit. Social reproduction in the form of families and communities is needed to produce well-trained and socially integrated workers willing to work (see Chapter 8). Ecological reproduction is required to provide raw materials and an environment for absorbing wastes (see Chapter 9). A stable system of money is needed to facilitate exchange and investment. And political institutions are required to give the whole process legitimacy, so that people accept the system and work with it, not against it.

At the heart of the surplus model are workers. This is evident in the 'labour theory of value' proposed by classical political economists like Marx, Smith and Ricardo (see Chapter 2). This theory was an important part of Marx's analysis of capitalism and his critique of classical political economy. He argued that successful accumulation was dependent upon workers producing more value than was returned to them in wages. The employment relationship means that business owners retain the new value created in production. They appropriate the 'surplus value' to pay rent and interest and to draw profit, giving them the choice to consume or reinvest in expanded production.

In emphasising the role of increasing value in production as the source of capital accumulation, Marx rejected earlier ideas about wealth as a 'zero sum game'. Neither plunder nor 'buying cheap and selling dear' explained the distinctive tendency to economic growth of capitalism. Trade or market exchange, he argued, did not change the nature or quantity of goods, it simply changed the pattern of ownership. By itself, exchange could not create value, it could only see winners gain at the expense of losers. While trade had long existed, the growth produced by capitalism was new and new theories were therefore required to explain it. Yet it was to the sphere of exchange that neoclassical economists turned to develop their own economic analysis.

## The neoclassical 'efficient' market

In the late nineteenth century economists increasingly turned away from the classical focus on production and the labour theory of value. Neoclassical economics focused attention on the sphere of exchange, the markets where goods and services are bought and sold. As introduced in Chapter 2, the neoclassical approach analyses the interplay of supply and demand under competitive market conditions. It emphasises the efficiency of markets in allocating scarce resources to their most useful end.

Following Lionel Robbins (1945 [1932]), neoclassicism rejects materialist definitions of economics. Instead of focusing on how value is produced, it focuses on how choices are made. Robbins claimed the main concern of economics was not increasing wealth, but dealing with scarcity. He (1945 [1932], p. 32) argued economics is 'the science which studies human behaviour as a relationship between ends and scarce means which have alternative uses'. This focuses on the process of choosing how resources are used. It is a process whereby resources are allocated to different people and different purposes.

This reflects a *subjective* view of value where commodities are valuable because people desire them and this is expressed in their willingness to pay. Thus, reallocating commodities through markets to those who value them most can increase value, even though the objective properties of the commodities do not change.

The neoclassical focus on allocation through markets, rather than production in the workplace, emphasises equilibrium, the point where supply and demand intersect. It explains how ownership patterns change – how firms or individuals buy the things they want most and sell those things they want less. Prices ensure that goods and services go to those willing to pay most for them. The tools of equilibrium analyse particular points in time rather than processes of change. Mathematically this is done through comparative statics, where different outcomes are compared.

Such neoclassical models have been influential in promoting measures that expand the role of markets in the economy, such as by privatising government-owned enterprises or removing taxes on trade. Comparative statics are used to argue that the allocation of resources after such reforms is superior to the allocation prior to reform because resources are allocated to people who value them most.

The tools of neoclassical economics are best suited to 'micro economics', the understanding of individual markets. During the twentieth century an important project within neoclassical economics was to extend this microanalysis to the economy as a whole, through general equilibrium theory. Leading economists attempted to prove that the equilibrium for each individual market (such as the market for wood or coal) coincided with a general (or economy-wide) equilibrium for all markets.

The project sought to demonstrate that markets left unimpeded by government intervention could deliver stable and desirable outcomes. It also sought to develop mathematical models that could be used to predict future economic outcomes. While many of these models remain useful for certain purposes and are widely used, more recent work has called the general equilibrium project into question (Ackerman 2002).

Concepts of increasing investment and capital accumulation were incorporated into the neoclassical research agenda by economists inspired by Keynes (see later in this chapter). Roy Harrod (1939) and Evsey Domar (1946) independently developed models that linked increases in the stock of capital (accumulation) to the rate of economic growth. Robert Solow (1956) expanded on this, incorporating improvements in technology as a separate variable.

However, these are 'exogenous' growth models. The drivers of growth are exogenous to (outside of) the model itself. The Solow model uses an equation to relate changes in savings and investment or technological innovation to growth rates. But the model does not explain why people save or invest, nor how technology improves. Instead, this is assumed to happen at a constant rate, determined by social, technical or political forces outside the economy.

These models have distinct strengths and weaknesses. By reducing complex processes to a few variables they are better suited to mathematical methods and can produce predictions of future economic behaviour. But they often fail to explain how economic, social and political factors interconnect. They also often explain complex processes through relatively simple means, thus obscuring other more complex processes.

## OTHER CONTRIBUTIONS TO UNDERSTANDING GROWTH

Criticisms of exogenous growth theory led neoclassical economists to develop 'new growth' models during the 1980s and 1990s. These models sought to explain growth endogenously – within the model rather than relying on changes in external variables that were not formally part of the model. Key to the new endogenous growth models is a focus on education and knowledge.

In the 1960s, Nobel Prize laureate Gary Becker focused attention on education with his theory of 'human capital'. Becker (1993 [1964]) argued that the skills and knowledge of workers contributes to productivity growth, helping to explain long-run growth in the United States.

Paul Romer (1986; 1990) and other new growth theorists added to this debate. Traditional growth theories are based on the principle of decreasing marginal returns. This means that as a producer uses more of a factor of production, the increase in output diminishes. If a firm employs more workers with the same machinery, then the output *per worker* will fall (although total production may rise). However, Romer argued that the opposite is true with knowledge. As new knowledge is generated, it interacts with existing knowledge, creating even greater productivity. This goes beyond simple economics. Romer argues that the culture of the economy can be conducive to knowledge creation, with institutions developing over time that encourage people to develop new ideas and new technologies.

Some critics argue the theory does not go far enough. Despite dealing with the issues of increasing returns for knowledge, the theory does not acknowledge how increasing returns may apply more broadly throughout the economy (see Arthur 1994). Although the new growth theory improves on traditional neoclassical models, it retains many of the same elements. It is heavily reliant on abstract mathematics making it difficult to capture the complexity of historical dynamics.

### Institutional perspectives

Other developments within economics have done more to integrate the economic and social dimensions of life. One closely linked to the development of new growth theory is the New Institutional Economics (NIE), mentioned in Chapter 2. Its approach seeks to understand the complex role of institutions – such as corporations and bureaucracies as well as laws and social norms – in shaping economic life.

In a similar way to Romer, NIE theorist Douglass North (1990) argues that growth is influenced by long-term social and cultural traditions. These traditions can enable free exchange or can lead to corruption and nepotism. Elinor Ostrom (1990) has shown how some economic problems can be solved by particular cultural traditions that promote cooperation. These theories also help us understand why some regions may struggle to grow over time (also see Chapter 4).

Another strand of NIE builds on the work of Austrian economists, particularly Joseph Schumpeter. Schumpeter's *Capitalism, Socialism and Democracy* (1943), rejects perfect competition, noting that many markets have few competing firms. But he argued monopoly could benefit the economy by increasing the scale of production. Instead of price competition, he emphasised competition in technical and organisational innovation. This contributes to growth because new inventions and the discovery of new ways of doing things leads to the production of new, or more, commodities at potentially lower prices.

Schumpeter argued that because capitalism depends on this process, it exists in a state of ongoing 'creative destruction'. Production technologies have a life cycle. They are superseded (destruction) by new (creative) innovations driven by competition. As time passes, firms that once revolutionised and dominated new industries see their profits and their dominance decline as competitors introduce new technologies or methods that make existing ones redundant. On this view, markets might be chaotic, but this is a strength.

Marxist theorists have also looked to institutions and social structures. The French *regulation* school (better translated as 'regularisation' (Jessop 1997) in English) argues that long periods of sustained economic growth arise because capital accumulation is facilitated by supportive institutions. These structures 'regularise' the accumulation process. They take time to establish and are the product of experimentation, negotiation and conflict resulting in institutional compromises.

The concepts of 'social structures of accumulation' (Kotz, McDonough & Reich 1994), 'regimes of accumulation' and 'modes of regulation' (Boyer & Saillard 1995) were developed to describe such regularising institutions. Emerging out of earlier Marxist theory, these approaches focus on how the interests of different social groups are reconciled over time, but also on how conflicts and contradictions within the supportive social structures can cause markets and production to break down. Thus, it combines a focus on increased production with the possibility of crisis. There can also be quite distinctive variations in the national contexts for growth (see Box 3.3).

### Box 3.3 Miracle growth and the 'Asian tigers'

From the 1970s a group of Asian countries rapidly industrialised, achieving high and consistent growth. Four of these 'Asian tiger' economies – South Korea, Taiwan, Singapore and Hong Kong – became the centre of an economic debate about which policies encouraged economic development (see Haggard 2004).

All four countries pursued export-orientated growth strategies. That is, they increased exports to help stimulate growth, rather than focusing on industries for the domestic market. Each specialised in a particular area – Singapore and Hong Kong in finance, South Korea and Taiwan in information technology. Reflecting the theory of comparative advantage, a World Bank (1987) report suggested that this more open trade stance might be responsible for a country's economic success.

Others argued the story was more complex. South Korea, for example, had strong industry polices whereby the government worked closely with large corporations and directed investment through control of the finance sector (see Wade 1990). This account is closer to Porter's (1990) theory of competitive advantage, emphasising that such advantage is consciously created, not an innate result of market processes. Industry policies also ensured a high rate of saving and investment, leading to a rapid expansion in industrial production – something that fits well with the surplus model.

Others claimed growth was promoted by cultural factors. In Asia this was associated with a 'Confucian ethic' (see Fukuyama 1995). In early capitalist Europe, Weber claimed it was due to a 'Protestant work ethic'. Both promoted a savings culture. East Asian countries played an important geopolitical role during the Cold War. All effectively bordered communist governments in Indo-China, and so were often granted preferential trade access by the West to support their development.

More recently, other Asian economies have had mixed experiences. The Asian financial crisis of the late 1990s dramatically increased poverty in countries like Indonesia (Krugman 1999). Malaysia argued that it survived the crisis by keeping greater government controls on investment. Now China and India are the next 'tiger' economies, but on a much larger scale. The experiences of the earlier Asian tigers may help us understand these new growth economies (see also Chapter 5).

## CRISES AND ECONOMIC GROWTH

The flipside of economic growth is economic crisis. Understanding the failure of the economic system to consistently and continuously increase production is a vital concern. Sometimes growth fails and economies shrink rather than expand. The history of capitalism is one of long periods of economic expansion, followed by often somewhat shorter periods of economic contraction. This regular pattern of economic expansion and contraction is generally referred to as the 'business cycle'. Periodically, more dramatic disruptions occur in the form of severe recessions or depressions.

The surplus model helps us think through some of the reasons for recession. At each stage of the circuit of capital things could go wrong. For example, interest rates may be high, raw materials may not be available, workers may strike or consumers may not spend (see Heilbroner 1978). The circuit of capital also highlights a key implication of recession. If businesses do not think they will make a profit, then they will not invest in the first place, and that means workers lose their jobs. Unemployment is one of the most important and socially harmful aspects of recession.

Sometimes periods of economic downturn are so severe they threaten the very foundations of the capitalist system. Growth remains negative or stagnant. Traditional methods of regulating the economy no longer seem to work. A combination of unemployment and low business confidence leads to a vicious cycle of economic contraction from which it seems difficult to break out. Such periods are often characterised as economic crises. Examples of economic crises include the Great Depression of the 1930s, the stagflation of the 1970s and for much of Europe and the US, the Global Financial Crisis (GFC) beginning in 2007.

## THEORISING CRISIS

There is considerable debate within economics over the nature of economic crisis. The neoclassical focus on equilibrium tends to emphasise the stability of markets. As economic conditions change, prices gradually adjust to ensure supply and demand remain in equilibrium. The tools of comparative statics suggest that markets will ensure all resources are employed efficiently.

As with theories of growth, the tools of neoclassical economics tend to produce exogenous theories of crisis – identifying the causes of crisis outside of the market economy. For example, neoclassical pioneer William Jevons argued in 1875 that recessions could be traced to the existence of sunspots which reduced the yield of agricultural production, driving up the price of basic staples, which had a flow-on effect through the rest of the economy (in Heilbroner 1980, p. 260).

Another well-known exogenous explanation of crises is Milton and Rose Friedmans's (1980, pp. 95–117) claim that the Great Depression, which began in 1929 and lasted well into the 1930s, was the product of state intervention by the US Federal Reserve System in the supply of money. Similarly, some claim that the GFC was caused by too much government regulation of the financial sector leading to irresponsible lending and the development of 'sub-prime' loans (Wallison 2009).

## Uncertainty

Most social scientists agree that crisis can be the result of exogenous factors, like natural disasters, wars or poor government policy. But other economic traditions differ from neoclassical economics in also identifying endogenous sources of crisis. They see systemic factors producing instability that is likely to lead to periodic downturns in economic growth and high unemployment. One source of endogenous crisis is uncertainty due to the time taken in production. Another is conflict stemming from people having different economic interests.

Two of the most significant theories of endogenous crisis come from the Keynesian and Marxist traditions. Both conceive of capitalist economies in ways that directly challenge the neoclassical notion of markets as harmonious coordination mechanisms. These approaches have influenced economic theory and, as discussed in Section 2, also the development of economic institutions.

The Keynesian tradition is inspired by the work of English economist John Maynard Keynes. Following the Great Depression, Keynes (1965 [1936]) wrote *The General Theory of Employment, Interest and Money*, arguing there was no reason to suppose that capitalist markets would tend towards the full employment of resources, whether labour or capital.

This argument directly challenged the neoclassical theory of efficient allocation which implicitly assumes that at equilibrium all available resources will be used, including the employment of all workers. Instead, Keynes argued that the operation of the labour market could produce ongoing unemployment even at 'equilibrium' (see Box 3.4). The labour market was not, therefore, inherently 'efficient'.

**Box 3.4 Wages and the labour market**

A crucial difference between neoclassical and Keynesian economics is their approach to the labour market, particularly the level of wages. For neoclassical economics, the labour market is just like any other market. Competition and the forces of supply and demand determine both the price of labour (the wage) and the quantity of labour (the level of employment).

On this neoclassical view, unemployment is likely to result from excess supply. As with other markets, this is corrected by allowing the price to fall, bringing supply and demand back into equilibrium. For the labour market, this means allowing wages to fall, thus increasing the number of workers employers are willing to hire, and potentially decreasing the number of people willing to work. Regulations that set a floor – like minimum wage legislation – can thus generate unemployment.

Keynesians disagree with this analysis. They argue that the labour market is a special kind of market. Unlike other commodities, labour is a factor of production and the price of labour (the wage) is also the main source of income for the majority of people in the economy. Wages therefore cannot fall below the level needed for subsistence. Keynes's argument has some similarities to Polanyi's (2001 [1944]) claim that labour is a 'fictitious commodity', because it is not produced in markets and therefore requires protective laws that are not necessary for other commodities.

Keynes's argument has implications for the relationship between individual economic agents and the economy as a whole. He argued that for the individual business owner, lowering wages was rational. This would lower their costs of production and thereby lower the price of goods. If demand was stable, this would allow the business to sell more of its product.

However, if all businesses lowered wages, this would lower the incomes of all workers and thereby reduce demand throughout the economy, making it *harder* to sell their products. The result would be further job cuts or wage reductions. This analysis supports economy-wide regulation of wages, sometimes called 'incomes policy' (also see Chapter 5).

Beyond the specific problems of labour market analysis, Keynes also identified the importance of uncertainty in economic life. Uncertainty here means more than risk. It suggests we simply do not know what the future holds. Keynes writes:

> By 'uncertain' knowledge... I do not mean merely to distinguish what is known for certain from what is only probable. The game of roulette is not subject, in this sense, to uncertainty... The sense in which I am using the term is that in which the prospect of a European war is uncertain, or the price of copper and the rate of interest twenty years hence... About these matters there is no scientific basis on which to form any calculable probability whatever. We simply do not know.
> (Keynes 1937, pp. 213–14)

If future economic conditions are uncertain, then prices cannot signal correct information about those future conditions. Instead prices signal the expectations of buyers and sellers. Such expectations are based on prevailing conditions, opinions and trends. Keynes argued that expectations were often the result of 'animal spirits' and group dynamics that led to both irrational exuberance and then panic. Unsurprisingly, this analysis has been revived since the GFC (see Akerlof & Shiller 2009).

For Keynes, the implications are profound. Expectations are volatile. Uncertainty, and the importance of trust, means that confidence can quickly disappear and so prices and markets can also be volatile. As with the labour market, Keynes believed this volatility was not solved by the equilibrating forces of the market.

If expectations are very low, firms may not expect to sell their products, and will not invest or hire workers. If this is widespread, incomes will fall, leading to precisely the outcome businesses feared. Keynes observed this 'self-fulfilling prophecy' at work in the Depression of the 1930s. Because of the interaction of expectations, production and demand, low or negative growth and high unemployment could be self-sustaining, with no mechanism to ensure growth returned.

## Conflict

Writing in the nineteenth century, Karl Marx developed an even more critical explanation of how capitalism is prone to economic crises. Marx identified the importance of imbalances between production and consumption. However, Marx differed from Keynes by seeing such imbalances not only as the result of complexity and uncertainty but also contradictions and conflicts between social groups within capitalism.

Marx argued that the very forces that drive capital accumulation and enable enormous increases in productive capacity under capitalism also produce economic crises. Two key sources of conflict are between workers and employers and between different businesses. In both cases this reflects conflict between different groups in the economy with different interests.

The imperative of capitalists to increase profits through the surplus value generated by workers can lead businesses to reduce wages. However, if wages are too low, then workers will not be able to purchase enough commodities for capitalists to clear their inventories. The result is a crisis of 'underconsumption' or 'overproduction' (Fine & Saad-Filho 2004, p. 93). This is similar to the macro economic approach of Keynes, seeing tensions between the behaviour of individual businesses and the outcome for the economy as a whole.

Marx argues when business is booming, capitalists will take on more workers. This can bid up wages, reducing profits. As a result, businesses may use machinery to replace workers, increasing unemployment and decreasing wages. But Marx was sceptical as to whether this process could work in the long term. His labour theory of value suggests that machines, unlike labour, cannot generate new value. He argued, controversially, that increasing mechanisation could lead to a falling rate of profit (Fine & Saad-Filho 2004, p. 95).

Because Marx focuses on conflict between social groups, he also identifies the importance of strategic action. The relative negotiating power of workers and employers is clearly influenced by their alternative options. Unemployment, Marx argued, could discipline workers and keep wages low because it presented an undesirable alternative to low-paid work. Marx (1976 [1867], ch 25) called the unemployed the 'reserve army' of labour, because employers could use the unemployed to replace recalcitrant workers.

This idea is similar to the efficiency wages hypothesis of conventional economics. This theory suggests that employers will often pay workers more than the equilibrium wage needed for full employment. Higher wages encourage greater work effort, but also produce unemployment. However, unemployment may be beneficial for employers because it reduces the chances that workers will shirk by increasing the cost of losing their job (Shapiro & Stiglitz 1984).

Similarly, different business sectors may have different priorities and these can also come into conflict. A boom in one sector of the economy may lead to more production goods (such as heavy machinery) but demand for final consumer goods may not justify this expansion. Because production takes time this may not be clear until too late, causing a crisis of 'disproportionality' (Fine & Saad-Filho 2004, pp. 92–3).

In each of these cases Marx highlights that the economy is rife with conflict, which is heightened at times of economic distress. People have different interests and they use every means to gain an advantage over rivals. Competition might fuel the engines of growth but it also leads to instability.

### Limits to growth

Another potential source of crisis comes from the interaction of the economy and the natural environment. Increased production within the economy relies on ecological reproduction of the conditions in which growth occurs. The environment provides important inputs into production, acts as a sink for various waste products and supports life through the operation of the biosphere. These environmental functions can be compromised. For example, the nuclear accident at Chernobyl in the former USSR contaminated much of northern Europe, while the recent oil spill in the Gulf of Mexico wiped out whole industries. However, there is also the possibility of broader global ecological crisis.

In 1972, *The Limits to Growth* (Meadows et al 1972) raised awareness of the ecological limits to natural resource use, which have since been echoed in numerous United Nations reports (for example, WCED 1987). While some aspects of the environment can be renewed, others, like fossil fuels, are finite or have limited regenerating capacities. Some argue the 'earth's billion-year-old sustainable support system' itself has been breached (Brown 1998, p. 270).

Economic concerns have been raised about the limited supply of some important economic inputs. Many claim 'peak oil', the point at which oil production can no longer be expanded, will lead to higher energy costs and potential crisis. Economists have also raised the potentially devastating costs of changes in the earth's climate caused by economic activity, particularly the burning of fossil fuels for energy. This has led to calls for radical changes to the economy to prevent a growing crisis (Stern 2006).

Some theorists argue that indefinite economic growth is fundamentally incompatible with a finite ecology (Trainer 2002, pp. 167–75). Others emphasise *qualitative* growth (or increased quality of life rather than increased quantities of GDP) under conditions of ecological protection (Daly & Townsend 1993). We discuss the crucial role of the environment in reproducing the conditions for economic life in Chapter 9.

Many environmental theorists are also critical of the impact of sustained economic growth on social relationships. The rise of a consumer society, where people's identity is increasingly linked to the products they buy, is clearly related to the remarkable increase in economic production (see Chapter 8).

The global nature of environmental challenges like peak oil and climate change highlights the need for international cooperation. This was acknowledged by the watershed United Nations World Commission on Environment and Development in its 'Brundtland' report (1987), and is the basis of international agreements over fishing, climate change and the use of damaging chlorofluorocarbons. Ulrich Beck and Anthony Giddens (see Beck, Giddens & Lash 1994) argue the global nature of environmental challenges and the uncertainty of environmental outcomes reflects a new type of problem unique to 'late modernity'.

This periodisation suggests the process of 'rationalisation' associated with 'modernity' has deepened with even greater emphasis on measurement, control and prediction to manage risk. However, the nature of the risks faced has changed requiring greater attention on the future and managing its uncertainty. The environment is an archetypal example of what Beck (1992 [1986]) calls the 'risk society' where risks that result from the complex interactions of human systems replace 'natural' disasters as a key challenge facing humanity.

## THE POLITICS OF CRISIS, GROWTH AND LEGITIMACY

Reactions to crises reveal how economic growth also serves important political purposes. The affluence brought by economic growth is one of the most powerful justifications for organising society according to market principles. Alternatively, when growth fails it generates unemployment, poverty and hardship. Because so many people's livelihoods are tied directly to the fortunes of markets, an economic crisis can also generate political crisis.

Past economic crises have generated significant political and social unrest. The Great Depression of the 1930s was a key factor in the rise of fascism in Germany and the success of the Nazi Party. In Australia the Depression of the 1890s gave birth to the Australian Labor Party and through it to significant social and economic reform. Alternatively, market advocates claimed that stagnation during the 1970s was due to excessive government 'interference' in markets and this justified significant economic reforms that sought to limit the size of the state.

Clearly, the health of the economy has implications for the popularity of governments. In many liberal democracies 'economic management' is an important election issue. However, political sociologists have identified the economy also plays a broader role in establishing *political legitimacy*. Legitimacy goes beyond the popularity of the government of the day, instead referring to the acceptance of political institutions themselves.

Max Weber was one of the first to explicitly discuss this sense of legitimacy. In *Economy and Society* (1978 [1922]) he argued that legitimacy was necessary to achieve predictability and order. Neither self-interest, nor social norms were enough to ensure order, he suggested. Rather, it was important that people accepted the right of leaders to govern.

Weber identified three sources of legitimacy: tradition, where people accept the system because of its history; charismatic leadership, where people see a leader as possessing extraordinary properties; and rational–legal authority, where people accept leadership because it flows from following agreed rules, such as a constitution. It was this final source of legitimacy that he saw as most common to rationalised, market societies.

Alternatively, many political philosophers have identified legitimacy with normative claims about the just use of power. They see governments as being legitimate because their authority comes from just processes – such as democratic election – or because they uphold individual liberties through the rule of law.

A more critical approach comes from the tradition of 'conflict' models of legitimacy (Zeldich 2001). Critical theorists such as Marx, and some other political theorists such as Machiavelli (1969 [1640]), believed that the interests of rulers conflicted with the ruled. Overt use of power by itself was costly and unsustainable and so myths or ideologies that justified the system as 'right' were also necessary. Other critical theorists have developed variations on this account, emphasising the role of ideology in maintaining market society (see Chapter 10).

Many social scientists see the success of political institutions as tied to the success of the economy (O'Connor 1973). Economic growth not only provides employment, it can also generate tax revenues that can be used to address other claims about the fairness of market society by redistributing income. In this sense, growth has a political as well as an economic dimension.

## CONCLUSION

The nature of economic growth is central to understanding market society. Historically, growth has enabled increasing living standards and social and economic transformation. It remains an important conventional indicator of an economy's success. It is also central to the healthy operation of capitalist economies. Without growth, unemployment rises and crisis can result. We can understand growth as the effect of the division of labour and the competitive pressures of markets. But growth is also the product of accumulation, where value is produced and re-invested to expand production. All of this takes place in an historical and institutional context that can aid, or frustrate, the growth process, and it is supported by ecological and social processes of reproduction. This creates tensions when growth undermines the environment or social relationships. Historically, however, another source of tension has proven even more challenging – the struggle over distribution and the implications of inequality.

## Questions

1 How is growth measured and what implications does this have for promoting human wellbeing?
2 In what ways might the expansion of markets contribute to economic growth?
3 What are the key differences between the Marxist surplus approach to growth and the neoclassical efficiency approach?
4 In what ways might conflict and uncertainty contribute to economic crises?
5 What is the relationship between economic growth and political legitimacy?

# 4 Inequality, distribution and conflict

THE LAST TWO chapters have explored key aspects of economic production. The market system is built on the commodity form and markets act as a coordinating mechanism, allocating commodities for consumption and between different uses in production. This coordinating role of the market has also been extended to the factors of production – land, labour and capital – making them 'fictitious commodities' and thus creating a 'market society'. The market system has proven to be highly productive with accumulation expanding the range, quality and quantity of goods available. Material living standards have also been lifted for many people. This process sometimes breaks down, creating hardship during periods of economic recession. For some people, this hardship is a persistent feature of their everyday lives, even through periods of economic growth. This is because the proceeds of growth are unevenly distributed.

Analysing economic production is therefore only part of the story in understanding market society. Looking at economic distribution is also an important and necessary counterpart in understanding and evaluating a commodity-based system. Historically, inequality was an essential part of how market society was constituted and such societies continue to be marked by pronounced inequalities in the distribution of economic resources. In this chapter we explore the nature of inequality and how it is measured, as well as how the onset of capitalism changed the nature of inequalities. The resulting patterns of distribution have also been highly contested as the values of modernity inspired many people to challenge the fairness of market distributions. We therefore also examine the struggles over economic distribution because such conflicts have profoundly reshaped the evolving character of market societies.

## THE DISTRIBUTION OF ECONOMIC RESOURCES

Inequality is a central feature of market society. It is both an objective feature of capitalism as well as the basis of normative claims for its legitimacy. Inequality in the distribution of economic resources both provides the incentives for economic action and reflects the social relations of capitalism. Historically, the transition from feudalism to capitalism involved restructuring the patterns of inequality, ending some forms of inequality while entrenching or creating others. Economic disparities were reinforced by allowing markets to be responsible not only for the distribution of commodities but also of income and wealth. Today, unequal distribution persists but the levels of inequality vary significantly between and within different market societies.

## INEQUALITY IN MARKET SOCIETIES

Economic inequality is at one level simply an objective measure of how people differ in terms of the economic resources they have available to them. Yet, we often have strong views on whether inequalities are fair. Many economists argue that the distribution of income produced by markets *is* fair because it reflects the contributions different people make to the economy. This position is contested. Thus, understanding inequality requires attention not only to how resources *are* distributed but also to different perspectives on how resources *should* be distributed. The two questions are linked. How we measure inequality, what resources we include, who we compare and what time period we use are all influenced by our understanding of why inequality matters.

Traditionally, there have been two main measures of individual inequality (see Box 4.1). The first is income, which represents a *flow* of resources a person receives over time. The second is wealth, which represents the *stock* of resources owned. For economists, most interest has centred on income as the measure of inequality. This is partly because we have better data for income than we do for wealth but also because it tends to be a more accurate indicator of living standards. A person may have substantial assets – housing property, for example – but without a flow of income they will not have the means to meet even their basic needs.

## Box 4.1 Measuring inequality

Income is an indicator of our standard of living but like the measures of economic growth discussed in Chapter 3, caution is needed. This is because knowing a person's level of income does not tell us about other relevant circumstances. For example, parents of young children often have high costs and need more resources than older retirees to achieve the same standard of living. Furthermore, 'income' may only include monetary resources, thereby excluding other beneficial resources. Having access to the unpaid labour of a spouse, or to free public services, or to the shared resources of a household are all resources through which an individual's standard of living can be enhanced.

Because of these complexities, social scientists have developed different measures of income distribution. Some studies focus on the distribution of individual income while others focus on the distribution of household income. Usually these figures reflect an *equivilised* distribution of household income. This means the income is adjusted to reflect the needs of different households, both in terms of size (how many people) and composition (children versus adults).

Measures of inequality are usually determined by lining up all the households from poorest to richest. The level of inequality can then be expressed in different ways, such as comparing different groups or determining an overall degree of inequality. The first approach involves dividing the population into 10 even groups, each representing 10 per cent of the population. These groups are known as deciles. This division allows comparison between the groups, such as comparing the income gap between the top decile and the bottom decile.

The Gini coefficient, developed by Italian sociologist Corrado Gini, is another measure of inequality. It is a score between zero and one, where zero corresponds to complete equality (everyone has exactly the same income) and one corresponds to complete inequality (one person receives all income). The Gini coefficient is a useful way to compare inequality between countries or over time within a country. For example, the Organisation for Economic Cooperation and Development (OECD) used Gini coefficients to establish that income inequality increased in most rich countries from the 1980s and that large differences remain between countries (see OECD 2010, Table 1).

An individual's pattern of income is a product of their economic participation and the variability in the type and level of participation can give rise to extreme inequalities at the social level. Incomes derive from both earnings – the 'returns' to different factors of production – as well as the sale of various assets. For example, we can earn income from work in the form of wages and salaries, or by investing money and receiving profit or interest, or by leasing assets such as land and buildings for rent. We might also receive 'windfall' income through the sale of assets at a higher price than we originally paid. This is known as capital gains.

Our stock of wealth can also influence our income. Indeed, earnings from the returns on assets, such as share dividends or property rentals, might be so substantial that participation in the labour market is not required! Generally though, this situation is applicable to only a very small proportion of people in society. Many people receive transfer payments, such as government funded family assistance or income support when they are unable to work. The unemployed, especially those who experience frequent or long periods of unemployment, often struggle to meet their basic needs and are at the highest risk of living in poverty.

### The existence of poverty

Whereas inequality refers to situations where some people have more than others, poverty occurs where a person does not have the resources necessary to live even a basic life. Although many economists claim that some degree of inequality is useful, the persistence of poverty across the globe and within otherwise wealthy countries has attracted much more attention. There are two common conceptions of poverty – absolute and relative – which tend to be used in specific contexts.

The concept of *absolute poverty* is primarily used in poor and 'developing' countries where many people do not have access to clean water, food or shelter. The World Bank equates this 'extreme poverty' with a level of resources equivalent to approximately US$1.25 per day. The proportion of people living in this condition has been declining globally, from over 40 per cent in 1990 to 25 per cent in 2005 (World Bank 2008). However, the recent global financial crisis placed an additional 64 million people into extreme poverty (Habib et al 2010). In the rich 'developed' countries, absolute poverty is a less useful measure.

Instead, the concept of *relative poverty* is often used, which suggests that the resources necessary to live a basic life varies between countries and over time. Relative poverty refers to measures that attempt to identify those that are unable to live a basic life by the standards of their own society. In Australia a Royal Commission into poverty during the 1970s established a 'poverty line' based on the cost of a basic set of goods and services (Australian Government 1975). This is often called the Henderson Poverty Line. Another commonly used measure is the proportion of people receiving less than 50 per cent of the median (or the middle) income, suggesting their access to resources is comparatively low.

Some economists have criticised measures of relative poverty as being too similar to measures of inequality. They argue that if the incomes of the rich increase but the incomes of the poor do not decline (although this *has* happened in some countries) then the presence of such inequality should not be a cause for concern. Other evidence suggests that large inequalities in rich countries should be a concern because they increase forms of social dysfunction associated with poverty, such as poor physical and mental health (see Wilkinson & Pickett 2009). The persistence of inequality and poverty despite the significant wealth produced in capitalist economies draws attention to the political and historical processes that shape the distribution of economic resources, something we discuss later in the chapter.

## HOW CAPITALISM CHANGED INEQUALITY

The development of market society coincided with significant political and cultural changes that also provided the foundations for capitalist commodity production. The traditional inequalities and power relations of feudalism were challenged by the new Enlightenment ideas about individual liberty and equality. Where a person's rights, income and wealth were based on their rank or social class as inherited from their parents, market society provided an opportunity, at least in principle, for 'mobility' where individuals could improve their relative position in the income distribution.

A new system of individual rights, based on equality before the law, gave citizens the same legal entitlements. Property rights were introduced and the establishment of constitutional government ruled by parliament provided a framework for protecting them through the rule of law. The rise of this *political* equality alongside market economies was seen as a mutually compatible process by many Enlightenment thinkers. John Locke's (1967 [1689]) support for the English revolution of 1688 combined a defence of individual rights with a defence of private property. Later, John Stuart Mill (1970 [1869]) combined his advocacy of free markets with calls for female suffrage.

The early liberals believed protection of private property was central to individuals pursuing their interests and that market society allowed the free interaction of individuals, regardless of race, religion or (in the case of Mill) gender. The new market system seemed to signal the end of old social divisions and the colonial society of the United States was dubbed a 'land of opportunity' precisely because it was free of the class system of the 'old world' in England. It appeared to give all (white) people the opportunity to succeed. However, Native Americans and Africans transported through the slave trade, for example, were often brutally excluded.

Indeed, the development of market societies along Enlightenment lines was slow and uneven and in many cases is still incomplete. The modern conception of equality – that all people are created equal – initially applied only to white, relatively wealthy, male citizens. Only later did other social groups claim citizenship rights for themselves. Some examples of significant progress towards equality in some countries include the end of legalised slavery and formal segregation between different races, recognition of indigenous people's rights and women's right to vote and own property. Market societies are clearly associated with an important conception of equality but it is one that is limited to 'formal' equality.

This means that people are 'equal before the law' with the same legal and political rights, including the right to buy and sell and have their property protected. But this legal equality emphasises 'due process' rather than substantive outcomes. Different people have different substantive choices determined either by their capacity to earn money in the market or control accumulated (or inherited) wealth. As a result, individuals who have legal equality may not have the same substantive access to a 'good life' with health services or fulfilling employment, for example. Indeed, the presence of economic inequality is a perennial feature of market societies and was particularly notable during the period of capitalist industrialisation in the seventeenth and eighteenth centuries.

Two important reasons for this have been identified by economist Simon Kuznets (1955). First, those with the greatest wealth have higher rates of savings, which in turn allows them to accumulate more wealth. This created significant inequality because the majority of people lived a bare subsistence lifestyle (and did not have income support during periods of economic recession as is the case today). Second, capitalism promoted urbanisation and while cities have higher average incomes than rural areas, those incomes are both less equal and more volatile. Kuznets suggested the competitive conditions of rapidly evolving industries meant markets produced not only unequal but also unstable income distributions. The result was that some people became very rich while many others continued to live in grinding poverty.

Confronted by these circumstances popular movements extended their claims from legal equality to economic equality, often linking this to the Enlightenment value of individual liberty. However, the meaning of freedom itself is contested. Isaiah Berlin (1969) argued Enlightenment liberalism involved the idea of *negative* liberty, where people were able to pursue their own 'good life' because their property was protected from theft, fraud or violence. In contrast, the idea of *positive* liberty means that people would be given access to resources, such as healthcare, food and housing, to reduce uncertainty and allow their full participation in society. In practice, securing either of these liberties could mean violating the other (Berlin 1969). Our judgements about whether the inequalities produced by market distribution in capitalism are fair tend to be shaped by whether we value positive or negative liberty.

## Distribution through markets

The economic inequalities that developed with capitalism were not incidental to the rise of market society but were its direct by-product. Markets play a central role in determining the distribution of income. This is because the commodity production system incorporates the factors of production (land, labour and capital) into markets as (fictitious) commodities (Polanyi 1944) (see Chapter 2). Such commodification ensures that the distribution of income (rent, wages and profit) to landlords, workers and business owners follows the rules of market competition. In turn, the level of such income determines the capacity of market participants to satisfy their consumption needs and wants.

In practice, the distribution of economic resources is also regulated by laws governing safety, environmental standards and monopolistic practices, by social norms and community standards and by taxation and government spending. However, the Nobel laureate and well-known market advocate Milton Friedman (see Friedman & Friedman 1979) argues the competitive dynamics that drive efficiency in markets can only be achieved if markets are also allowed to determine the distribution of income. Market prices, he claims, serve two functions. They provide information about costs of production and consumer desires, allowing producers to more efficiently match resources to consumer demand. But they also provide incentives to act on this information, by rewarding those that act in accordance with the price signal. This second function can only be achieved if people's incomes reflect their participation in the market.

If businesses that are efficient are not rewarded with high profits or workers who are skilled and diligent are not rewarded with high wages then market incentives will not function. On this account, the unequal rewards offered by the market reflect the relative contributions of different people to production (see Box 4.2). Friedman acknowledges that this is the result of both *choice* and *chance*. People's employment, investment and education decisions impact on the rewards they receive, but people are also borne with differing capacities and resources and their choices can be affected by chance events. Nevertheless, Friedman claims, interfering too much with market allocations in an effort to correct the unfairness of chance threatens to undermine market incentives.

### Box 4.2 Value and inequality

In the previous chapters we discussed two important economic approaches that attempt to explain how price and value are set in a competitive economy. But the neoclassical and Marxian theories are not just about economic growth or prices; they also help to explain the distribution of income and to justify (or critique) the fairness of that distribution.

The neoclassical focus on the forces of supply and demand suggests that prices of consumer goods reflect the 'marginal' utility that consumers enjoy. Likewise, it argues that in production, workers, landowners and business proprietors receive incomes that reflect the 'marginal' productivity of their labour, land or capital (see Chapter 2, Box 2.2). Thus, the incomes earned seem justified because they are said to reflect the value of contributions to production.

Alternatively, the labour theory of value used in classical and Marxist economics, suggests that all value ultimately comes from labour. This provides the basis for a critique of market distribution because the incomes of landowners and business proprietors are not justified by their contributions but rather result from their control of important resources. This is particularly concerning because workers, who contribute the most effort, often receive the least return.

Because theories of value matter to our evaluation of inequality they have been the subject of significant debate and criticism. Many economists, starting with Eugen von Bohm-Bawerk (1949 [1896]), have rejected the labour theory of value on the basis of the 'transformation problem'. They demonstrate that outside very specific conditions, prices do not correspond to the value of labour embodied in them. Similarly, Joan Robinson, Piero Sraffa and others showed that the neoclassical theory of marginal productivity could not be sensibly applied to capital. Indeed, the 'Cambridge controversy' suggests profit cannot be understood as the marginal return to capital (Harcourt 1972).

Both neoclassical and Marxist economists have struggled to respond to these specific criticisms and although the debates are technical in nature, they have important implications. While these theories of value remain useful in highlighting important dynamics in how value and price are determined, neither provides an entirely convincing and complete account. This is unsurprising. Explaining value is complex, and related to both political and cultural factors, as much as economic ones.

More strongly, the libertarian Robert Nozick (1974) argues that market outcomes are the result of free and voluntary exchange and any attempt to redistribute them is a violation of justice. Such arguments against the state's role in redistribution have been supplemented by the sociologist Laurence Mead (1997) who suggests that government programs designed to help the disadvantaged often have perverse effects. They can reward bad behaviour – such as being disruptive at school or shirking at work – and over time create a 'culture of dependency' where government assistance is preferred to seeking greater rewards in the market. For Mead (1997), any government assistance should be conditional upon demonstration of 'desirable' behaviours. This paternalism supports the anti-redistribution arguments of neoliberalism which we discuss further in Chapter 5.

## CLASS AND INEQUALITY

In market societies, those who own significant business assets (capital) have higher average incomes than those who derive most of their income from wages. Those with high levels of formal education tend to earn more than those without formal education. While capitalism makes it possible for people to move up (or down) the economic hierarchy, amongst the developed market economies those with the least equitable distribution of income have the least social mobility (Andrews & Leigh 2009). This suggests that allowing markets to distribute income unevenly can entrench advantage and disadvantage. While the neoclassical approach to inequality focuses attention on individuals and the incomes they receive from the market, other theoretical traditions have focused on the inequality between different social groups. Historically, a new language of 'class' developed to explain the patterned inequalities evident in the unequal distribution of society's resources.

## THEORISING CLASS

Class was a prominent feature in the work of the early political economists such as Adam Smith, David Ricardo and John Stuart Mill. They understood the functioning of the capitalist economy in terms of the interactions between three different 'classes' or 'constituent orders'. Each class was defined by its role in the production process stemming from the resources it controlled. The class of capitalists owned the means of production and received income in the form of profit (or interest if lending money for investment). The labouring classes who performed the work associated with producing commodities received wages. Landlords received rent for the use of the physical space (the land and buildings) in which production took place.

Class was important to the classical political economists for two reasons. First, the changing income levels of the different classes reflected the changing stock of funds available for economic activities such as consumption and investment in expanding productive capacity. The levels of wages, profit and rent all had implications for economic growth and the wellbeing of society. Second, because each class received a different form of income, they had different interests. Landlords had an interest in raising the level of rent, which would be at the expense of profits. Capitalists had an interest in increasing their profits, and one way to do this was through lowering wages. Yet workers had an interest in maintaining, if not increasing, their wages which tended to be at mere subsistence level throughout the classical period.

Adam Smith (1904 [1776]) argued that the different interests of each class would lead members of the same class to join forces, or 'combine', either to get favourable treatment from government or to enforce their interests on members of another class. For example, according to Ricardo, landlords derived benefit from the 'corn laws' which put a tariff (tax) on foods imported to Britain. This boosted the rents of local landowners while reducing the profits of capitalists who had to pay higher wages to workers so they could meet their increased food costs. The theme of 'conflict' was taken further by Karl Marx who famously used the concept of class to analyse the systematic inequalities present in industrial capitalism.

## The Marxian account of class

Marx used the concept of class to explain the structure and evolution of economic organisation in different social systems. Slave, feudal and capitalist societies all reflected specific social relations around which the economic process was organised. In each of these systems, Marx suggested, the economic surplus required for the reproduction of society was produced by one class but appropriated by another. This created tensions and conflict that would ultimately lead to social change. Acknowledging the unfairness present in feudal or slave societies is relatively uncontroversial. However, the bondage of such societies is not apparent in capitalism where people's freedom and equal legal status is protected in law and an 'impersonal' market mechanism determines the distribution of income.

For Marx, though, the private ownership of society's productive resources ensured that the new legal equality remained a class-based system where the majority of people were forced into waged labour. In contrast to the distinctions between slaves and their owners, or serfs and their lords, Marx argued that capitalism produced classes based on legal entitlements to resources. The 'bourgeoisie' (capitalist class) owned the means of production such as factories, machines, tools and raw material inputs. They also have rights of legal ownership over the outputs of production (the finished commodities) and the proceeds from their sale. This provides the owners of capital with income which they can use to reinvest, continuously expanding their incomes and accumulating wealth.

Members of the 'proletariat' (working class), on the other hand, do not own productive property. In order to survive, they must enter the exploitative conditions of waged labour by selling the one input of the production process they own: their labour power or capacity to work (Marx & Engels 1977 [1848]). For Marx, production reflects a process of 'exploitation' whereby workers create *surplus value*, that is, value (in the form of commodities) greater than that returned to them in wages. 'Exploitation' is a technical term describing the process of surplus value creation and appropriation (Wright 2009) but it also has moral connotations. For some, it suggests the higher incomes of wealthy business owners were illegitimate when wage earners barely had enough income to survive.

While capitalists have an interest in keeping wages low and generating as much surplus value as possible to enhance profit, workers have their own interests. These include having enough time to spend with their families, ensuring a safe and healthy work environment and increasing their wages to purchase commodities. Because of these opposing interests, Marx claimed, the class relationship is antagonistic. Workers and capitalists are mutually dependent on each other for their existence yet will struggle over workplace organisation, the nature of working conditions and the wage rate.

As capitalism expands through periods of growth and crisis, concentrating wealth in fewer hands and increasing inequalities, class conflict would intensify. Marx suggested this may create the basis for a new socialist economy (Marx 1976 [1867]). While this emancipatory aspect of Marx's work is controversial, even his critics acknowledged the working class was growing (numerically and politically) during the nineteenth century.

Hence, there are two dimensions of 'class' associated with Marx. The economic or 'objective' definition of class as the relationship one shares with others to the means of production. This category is central to Marx's analysis of the logic of capital accumulation. The 'subjective' dimension of class is political in character. It manifests when wage labourers develop an awareness of themselves and their own power as a class and then organise themselves politically. When this occurs a 'class for itself' is formed where previously only 'a class in relation to capital' existed (Marx 1963 [1847]). The success of worker movements in the late nineteenth and early twentieth century reflects such awareness and subsequent organisation (see Thompson 1980).

### The weberian account of class

German sociologist Max Weber developed an account of class for the context of the early twentieth century. He viewed economic classes as important structural features of capitalism but he disagreed with Marx about their significance in people's lives. Weber thought that other social groupings were also important signifiers of individual identity in modern market societies and that ultimately these may be more important than economic class for understanding people's attitudes, behaviours and affiliations.

For Weber, like Marx, class was relational (Wright 1997). Those who owned productive property or had technical skills enjoyed greater 'life chances' than those who did not. Similarly, other attributes such as education or membership of a profession also give people an advantage in the economy. Moreover, the privileged classes could only maintain their position by excluding others. Such exclusion occurred through, for example, the legal system, which protected private property ownership and through standards and quota systems for entry into educated professions. For this reason, Weber's approach has been referred to as an 'opportunity hoarding approach' (Wright 2009).

Despite some similarities in their analyses, Weber differed from Marx in his view of class conflict and class behaviour. He argued that while class antagonisms could occur, they need not be a necessary feature of capitalism. Furthermore, it was not possible to infer the objective interests or consciousness of individuals from their economic class position. In this context, Weber distinguished between classes and the more subjective nature of 'groups'. Where classes were given by the distribution of property and conditioned life chances, groups were formed deliberately by people and helped to structure social action, including conflict.

For Weber, 'status' – the identification with others based on a particular 'style of life' – was the most important factor that led to group formation. The important point about 'status' is that members of different economic classes can belong to the same status group. Religion and ethnicity were two important status groups mentioned by Weber. The implication of this is that economic class is intersected by other social factors which are, in some cases, more important than economic class in determining one's identity and consciousness, and therefore political propensities.

## CLASS, POLITICS AND INEQUALITY

Historically, class became one of the central divides in the political practice of market societies. In some countries this was expressed through radical revolutionary movements, such as in Russia (see Chapters 5 and 10). But more often, class was incorporated into conventional politics, coming to define policy and electoral choices. Trades and labour unions were at the centre of emerging social movements that demanded economic and political reform. These movements gradually expanded the franchise (vote) beyond property holders to include most of the adult male (and later female) population in most industrialising societies.

From the late nineteenth century, unions organised political parties, either directly as with the labour parties of Australia, New Zealand and Britain or indirectly through close alliances with social democratic parties, as in much of Europe. These mass parties, with large memberships, transformed politics. Progressive parties promoted policies that modified the operation of markets through regulating wages and working conditions, through taxation to fund public service provision or make transfer payments and even through nationalising industries. Political sociologists saw these political developments as the expression of social dynamics between groups with different interests (Lipset & Rokkan 1967).

Change often followed periods of economic crisis, such as the 1890s depression or the Great Depression of the 1930s. This has led some to see the incremental reforms leading to development of the welfare state as attempts to retain political legitimacy in the face of challenges from below. However, the extent and nature of reform also varied between countries, often reflecting alliances between different social groups (see Chapters 5 and 10). Political reforms had important implications for economic distribution. Inequality in many countries declined during the middle of the twentieth century as the modern welfare state took shape.

### The end of class?

Political interventions have influenced the market distribution of income and the overall level of affluence in market societies has expanded. In this context, political sociologist Ronald Inglehart (1972; 1990) used extensive survey data from across the developed world to show that people's understanding of inequality and politics was changing. He described a new 'post-materialist' politics in which younger people in the 1960s and 1970s were less interested in traditional class issues of wages and working conditions. With income redistribution institutionalised in the welfare state, their concerns were now more focused on non-material issues such as gender, human rights and the environment, themes that have clearly influenced political developments since that time (see Chapter 9).

In contrast to the historical struggles of the working class, these trends signalled a convergence on 'middle-class values' leading many authors to proclaim the 'death of class' (Pakulski & Waters 1996). A strong focus on 'class' explanations of inequality no longer seemed appropriate, especially with the rise of postmodern thinking which rejected singular factors or 'grand narratives' for explaining social phenomena. They looked beyond the ownership of economic resources to notions of ideology and the power of language and ideas to structure the way people act. This did not necessarily deny the importance of economic power but it shifted the focus to other dimensions of inequality, such as gender, race and sexuality (discussed later in this chapter).

However, there remains evidence of economic class inequality as many of the hard-won political arrangements that tempered inequalities through redistribution have been challenged in recent decades. The overall level of inequality has been rising since the 1980s in most rich countries and the proportion of income received in wages has been falling, while the proportion received in profits has been rising (OECD 2010, p. 35). In his examination of the changing patterns of inequality in the US, Nobel laureate Paul Krugman (2009) concluded they were primarily the result of political forces, especially the impact of changes to labour market regulation, taxation and social spending. These trends have prompted some reconsiderations of class.

In the context of globalisation and the growing dominance of transnational corporations (see Chapter 7), Michael Hardt and Antonio Negri (2004) have drawn on the normative aspects of Marxian theory to 'renovate class'. They have developed the concept of 'the multitude' as the agents of change in a world marked by increasing inequalities between developed and developing economies. This expands class to include the unemployed, students, domestic labourers and peasants. In this way they incorporate both the rich world and poorer groups in the developing world. The multitude, Hardt and Negri suggest, can collectively resist transnational capital and the processes of commodification.

Drawing on both Weber and Marx, Erik Olin Wright (2009) argues that the ownership of economic capital remains central to explaining economic inequality. However, as affluence has spread, other factors are also important. For example, access to resources such as knowledge, skill and education, provide opportunities for greater bargaining power in the labour market and greater autonomy at work. The focus on education is also reflected in Pierre Bourdieu (1986). However, he sees training and education as a source of class privilege. The way knowledge is recognised through qualifications reflects the interests of powerful social groups. In turn, the privilege associated with qualifications and cultural knowledge is reproduced through the education system. Like economic capital, this 'cultural capital' is passed on between generations. For Bourdieu, class is related to social, cultural and economic advantages.

## STRUGGLES BEYOND CLASS

Many of the criticisms of traditional class theories reflected a growing recognition that class was not the only important form of inequality in market societies. Other distinctions existed with equally profound implications. In practice, inequality reflects a more complex picture of social, political and economic interactions stemming in part from the historical failure to extend the legal equality promised by the rule of law.

As market societies developed across Europe and the Americas women were denied the vote and were unable to own property. Indigenous populations were actively expelled from their lands. And those living under colonialism were denied self-determination, had their resources appropriated by foreign powers and were often forced into slavery or slave-like conditions. Although formal legal inequalities have gradually been eliminated, large economic inequalities remain. The most profound are between nations but significant inequalities also remain between men and women, between different racial groups and between the native born and migrants within developed economies.

## INEQUALITIES AND GENDER JUSTICE

Formal legal inequalities between men and women in market societies persisted well into the twentieth century. Alongside this, and to a much greater extent than other forms of inequality, gender disparity reflects the organisation of economic activity outside of commodity production. Gender inequality is related to the reproductive labour of raising children and the social and cultural forces that shape people's relationship to production. It has therefore been less prominent in economic analysis (see Chapter 9). However, like class inequality, it has prompted political struggle. A number of 'waves' of both the women's movement and feminist theory have made a significant contribution to addressing gender injustice in the distribution of economic resources.

### The waves of feminism

'First wave' feminism is associated with groups such as the suffragettes who focused primarily on addressing the legal inequalities between men and women that, among other things, denied women the basic democratic right to vote. Women were also not permitted to own property, indeed they were often classed *as* 'property' – either daughter or wife. Theorists like Mary Wollstonecraft (*A Vindication of the Rights of Woman*, 1978 [1792]) and John Stuart Mill (*The Subjection of Women*, 1975 [1859]) pointed out that such treatment of women went against the Enlightenment principles of universal freedom and equality and implied women were somehow less than human.

The restriction on women's political participation was echoed in the economic sphere. With the growing dominance of factory work outside the home the household was designated as the place where women would raise children and reproduce families (see Chapter 9). Women's participation in paid work was thereby limited by formal laws and also by social norms that reflected 'middle class' values rather than the financial needs of poor families (see Chapter 9). Women were also excluded from educational institutions and many occupations. When they did work, it was for a much lower wage than men and often in jobs segregated by sex.

Women were effectively marginalised from the market, producing a 'gender division of labour' in which men were concentrated in paid employment and women provided unpaid labour in the home. Such roles meant women were economically dependent on men. The situation of dependence was, in part, addressed by the idea of a 'family wage', where men received higher wages in order to support their families. However, wives were not formally entitled to such income and their access to it depended on the nature of their personal relationship with their husband.

This reflected what feminists referred to as 'patriarchal power', where women's dependent position was the product of the organisation of social structures – particularly the labour market and the family – rather than the actions of any individual man (Matthaei 1999). Regardless of the benevolence or belligerence of their husband, women's dependent status denied them autonomy and exposed them to particular risks. If a man died young or was disabled – for example in war or in a workplace accident – then his entire family was denied income. Some of the first forms of government support, such as payments to the widows of war veterans, reflected this insecurity (see Skocpol 1992).

After World War II, 'second wave' feminism emerged, along with other 'new social movements' (see Chapter 10). Their emblematic chant was 'the personal is political' as they sought to draw attention to the inequalities and injustice associated with the 'private sphere' of home and family as it had been socially constructed. In part their concerns related to women's rights as women. They campaigned to have control over their bodies and reproductive capacities, including birth control, abortion and the right to be free from sexual violence. But the movement also turned its attention to the economic inequalities arising from job segregation, discrimination and unequal wages in the 'public sphere'.

As a consequence, significant gains were made for women in the second half of the twentieth century, at least in the first world. Female participation in work and education increased significantly as their formal equality became socially sanctioned. Legal changes removed official wage discrimination that had set women's wages below that of men doing the same work. It was also made illegal for employers to discriminate on the basis of sex when hiring employees.

Yet despite these efforts to address economic injustice, women continued to experience marked income inequalities. This stemmed, in part, from ongoing separation between 'men's' work and 'women's' work which had the effect of disguising institutional discrimination (Game & Pringle 1983). Work associated with women, particularly care and emotional labour, came to receive lower pay. This partly reflects the lower value placed on 'women's work' and the belief that women required less income because they did not support dependents. Equal pay cases now often focus on ensuring different jobs requiring similar complexity of skill are paid equitably, rather than 'masculine' jobs (like mechanics) being paid more than 'feminised' jobs (like nursing). However, despite legal changes to promote equality, women remain more likely to receive lower incomes and are more likely to live in poverty.

This is primarily because women continue to perform the majority of unpaid care work. This limits their access to paid employment and workplace benefits like superannuation and pension schemes (see Jefferson 2009). It also leaves women more vulnerable when relationships break down, as evidenced by the high rate of poverty amongst single mothers. Many recent changes to social and employment policy, such as higher family benefits and access to parental leave and childcare, reflect the tensions between paid and unpaid work. Yet these positive policy developments sit alongside continuing examples of open sexism where people (such as employers) treat others differently on the basis of sexual prejudice.

A 'third wave' of feminist theory, and its extension in 'queer theory', emerged in the 1990s. Its preoccupations centre on the way language is used to recreate stereotypes. It rejects the 'essentialism' of gender categories, instead emphasising 'difference' in light of the diverse identities associated with race, class, gender and sexuality. From this perspective, economic inequalities and social oppressions are too complex to be understood through a single identity such as 'gender' or class (Rudy 2001, p. 207). However, if the unequal material condition of women is to be addressed, then efforts to understand and address the complexities of inequality continue to be important.

## RACE, COLONIALISM AND EMPIRE

As well as gender inequalities, market societies have also been associated with inequalities based on race and nationality. Historically, the rapidly increasing wealth experienced by the core European countries, and later settler colonies like the US and Australia, did not extend internationally. Much of the world was instead incorporated into the new global market system through imperialism and colonialism. This was often a brutal process and one that concentrated the gains of economic growth in a small proportion of the world's population. Distinct patterns of economic inequality were also reproduced within the developed North where people of colour, local indigenous peoples and migrants continue to have lower than average incomes. These inequalities reflect a complex interplay between economic forces, migration and racial dynamics.

## Imperialism

The rise of capitalism also coincided with growing imperialism as numerous European countries sought to extend their control over parts of Africa, Asia, the Americas and Oceania. This was supported by the prevailing economic doctrine of mercantilism which emphasised expanding exports because trade surpluses were thought to reflect the nation's growing wealth (see Chapter 3). This profoundly shaped economic development in both the colonies and the imperial nations. In England, the policies to promote trade included an emphasis on obtaining raw materials for production. This partly involved restrictions on the export of raw materials, but it also drove expansion of the British Empire.

Industrial development in the colonies was weakened by regulations that promoted the export of raw commodities to fuel imperial industries. For example, in India, an advanced textile industry was destroyed and replaced with cotton exports (Hobsbawn 1987). Colonialism involved the use of indentured labour, including slavery and unequal tax arrangements (this contributed to the American War of Independence and other nationalist movements). In turn, such practices aided growth in the imperial economies. Manufacturing benefited from a lack of competition from the colonies and from cheap raw material inputs. White colonial countries, such as the US and Australia, benefited from a direct seizure of resources from indigenous populations as well as indentured slave and convict labour.

Rather than being incidental to the rise of market economies, many theorists saw these developments as central and the racism involved as 'systematised oppression' (Boggs 1970). However, within the North these policies gradually became less popular. Many liberals objected to slavery on moral grounds. Political economists such as Adam Smith and David Ricardo rejected the mercantilist thesis, arguing instead that free trade would increase wealth in all nations and particularly for the domestic population. By the late nineteenth century England was increasingly advocating free trade on the basis of gold as the international currency (gold standard) reflecting its industrial dominance. Even so, colonialism continued with a dramatic expansion of empires in Africa which involved considerable violence within the colonies (Hobsbawm 1987).

Some political geographers have argued this expansion was motivated less by economics and more by an ideology of progress and white superiority where Europeans brought 'civilisation' to people they deemed to be less 'advanced' (see Painter & Jeffrey 2009). Alternatively, critics of capitalism continued to link colonialism with economic themes, especially the practice of 'free trade'. Vladimir Lenin (leader of the Russian Revolution) argued that the rise of large monopolies in Europe had changed the dynamic of capitalism. These firms produced large surpluses, and sought to gain state backing to invest this surplus in new markets where labour was less organised and profits were higher. This analysis proved influential with historians who saw this imperialist dynamic driving the conflict of World War I (Hobsbawm 1987).

Nevertheless, in the aftermath of two world wars, the international order changed considerably. Colonialism and theories of racial superiority were discredited, while national liberation movements saw colonies gain political independence. An international framework of institutions was also established to promote trade, investment and growth internationally (see Chapters 5 and 6). These institutions, including the International Monetary Fund (IMF) and World Bank, were instrumental in the reconstruction of Europe and Japan after World War II, and in promoting economic growth in the South. Yet racial inequalities, both between nations and within nations, persist.

## Contemporary challenges

The desire to promote economic growth within the South reflected a modernisation perspective dominant in European social science. Theorists such as Emile Durkheim (1984 [1893]) saw the rise of market society as a form of social evolution and argued that poorer countries were likely to undertake a similar path. World Bank policies reflected this belief, promoting large-scale capital investment that would aid industrialisation along largely European lines. Theories of 'development' thus reflect theories of economic growth (see Chapter 3).

More recently, the globalisation debate has echoed the modernisation theme. Market advocates claim poor economic growth in the South stems from a lack of engagement with the international market. By allowing foreign investment and greater international trade, they argued, poor countries would benefit from the international division of labour and grow more rapidly. This would lead to convergence, where more rapid growth in the developing world would eventually lead to similar average incomes across the globe.

However, dependency theorists challenge the view that poor countries were simply less advanced in a common journey to wealth. Instead, they argued the former colonies had developed differently because of their role as sources of cheap labour and raw materials in the international economy. They argued international trade was asymmetric. Poor countries were highly dependent on a few rich countries for trade and investment, but poor nations represented only a small proportion of trade or investment for the rich countries. Thus, poor countries had little bargaining power. Because of this, many dependency theorists promoted development on the basis of 'import substitution' that prioritised production for the local market. Such policies have since been challenged by the success of export-orientated growth strategies in East Asia (see Chapter 3).

Nevertheless, dependency theory has influenced a number of contemporary approaches, including world systems analysis. This takes the entire international economy as a unit of analysis, rather than focusing on individual nation states. Its foremost proponent, Immanuel Wallerstein (1974), argues that the rise of capitalism in Europe allowed European powers to shape the economic system for their own benefit. This has concentrated industries that 'value add' in the core, rich countries, while labour-intensive manufacturing and resource extraction dominate in the South. More recently, other theorists have drawn upon network analysis to better understand how elements of the global economy link together. This has highlighted an international division of labour and the export of dirty and polluting industries to the global South (see Chapter 7).

For example, drawing on theories of accumulation, Sasskia Sassen (1988) has used a network approach (see Chapter 10) to identify how corporations seek to restore profitability by reorganising the labour process internationally. The North has become the centre of numerous financial, social and political networks concentrated in 'global cities' where elite knowledge workers enjoy high wages, while other service workers, often migrants, are pushed to the periphery (see Sassen 2006). The limited social networks of recent migrants also help to explain why they are often confined to low-wage jobs. These network approaches highlight how production is reorganised both locally and globally as part of an international system and how the rewards of the international economy are unequally distributed along racial lines (see Box 4.3).

## Box 4.3 Coffee and colonialism today

Coffee is one of the world's most traded commodities and most profitable markets with approximately two billion cups of coffee consumed worldwide each day. However, the significance of coffee is very different in the wealthier countries of the global 'North' where most coffee is consumed, compared to the poorer global 'South' where most coffee is produced. Much of the world's coffee is grown in poorer countries in Africa, the Asia Pacific and Latin America. Production in these countries has been expanded in response to international pressures to increase production for export rather than subsistence for local consumption.

A small number of large multinational corporations dominate coffee sales. These corporations exercise considerable market power, while both workers and governments in the South have relatively little market power. The result is often low wages and exploitative conditions. Only a small fraction of the end price of a cup of coffee in the North is actually paid to those who produce the beans. In turn, this has led many Northern consumers to campaign for 'fair trade' coffee production where workers are paid a living wage in decent working conditions.

Alternatively, increasing attention is being paid to the role of institutions in explaining unequal development. Douglass North (1990), for example, has argued that early developments in a country's transition to a market economy can profoundly shape its future development. Evidence also suggests indigenous communities in North America have developed more rapidly when they enjoy substantial self-government, rather than having economic and political decisions made by non-indigenous authorities (Cornell et al 2005). Similarly, the lack of a formal Treaty or self-determination helps explain the poor development outcomes amongst Australia's indigenous population (Brennan et al 2005).

Continuing indigenous disadvantage also highlights substantial racial inequalities within nations. In part this reflects formal discrimination. Many countries deny citizenship rights to migrant workers or tolerate large 'illegal' migrant populations working in the informal economy with few legal protections. There is also evidence of overt discrimination. US evidence, for example, suggests employers are less likely to employ African American applicants than equally qualified white applicants (Page et al 2009). Furthermore, labour markets are often segmented in ways that concentrate some racial groups in particular occupations. Recent migrants may be less likely to have formal qualifications or to have their qualifications recognised. Migrants are thereby denied 'cultural capital' (Bourdieu 1986) when their experience is not culturally recognised even though their technical skills are similar to native born people.

In the political economy tradition, a number of theorists developed accounts of 'cumulative causation' (Myrdal 1944), in which different modes of inequality, such as gender, race or nation reinforce and affect each other (Dugger 1996). People who live in poverty, for example, are more likely to have ill health, be poorly educated and lack the skills necessary to get a job. This traps them in a 'vicious circle of poverty' that extends between generations even after formal equality is achieved. This situation is exacerbated for people in marginal ethnic groups who also suffer from discrimination based on racial stereotypes (Myrdal 1944).

## CONCLUSION

Economic inequalities are a constitutive aspect of market societies because markets are the primary institution determining the distribution of incomes. This is necessary to allow the incentives of the market to structure economic behaviour and to constitute the social relationships that define capitalist production. The centrality of commodity production within market societies produces inequality based on access to economic resources, such as capital and education and also generates inequalities based on access to the paid labour market. Those with unpaid care responsibilities, or those in countries or regions with poorly developed labour markets, are also disadvantaged. Alongside this, social and cultural norms regulate what roles different people play in the economy, based on characteristics such as race, sex and nationality.

However, the nature of economic distribution continues to change over time as campaigns to address inequalities have reshaped the economy. But the constitutive elements of market society itself also produce ongoing change. Commodification and the extension of markets, new technologies and forms of production, economic growth and crises in accumulation are all dynamic processes that generate opportunities for conflict and change as well as the need for management. In Part 2 of the book, we turn to examine how these ongoing processes are regulated. We focus on three of the most important institutions in the regulation of market societies – the state, the market and the corporation. Each is responsible for influencing the way production and distribution take place. We begin in the following chapter with the state.

## Questions

1 What are the differences between economic inequality and poverty?
2 What is the difference between economic equality and political equality and how is this related to positive and negative liberty?
3 How do the theories of class developed by Marx and Weber differ? Are they relevant today?
4 How does women's access to paid employment impact on gender inequality?
5 How might the persistence of racially based inequalities in the global economy be explained?

# Part 2
# Regulating market society

# 5 States, politics and welfare

THE STATE PLAYS a central role in economic life. It creates the rules in which markets operate and produces some goods and services directly. The state also facilitates private sector production and service provision through financial support. It redistributes income, both directly through taxes and transfer payments and indirectly through regulating wages and industry. It also performs many functions that help reproduce the economy, such as establishing education and health systems and governing the use of the environment. In all of these ways the state is a key economic institution of market societies.

This chapter is concerned with the interrelated economic and political developments of the capitalist state. Having arisen from the uncertainties of medieval conquest and war, the state has been shaped by challenges to its legitimacy arising from the periodic economic crises and conflicts discussed in Chapters 3 and 4. There remain diverse attitudes towards the state and different understandings of what the state is which have, in turn, influenced what states do. We look at how states differ across time and between countries and the recent effects of neoliberalism.

## STATES, LEGITIMACY AND THE ECONOMIC PROCESS

The modern state is a complex of institutions. As well as the government and parliament, the state also includes the armed forces and the police, the courts, the bureaucracy, authorities like the central bank and often also institutions providing a range of services such as education and healthcare. All of these institutions share important functions in regulating our lives. While the state predates the existence of market society, the state has changed alongside the rise of market society. Understanding these transformations is important for understanding the economic role of the state.

## ESTABLISHING THE CAPITALIST STATE

Changes to the nature of the state were important in facilitating the rise of market society. From around the sixteenth century, new ideas about political authority, its limits and how it should be exercised, began to circulate. They transformed medieval conceptions of sovereignty away from the personalised rule of monarchs towards a view of the state as an 'impersonal institutional entity' (Wood & Wood 1997, p. 30).

These changes in thinking coincided with ideas about legal rights and liberties which gave 'free men' protections and claims against the state (Hilton 1985, p. 152). Political conflict moved the state away from the absolute power and arbitrary law typical of medieval feudal social systems. In England, by 1688 the so-called 'glorious revolution' cemented the power of parliament, ending the 'divine right' of Kings in favour of a constitutional state overseen by an elected parliament and underpinned by a set of rules and laws.

England's constitutional state did not immediately grant political rights to all its people. Initially only the aristocracy and wealthy landowners achieved parliamentary representation and voting rights. Importantly, however, for the development of market society, this enabled the creation of private property rights, which had immediate benefits for those who controlled parliament. In ratifying enclosures, for example, political elites instituted and protected private property through the rule of law thereby furthering their interests as landowners and enhancing the importance of markets in the English economy.

Max Weber would later link the rise of the state to the broader historical process of rationalisation with its bureaucratic, legal and administrative authority (1978 [1922]). This was central to the impersonal authority of the state which comes from following a set of rules rather than the commands of an individual, such as a monarch. Thus, the shift from 'personal' monarchical rule to an 'impersonal' rules-based state in many ways mirrored the shift from the localised, personal and face-to-face markets of the medieval towns, to the impersonal markets of capitalism.

The rise of the capitalist state thus raised questions about who benefited from new economic and political liberties, and what role the state had in distributing economic resources, which, in turn, raised questions about the state's legitimacy. These questions were taken up by the early theorists of political economy.

Liberalism and laissez-faire

Early liberal thinkers like John Locke and Adam Smith laid the basis for the 'small government' perspective of classical or 'economic' liberalism where state legitimacy is based on 'limited government' and on the consent of its people. On this view, the purpose of the state is to protect private property rights and uphold individual liberty through the rule of law. The state is also required to provide national defence and maintain civic rights. However, it is expected to adhere to a general principle of 'non-interference', known as *laissez-faire*, with respect to the economy. Only where markets fail may the state provide public goods (see Box 5.1).

**Box 5.1 Market failure**

Orthodox economists generally agree that, given 'perfect competition', the market mechanism is the most efficient way of allocating resources. This is based on the assumption that all costs and benefits associated with the production of a good are reflected in its price and that the owners of the good enjoy exclusive property rights over it. However, the concept of 'market failure' acknowledges there are some circumstances where markets fail to ensure 'efficient allocation'.

There are three main examples of this. The first is in the provision of public goods. These are goods or services where there is little or no profit incentive for private firms because they cannot exclude non-payers from use. For example, a lighthouse cannot be restricted to paying users. Second, imperfect competition may give rise to market power in the form of monopolies or oligopolies. These prevent markets from allocating resources efficiently if firms reduce production and increase prices.

Related to this idea of price 'distortion' is a third category of market failure known as 'externalities'. Pollution, for example, creates potential clean-up. Markets fail when society, rather than the producer, bears this cost. According to the high-profile Stern Review (2006) climate change might be considered 'the greatest market failure the world has seen'.

Externalities represent costs (or benefits) that are not reflected in a market price. Under such circumstances, it is considered appropriate for governments to restore 'equilibrium' through price-based mechanisms such as taxes (Pigou 1938 [1920] p. 192) or rights-based mechanisms such as emissions trading schemes.

However, some orthodox economists, such as Milton Friedman, reject the policy implications of market failure, suggesting government intervention causes additional problems. Public choice theorists (see below) argue that 'government failure' – or inefficiencies coming from poor policy making – may be worse than the market problems they seek to address (Tullock et al 2002).

Beyond its specific meaning in economic theory, the term 'market failure' is also used by Marxian and other critics to refer to recurring problems of capitalism. These include, for example, the inequitable outcomes of market distribution, and the idle resources (including unemployed workers) that stem from periodic economic crises.

By outlining the central principles of *laissez-faire* in classical liberalism, Adam Smith is often considered the 'father of [both] economic science and of modern liberalism' (Screpanti & Zamagni 1993, p. 56). Smith (1904 [1776]) argued that by allowing propertied individuals to have freedom in relation to their own 'industry and capital', it was possible to achieve both social order *and* prosperity. He suggested it was not necessary for the state to direct economic decisions in competitive markets where productive assets were privately owned. Instead, individuals could freely pursue their self-interest which would expand employment opportunities and contribute to the nation's progress (Smith 1904 [1776). These ideas are captured in Smith's metaphor of the 'invisible hand':

> As every individual... endeavours as much as he can... to employ his capital in the support of domestic industry... every individual necessarily labours to render the annual revenue of the society as great as he can... he is... led by an invisible hand to promote an end which was no part of his intention.
>
> (Smith 1904 [1776], book IV, chapter II)

Such ideas about the relationship between the state and the economy became widely accepted among policy-making elites during the nineteenth century, particularly in England. Smith wanted to limit the state's 'interference' with private business activities. However, he also believed that unregulated private interests could, 'as much as governments', interfere with national progress (Barber 1967, p. 49). This was especially so if collusion resulted from the absence of economic growth and competition.

He therefore made numerous qualifications to *laissez-faire* (Viner 1958). Smith also argued the state should provide education to workers to offset the negative effects of monotonous labour because workers' low incomes would never induce businesses to provide such services.

John Stuart Mill (1909 [1848]) further modified the classical position on *laissez-faire* as it became evident that economic growth did not guarantee social order and prosperity. On its own, growth could not remove poverty and hardship which were made even worse during economic crises. Mill suggested that governments should not direct investment or production decisions, but could play a role in promoting a more equitable distribution of income (Barber 1967, p. 100). Later in the nineteenth century, Mill's ideas supported social reformers campaigning for policies of redistribution through taxation.

In contrast, a more extreme uptake of classical liberal ideas promotes a minimal or 'night watchmen state'. This extreme *laissez-faire* position argues that the state's role is merely to ensure people are free to enter into voluntary transactions. Its core concern is that the state should not use its coercive powers to interfere with such transactions including through taxation which, on this view, is considered 'theft'. This philosophy is typically found in the work of libertarians, such as Robert Nozick (1974), and is also a feature of the Austrian School of economics. Beyond Liberalism there are alternative challenges to the state, which have also had a significant impact on the state's development.

## QUESTIONING THE STATE'S LEGITIMACY

Despite the advances of constitutional government and the gradual democratising of parliamentary rule, the majority of people continued to live in very poor conditions throughout the eighteenth and nineteenth centuries. In England, despite electoral reforms and extensions to the franchise in 1832, workers remained outside the parliamentary system (Thompson 1980, p. 11). They were doubly disadvantaged because their employers exercised power in the workplace *and* through their political participation, setting the rules governing the economy.

Max Weber (1918, p. 78) argues the defining aspect of the state is its 'monopoly of the legitimate use of physical force within a given territory'. This authority, even when it is seldom used explicitly, lies behind the power of the state to regulate social and economic life. The importance of the state's coercive and regulatory powers was evident during the rise of market society. Capitalism was advanced both through the state's active repression of dissent against social and economic changes as well as through the legislative power of parliament.

For example, in addition to enclosures and the codification of private property rights, the English parliament introduced other laws helping to secure an available and quiescent industrial workforce. It legislated against trade unions and the collective bargaining of workers (Combination Acts 1800 and 1825), it outlawed unemployment and poverty from idleness (Vagrancy Act 1824) and it introduced new poor laws built around a system of workhouses that were meant to serve as a deterrent to unemployment (Poor Law Amendment Act 1834).

Furthermore, low wages meant workers had little in the way of surplus funds for saving so they lived a very precarious existence. Inflated food prices together with the practice of reducing wages (or loss of income altogether through unemployment) had devastating effects on families with no other source of income. Hence, the recurring depressed economic conditions coincided with waves of violent political protest.

These volatile conditions led many to question the legitimacy of the state. More radical views had varying degrees of influence within the worker movements that gathered momentum in the nineteenth century. For some, the state had become an illegitimate institution. They sought to transform the state through immediate and, if necessary, violent revolution.

### The Marxian challenge

The vibrant workers movement of the 19th century was the main arena for developing and circulating radical ideas. Although united in its opposition to exploitation, this movement was diverse, with several distinct intellectual and political currents. One area in which divisions emerged was over the nature of the state and the movement's relationship with it. Anarchists, for example, rejected the legitimacy of both government authority and private property. Some anarchists experimented with small communities where the tools of production were collectively managed. Pierre-Joseph Proudhon, an early philosopher of anarchism, thought private property a form of 'absolutism' (Nettlau 2000). Although anarchists had many synergies with Marxists and other socialists, there were also significant differences.

Some anarchists were considered 'utopian' in their ideas about worker control in decentralised, non-hierarchical communities. This seemed naive in a world where industrialisation had changed forever the scale and nature of production. Many Marxists thought those against the goal of centralised or state control over economic production merely served to divide the workers' movement. Marx (1871a) himself thought workers should become members of parliament and criticised the anarchist rejection of political participation. He argued that the purpose of a working-class movement was 'the conquest of political power for the working class' (Marx 1871b).

Hence, while Anarchists reject the state and organised political authority as such, Marxists tend to problematise the capitalist nature of the state. They argue that the modern state must be understood in the context of the class-based organisation of production (as discussed in Chapter 4). While there is a formal separation of those who own capital from those making laws in parliament, Marx and Engels argued in *The Communist Manifesto* that 'the executive of the modern State is but a committee for managing the common affairs of the whole bourgeoisie' (1977 [1848]). This is because those who own capital control economic production, giving them enormous political power.

For Marxists, there is abundant evidence of the state acting in the interests of the capitalist class. Recently, for example, states have limited the rights of workers to take strike action, lowered corporate tax rates and spent billions bailing out the finance sector during the global financial crisis. However, some Marxists also argue that the state is a force for cohesion within capitalist society. Conflict between classes is socially and economically destructive. Marxist scholars argue that by mediating such conflict, the state promotes the interests of capitalists as a group, by ensuring production can take place smoothly. It does this through, for example, providing environmental protections, health and safety standards, regulating the labour market and provision of social security.

For many Marxists, though, such piecemeal reforms can never abolish the exploitative character of capitalism nor the capitalist nature of the state, which they expect to 'wither away' with the transition to socialism. This thinking has directly influenced the development of states around the world by inspiring millions to challenge the state's legitimacy. The Bolsheviks, for example, used such ideas during the Russian Revolution in 1917 which began a period of communist rule lasting 64 years (see Box 5.2). Elsewhere too, Marxist ideas became influential during the late nineteenth and early twentieth centuries. Marxism seemed to offer an answer to why economic conditions were so unequal and how things could be made better.

## Box 5.2 The Russian Revolution

In Russia, Marx's ideas provided the inspiration for the Bolsheviks, a small revolutionary group which seized political power in 1917. This was despite Russian capitalism being far less developed than in many other European countries, meaning the preconditions Marx predicted for communism (enormous productive capacity and a large proletariat) did not exist.

Nonetheless, unique domestic factors helped the Bolsheviks gain control of the levers of political and economic power. These included the inability of the Tsarist regime to solve problems of land and food distribution and Russia's involvement in World War I against Germany. However, when they took control, the Bolsheviks were confronted with the problem of what to do next because Marx provided few detailed blueprints about what a communist society should look like. Furthermore, to maintain power the Bolsheviks had to fight off challenges from various armed forces loyal to the old political regime.

While the Bolsheviks collectivised land and factories, in practice production became controlled by the new communist bureaucracy. Russia was able to industrialise rapidly but by the 1960s the system began to deteriorate. The centralised coordination of production decisions was unable to meet the needs of Russia's vast population and geography. Ongoing threats from the capitalist countries meant resources were diverted from economic production to military production. This occurred against the backdrop of a violent, authoritarian state that did not tolerate dissent and strictly regulated both politics and culture. By the early 1990s, these conditions contributed to the collapse of the communist state in Russia.

The experience in Russia points to the complex relationship between economic theory and practice. The extent to which communist Russia was 'Marxist' is difficult to determine. The Bolsheviks and their successors claimed they were implementing the visions outlined by Marx and Engels and they managed largely to abolish production for profit in Russia for much of the twentieth century. However, this did not lead to the distribution of economic resources as advocated by Marx (1971 [1875]): 'to each according to their needs'. Nor did it lead to the withering away of the state – quite the opposite.

Revolutionary forms of socialism inspired conflict and activism in many different countries. While this had its most profound implications in

Russia, in other parts of the world less radical forms of socialism aimed at gradual social transformation were influential. In many countries, the interest in socialism and universal suffrage was ignited by workers' wretched living conditions and their lack of political power. However, this led to reform not revolution and ultimately to the compromises of the welfare state that sit at the core of contemporary market societies.

## THE POLITICAL ECONOMY OF THE WELFARE STATE

Throughout most of the nineteenth century, the liberal principle of *laissez-faire* was used to justify government policies aimed at deepening the role of markets in society. However, resistance and the push for reforms gathered momentum as social and economic conditions significantly deteriorated and open class conflict between workers and employers developed. Social liberals and other 'middle-class' reformers, such as the Fabian Society, supported workers in calling for systematic social reform through government.

The enduring legacy of the nineteenth century reform movements was the birth of social democracy. This effectively meant seeking socialist goals through parliament rather than revolution. Political parties influenced by social democracy evolved with close links to labour unions and transformed many capitalist societies. Their policies reflected the interests of workers in supporting higher wages, better working conditions, pensions for older workers, housing and healthcare.

Social liberals argued that while the principle of 'limited government' remained central to safeguarding individual rights, the state could, and should, be harnessed for social purposes. The interplay between economic crises and political reforms during this period indicate that, in one form or another, political and economic compromises are a necessary part of maintaining legitimacy both for the constitutional state *and* the capitalist economy. This dynamic is reflected in the emergence of the welfare state.

## THE GROWING ROLE OF THE STATE

The gains of the nineteenth century reform movements were hard won, often involving significant conflict. However, they reinforced the state's regulatory role in economic activity and laid the institutional basis for extending its form and reach. Conflict was also reflected in economic theory. While the emerging neoclassical approach supported the principle of *laissez-faire*, favouring market competition to return the economy to 'equilibrium', institutionalist and Keynesian economists favoured a greater role for the state.

Institutionalists focus attention on the way key institutions in the economy develop and evolve historically. They argue that the institutions we inherit shape the economic choices available to us. Institutionalists recognise that states play an important role in establishing markets and shaping their operation. However, they also seek to understand the broader implications of institutional development on social and economic activity. As well as the evolution of 'big government', they analyse the evolution of 'big business' in the form of the corporation and 'big labour' in the form of trade unions.

Several institutionalists played key roles within the state. Wesley Mitchell, for example, founded the US National Bureau of Economic Research in 1920. This provided the state with the statistical information about production, employment and prices it needed to better manage economic growth. John K Galbraith also played an important role in regulating prices during World War II. His insights led him to understand how corporations often behaved in similar ways to governments, using planning to manage their own production.

The institutionalist focus on history and the detail of real world markets contrasted to neoclassical theories that focused on abstract and mathematical explanations of economic behaviour. For some decades, institutionalism rivalled neoclassical economics for influence. Even as neoclassical economics began to gain dominance, it was challenged further by the Great Depression. This led many to question the ability of markets to function according to a 'self-regulating' logic. It was in this context that John Maynard Keynes wrote his influential *General Theory*.

As discussed in Chapter 3, Keynes argued that markets could produce large-scale sustained unemployment and that there was no automatic mechanism to correct this within the capitalist system. He therefore examined the economic role governments needed to play in market societies through periods of recession and recovery. These ideas were important in shaping government policies beyond the Great Depression.

Keynes was also the British representative at the Bretton Woods negotiations in 1944 that shaped the institutional character of the post-World War II economy. The international economic system that emerged out of the Bretton Woods conference operated until the 1970s, underpinning a 'golden age' of capitalism. This was an unprecedented era of growth in the global economy and a period of close to full employment in the advanced capitalist economies.

Domestically, national governments were given a strong hand in the regulation of markets. Internationally, the US took a leading role in the post-war reconstruction effort, providing aid and favourable trading policies to the war ravaged economies of Europe and Japan. It was also central to the 'Bretton Woods' financial system which established the World Bank and International Monetary Fund (IMF) (discussed in Chapter 6). This system was based upon the principle of restricting international finance and imposing currency stability in order to achieve global economic growth.

Currencies were set at a fixed value in relation to the US dollar, which in turn was linked to the price of gold. One ounce of gold was equivalent to 35 US dollars, and dollars were redeemable for gold on request at banks. This meant that the US dollar became the global reserve currency (as the British pound had been in the previous 'gold standard' era). To support this system, the IMF provided states with loans when necessary to maintain the value of their currencies. The cross-border movement of capital was also restricted through what has been called 'financial repression'.

Keynes also pioneered the concept of macroeconomic management whereby the state managed national economic growth. This was seen as an important element in funding the welfare responsibilities of the state. Both Keynes and the institutionalists also thought the state should invest directly into infrastructure, such as railways, hospitals and schools. These ideas shaped national policies around the globe throughout the long post-World War II boom. They underpinned an era in which states played an active role in shaping the direction of economic development.

## Keynes and macroeconomic management

Keynes argued that confidence played an important role in the growth of the economy. As businesses or households lose confidence they invest and spend less, producing a 'self-fulfilling prophecy' and potentially producing crisis (see Chapter 3). These results stem from individual consumers and businesses acting in ways that seem rational to them personally. However, they are irrational from the perspective of the economy as a whole. Hence, Keynes believed governments should take action to stimulate economic activity and prevent deepening recession. This is the basis of macroeconomic policy which is directed at maintaining the 'aggregate' level of economic activity, rather than focusing on individual markets. Keynes believed that if the state could start people spending again, then businesses would start to hire and the economy would start to grow.

The two most common policy mechanisms used by governments to manage the 'macro economy' are fiscal policy and monetary policy. Fiscal policy uses the government budget to raise or reduce taxes and allocate spending while monetary policy involves setting interest rates and the overall supply of money. Both sets of policies are designed to be 'counter-cyclical', meaning they push the economy in the opposite direction to markets, creating jobs in a recession and reducing inflation in a boom.

According to Keynes, during recessions governments should spend more in order to make up for decreased consumer spending and business investment. This would stimulate demand and increase economic growth. When this happened the government would benefit from higher tax receipts, meaning that any budget deficit would actually finance itself through higher production. In good times a government budget surplus would take money out of the economy thereby reducing the risk of inflation.

Keynes argued fiscal policy was more effective at stimulating the economy than monetary policy. He suggested monetary policy was a bit like a string – you could pull it (raise interest rates to stop the economy from overheating) but not push it. In bad times, even low interest rates might not encourage investment because businesses do not think they will make much profit while households are afraid they will lose their jobs and be unable to repay a loan. This was precisely the situation that occurred during the Great Depression.

Nonetheless, since the 1990s monetary policy has often been viewed as the main macroeconomic policy tool. Raising interest rates reduces business investment and household spending by increasing the cost of borrowing money. This is usually done by the central bank (Australia's Reserve Bank or the Federal Reserve in the US, for example). Businesses borrow money to invest but only when they think their profits will be large enough to pay back the interest. Likewise, households need to be confident they can pay back a mortgage.

Keynesians also advocate other policy measures that have been the basis of some welfare states. For example, these theorists note that those on low incomes spend more of their money than the well off because they cannot afford to save. Keynesians therefore advocate income policies involving redistribution to increase consumer spending.

The welfare state also provides a safety buffer to the economy called 'automatic stablisers'. During recessions, tax revenues fall and welfare payments increase thereby creating a budget deficit. In times of economic boom, tax revenues rise and welfare payments fall creating a budget surplus. This happens 'automatically', stabilising the economy without any change in policy settings.

The basic principles of macroeconomic management continue to underpin what states do in practice. However, from the late 1970s the overall extent of government activity in the economy came under question. Keynesianism and advocacy of an active economic role for the state has since been marginalised by the promotion of neoliberalism, especially at the 'microeconomic' level, something we explore in the next chapter.

## WELFARE STATE REGIMES

The modern welfare state matured in the post-World War II period, having first emerged out of the periods of economic crises and conflict in the late nineteenth to the mid twentieth centuries. Karl Polanyi (2001 [1944], p. 138) understood this as society protecting itself against the perils inherent in a self-regulating market system. These 'protections' took different forms in different countries and continued to expand and evolve in response to political and economic events throughout the twentieth century.

Welfare regimes represent a shift to the public provision of services which were previously met privately on an ad hoc basis by charities, mutual aid societies, private insurance schemes, the family, or not at all. The idea of 'social insurance' developed out of the need to systematically decrease the impact on workers of economic fluctuations, providing assistance to ensure they could survive periods of unemployment when they would otherwise have no income. This reflects a logic of 'decommodification'. Basic services are provided to citizens as a 'right', rather than on the basis of their ability to pay (Marshall 2009 [1950]). However, such developments were not without significant political struggle.

Welfare state theorists see policy developments reflecting compromises between different classes or social groups, which vary across countries. In Britain and Scandinavia, for example, the post-war developments in welfare may have served the interest of the poor but they also benefited the middle-classes. However, in parts of Europe reforms failed as the better-off, who were not destined to benefit, mobilised against the states' efforts at redistribution (Baldwin 1990, p. 290). Hence, an important enabling factor in welfare state formation was cross-class 'solidarity' in spreading the burden of risk across society more broadly (Baldwin 1990, p. 288).

A particularly influential analysis of welfare regimes is that by Gosta Esping-Andersen (1990). While his investigation initially aimed to explain differences in social policy, the framework has much broader implications, highlighting how state economic and social policies are linked and reflect a broader approach to organising the economy.

## 'Three worlds of welfare'

Esping-Andersen's work on welfare states contrasted with previous approaches that focused primarily on the size of the state, as measured by indicators such as the proportion of total income spent on social policies. He argued the object of spending, not just its size, was also important. For example, some governments give generous benefits to relatively high-income public servants, while countries like Australia emphasise the very poor or needy.

Esping-Andersen shifted attention away from the size to the *effects* of state policy. For Esping-Andersen, the most important question was the role the state had in commodifying or decommodifying social life. By this he meant the extent to which access to the basic necessities of life was dependent on earning income through markets. On this test he found three broad categories of state: liberal, corporatist and social democratic.

The liberal model of state provision is the most limited and is associated with the Anglo-democracies, like the United States, Canada and Australia (but see Box 5.3). Benefits are generally modest and means-tested so only those on low incomes can access them. Benefits are also often stigmatised, meaning people have negative associations with those receiving benefits.

### Box 5.3 Australia's wage-earner model

From the early twentieth century Australia developed a unique 'regime' of welfare. In *The Working Class and Welfare* (1985), Francis Castles described this model as a 'wage earners' welfare state. This distinguished Australia from other 'liberal' and 'residual' welfare states. Although Australia is amongst those countries with the lowest social expenditure, typically half as much as the Scandinavian countries, Castles argued it was misleading to characterise Australia as a 'liberal' welfare regime (at least until the 1980s when welfare underwent significant changes).

Historically, despite its comparatively small welfare expenditures, Australia had relatively low levels of inequality and waged poverty, giving it more egalitarian economic outcomes than might have been expected using the criterion of direct social expenditure. This is because Australia had established a broader institutional basis for social protection with a unique system of wage regulation at its core. The 'Australian settlement', which also included a restrictive immigration program and tariff-based industry protection, had grown out of economic crises and conflicts of the 1890s after which labour organised as a political party and was able to use the state for progressive purposes.

In 1904 Australia established a compulsory system of conciliation and arbitration for industrial disputes, allowing courts to influence market wages. In 1907 the 'Harvester Case' provided a benchmark for ensuring workers were paid a 'fair and reasonable wage'. Rather than using taxation and social spending, Australia promoted equity by regulating wages.

The Australian system featured an 'award system' which guaranteed a minimum wage for workers doing similar jobs. Because unemployment was generally low, this system provided the core of Australian 'welfare'. The state also facilitated access to owner-occupied housing and other selective universal welfare state benefits. At its peak, the wage levels of approximately 80 per cent of Australian workers were protected by the centralised wage arbitration system (Castles 2001).

This type of regime often creates a sharp divide between perceptions of the deserving and undeserving poor, with strict rules that cut off payments for those deemed undeserving. Often these rules are linked to participation in the labour market and are designed to force people back to work. As a result, state benefits do not really act to decommodify life but only serve as a safety net to prevent severe poverty.

The corporatist model has a more extensive role for the state than in liberal regimes. However, benefits often reflect the status of occupations, so that those in higher status professions gain greater benefits. This does partly decommodify social life in that access to essential services and income is not fully market-dependent. But it also means the state does not act to redistribute income.

This approach is typical of many continental European countries like Germany, France and Italy. The role of the state often reflects the influence of the church. This means welfare rules promote the traditional family, limiting benefits available to non-working married women and encouraging provisioning within the family from the male breadwinner.

The social democratic model is found in the smallest number of countries. Here benefits are both generous and universal. This regime is associated with the Scandinavian countries like Sweden. It has the greatest decommodifying effect of the three types of welfare state. This is because it attempts to break down the distinction between social classes based on their ability to pay for good quality services. Instead, the state provides a wide range of essential services, from healthcare to education and childcare but does so at the level demanded by those on high incomes. It then extends access to all.

As a result, access to health, education and other services is not determined by a person's ability to pay nor is the quality of the service influenced by being able to 'opt out' into a better funded private sector. Social democracies also have generous unemployment and other payments and a strong state commitment to helping workers from declining industries retrain and find new work in emerging industries.

The welfare state taxonomy offered by Esping-Anderson is a useful way of thinking about welfare regimes in market societies. However, it misses much of the individual complexity present in different cultural contexts. The 'exception' of Australia's 'wage earners' welfare state provides a good example of the potential institutional diversity that might be found in different countries.

## DIVERSITY, CHANGE AND CONTINUITY

We have seen how the role of the state has changed and evolved over time. These changes were influenced by war, economic crises and social movements as well as by thinkers and ideas. The role of the state does not only change over time, it also varies across space. Historically, different countries have developed different welfare-state institutions, with different traditions of regulation.

The idea that states reflect different institutional and cultural histories marks a departure from many ideas about 'globalisation'. This was believed to be a powerful homogenising force, likely to compel all states to adopt similar policies and approaches. However, important differences persist between states in areas such as the level of taxation, levels of state ownership and degrees of inequality.

To explain this, theorists from across a range of disciplines and traditions have examined the historical development of the state in different areas. This marks a renewed interest in institutional political economy, alongside the development of New Institutional Economics (NIE) within the neoclassical and rational choice traditions.

While NIE shares the neoclassical focus upon rational individual agents, it departs from neoclassical economics in its recognition of transaction costs (discussed more in Chapter 7) which highlights the cost of changing the way things are done. Such an analysis shows that small differences in the early phase of state development can have lasting consequences because the 'costs' of subsequent change can be great. This helps to explain how differences remain in national economies despite the homogenising force of globalisation on the one hand, and the policy prescriptions of neoliberalism on the other.

## VARIETIES OF CAPITALISM

Drawing together aspects of both political economy and the new institutionalist tradition, Peter Hall and David Soskice (2001) developed a 'variety of capitalisms' approach centred on two basic models: liberal market economies (LME) and coordinated market economies (CME). This approach acknowledges that market societies and their states vary across nations.

On this view, the economic activity in LMEs is guided by either by markets, through contracts, or by firms who control internal production. In CMEs, the state plays a more important role in either directing economic activity itself or promoting coordination between firms or economic sectors.

Beyond the 'welfare state' regimes of the West, the varieties of capitalism literature points to other models of state-economy relations that have emerged in different countries. Most notably, in the second half of the twentieth century the rate of industrialisation began to accelerate in some Asian economies and the evident role of state support in this process gave rise to the notion of the 'developmental state'.

### The East Asian development model

The term 'developmental state' implies a situation where the state actively pursues industry policies in promoting economic development. This was the case with Japan in the post-World War II boom period but also the later East Asian 'tiger' or 'miracle' economies of Hong Kong, Singapore, South Korea and Taiwan. These countries gradually transformed themselves into high-income economies, maintaining rapid industrialisation and high rates of economic growth from the 1970s when advanced economies were generally experiencing stagnation. In the 1980s, Malaysia, Thailand and Indonesia followed on the development path, also experiencing rapid economic growth.

In all of these cases, governments took primary responsibility for promoting economic growth (Stiglitz 1996, p. 151). South Korea, following the example of Japan's Ministry of International Trade and Industry (MITI) (see Chapter 6), nurtured specific sectors and the growth of particular firms, transforming them into the big business conglomerates – the 'chaebol' – which drove economic growth (Park 2002, p. 339). However, in the case of the Taiwanese 'miracle', private small-to-medium-sized firms producing goods for export played a crucial role in growth and development alongside public sector companies which, supported by state banks, focused on industrialisation through domestic production (Baek 2005, p. 494).

While there is significant diversity in the policies used to encourage development and growth in different Asian contexts, the underlying commonality is the centrality of the state to the development path. However, this situation is not necessarily unique to Asia. Institutionalists argue it is something that characterised the development of all industrialised market societies including 'free trade' Britain where, despite the ideology of *laissez-faire*, early industrialists also enjoyed the protection of the state in trade (see Polanyi 2001 [1944], pp. 141–2).

## WINDING BACK THE STATE?

Despite the centrality of the state to the history and development of market societies, recent decades have witnessed the rise of efforts to 'wind back the state'. These efforts have rendered many institutional changes, successfully invoking the ideas of nineteenth century *laissez-faire* to effect a transformation in the form and function of the state. The genesis of this 'small state-free market' movement goes back to the birth of the welfare state itself.

As many countries adopted Keynesian forms of state-based economic management in response to the Great Depression of the 1930s, a small number of intellectuals began to develop a forceful critique of the state. From the 1940s economists such as Friedrich von Hayek and Milton Friedman argued that the growth of the state threatened both individual freedom and economic efficiency. Drawing on the ideas about *laissez-faire* developed by the classical political economists, these theorists took such ideas in new directions creating what is now called 'neoliberalism' (although they rarely used this term themselves). (See also Box 5.4.)

### Box 5.4 Neoliberalism and the war of ideas

In 1947, a small group of intellectuals met at Mont Pelerin, Switzerland, to discuss ways of combating what they viewed as the growing threat to freedom posed by 'collectivism'. The group comprised some of the world's leading economists and philosophers, including Milton Friedman, Friedrich von Hayek and Karl Popper. Later named the Mont Pelerin Society, it became the nucleus of a growing neoliberal movement.

At the meeting Hayek told his colleagues '[w]e must raise and train an army of fighters for freedom' (Hayek in Cockett 1995). Since then, the Mont Pelerin Society has supported the establishment of various 'think tanks' around the world to promote neoliberal ideas. These include the Institute of Economic Affairs in England, the Centre for Independent Studies in Australia and the Heritage Foundation in the US.

During this time, neoliberals have moved from the margins to the mainstream of debates about politics, society and economics. Key intellectual figures from the Mont Pelerin Society went on to become advisers to, and guests of, powerful political leaders. Most notably, this included the Prime Minister of Britain, Margaret Thatcher and the US President, Ronald Reagan, both of whom implemented neoliberal policies.

By the 1990s, neoliberalism had supplanted Keynesianism as the dominant orthodoxy of state economic management. The Mont Pelerin Society could justly lay claim to playing an important role in this change.

### The age of neoliberalism

Neoliberalism is an important and pervasive influence on government policies today. The movement's ideas first gained traction in the 1970s when economic crises signalled the end of the 'golden age'. Keynesian theory appeared to offer few solutions to the economic problems of the time. Capitalist economies were experiencing low growth, high unemployment and high inflation, which together became known as 'stagflation'. Many governments looking for policy alternatives turned to the prescriptions of neoliberals.

Neoliberals argue that society is comprised of individuals who should be free from coercion. Hence, they argue the most efficient way of organising the economy is through a system of free markets which, given the forces of competition, enable individual preferences to be satisfied while upholding individual liberty. Because market transactions are 'voluntary', and no one would voluntarily enter into a contract that disadvantaged them, free markets are said to produce mutually beneficial outcomes without the need for external interference or coercion. In this way, free markets are claimed to be the most efficient and the most moral form of economic organisation.

For neoliberals, the growth of the state that occurred after the Great Depression threatened individual liberty and economic prosperity. Friedrich von Hayek, a leading neoliberal theorist, argued that Keynesian welfare states, such as in Britain, and the authoritarian states of fascist Germany and communist Russia were all forms of 'collectivism'. Rather than creating a framework which allowed individuals to pursue their own interests, collectivist states pursued politically determined goals which inevitably infringed individual liberty. Thus, he (1994 [1944]) argued, such states were on 'the road to serfdom'.

To avoid this situation, neoliberals argued that 'big government' had to be wound back. They advocated devolving most state-provided goods and services to the private sector. This process of 'privatisation' involved state-owned enterprises being sold to private for-profit providers. They also promoted 'deregulation' which would remove restrictions on the ability of firms to trade within an economy. Finally, they supported 'marketisation' which created competitive markets for the provision of services that had previously been delivered by government.

One influential strand of neoliberalism is 'public choice' theory, developed by James Buchanan and Gordon Tullock (1962). It shifts attention from the state's involvement in the economy back onto the state itself. Here, the model of the self-interested utility maximising individual is applied to the government sector.

It is said that politicians, bureaucrats and lobby groups that claim to act in the public interest are in fact motivated solely by self-interest. Hence, it is argued that politicians increase government expenditure to win votes, bureaucrats expand departmental budgets to increase their power and prestige and pressure groups lobby for special treatment from government. Public Choice theorists therefore claim that states have an inbuilt tendency to deficits which should be addressed through constitutional limitations on government expenditure.

Over the past four decades governments have implemented many policies that resemble the broad agendas advocated by neoliberals, although the extent of their influence is debated. While the Global Financial

Crisis of 2007 witnessed a resurgence of interest in Keynesian ideas about financial regulation, this does not seem to have dislodged neoliberalism as the dominant policy approach. Having said that, neither has neoliberalism succeeded in abolishing the institutions of the 'welfare state' (discussed below).

## Underlying continuities

The size and role of the state in market societies has come under intense pressure from the rise of neoliberalism. Yet, as market competition is extended, new state agencies are created to oversee these markets (Levi-Faur 2005). Indeed, the size of the state continued to expand in many countries from the 1970s into the 21st century – during the supposed neoliberal era of governance. We discuss how this process worked in the next chapter, but some theorists suggest it reflects the dynamics of the welfare state.

Paul Pierson (1994) argues that the process of expanding state spending is different from the process of 'retrenching' (reducing) spending programs. Pierson examined the impact of neoliberal governments in the US and UK during the 1980s. In both cases, the incoming governments promised to reduce the size of the state and to retrench significant parts of the welfare state. But Pierson found the rhetoric did not match the reality; after a decade of reform the size of the state continued to be much the same.

His explanation focused on the politics of policy-making. New spending programs, he claimed, created new constituencies supportive of spending. A payment (such as the aged pension or disability support payment) created a group of beneficiaries with common interests who would organise to protect their entitlements. Pierson's work both anticipated and reinforced many of the themes of the various institutionalist schools in identifying the impact of history on future events.

Some claim the nature of neoliberalism itself explains the failure to shrink the state. In *Freer Markets, More Rules*, Steven Vogel (1996) argues that even deregulated markets require a framework of rules and administrative bodies to enforce them – and these are typically provided by states. While the state has changed the mode by which it delivers services – relying increasingly upon private rather than direct public provision – this has not reduced the total public cost of such services. This is consistent with the arguments of the institutional tradition of political economy that state institutions provide some of the necessary foundations of market societies. One important conclusion which flows from this argument is that markets and states are not antithetical. Rather, markets depend upon states for their very operation.

### Box 5.5 The free market and the repressive state

States in capitalist economies take many forms, including the repressive and authoritarian. This is often overlooked by those who assume that the 'invisible hand' of markets can only operate when governments apply a 'light touch' to regulation. Some striking examples of this are provided in Naomi Klein's (2007) *The Shock Doctrine*.

Klein describes how economic and political crises were used in the 1970s and 1980s in developing countries as opportunities to implement extensive 'free market' (or neoliberal) policies such as privatisation, cuts to welfare services and the removal of tariff protections. However, as Klein points out, this occurred alongside the seizure of political power by the military and the establishment of dictatorships. These governments used violence, torture and the disappearance of opponents to maintain power.

Earlier in the twentieth century, a similar phenomenon was evident in Germany with the rise to power of Hitler's Nazi Party. Fascism was highly centralised, authoritarian and nationalistic. The Nazis were responsible for the imprisonment and murder of millions of people. Yet, private enterprise survived in Nazi Germany. In fact, many large capitalist firms benefited from the regimented labour force imposed by the Nazis, and from Nazi contracts.

This suggests that a capitalist economy, and the pursuit of profit, can sit quite comfortably alongside a range of government types, including the authoritarian. It should also caution against assuming simplistic associations between markets and freedom.

## CONCLUSION

States are an important institution in market society. They have fostered the rise of markets by establishing private property and the rule of law. They manage conflicts that arise from the operation of markets and continue to regulate market activity. But the nature and role of the state is contested. Different theorists and groups within society believe it should play different roles. States are also shaped by events, particularly economic crises, and by the specific history of each nation. This leads to diversity between countries and over time. Where Keynesian welfare states dominated following World War II, more recently neoliberal ideas have influenced the state. Neoliberalism has reinforced the role of the market in regulating economic activity (the subject of Chapter 6).

Questions

1 What is meant by *laissez-faire* and why was it promoted by classical liberals?
2 Why are Marxists critical of the capitalist state?
3 Why do many welfare state theorists see a link between the growth of welfare state spending and Keynesian economic management?
4 How does the size and structure of the state differ between countries and how might this be explained?
5 Why are neoliberal advocates critical of the state? What impact have their ideas had in practice?

# 6 | Markets, risk and globalisation

MARKETS ARE MORE central to capitalism than to previous ways of organising the economy and are themselves a form of regulation. We have already seen how through commodification much of life becomes subject to the competitive pressures of markets. Because most people earn their income and purchase many of the goods and services they need through markets, the price mechanism is central to our lives. Since the 1970s markets have become even more central as state policies around the world have been transformed under the influence of neoliberal politics. Globalisation and policies of privatisation, deregulation and marketisation mean that many aspects of life that were not previously coordinated through the price mechanism are now subject to it.

Whereas states use law and regulation to exert direct control over the economy, market prices create incentives that 'regulate' and influence our behaviour. Thus, economists often talk about markets providing 'decentralised' rather than 'centralised' forms of decision-making. Market incentives also involve a greater degree of uncertainty than is typically the case with direct state regulation because they allow greater flexibility in behaviour and outcomes. A key feature of market societies is therefore the presence of risk. In this chapter we look at the increase in risk and other changes resulting from economic restructuring and explore key theoretical perspectives that seek to explain both the forces driving restructuring and its implications.

## THE REGULATORY FORCE OF MARKETS

Markets are a mechanism of distribution but they are weak in terms of prescribing outcomes. Governments create specific forms of entitlement, such as those provided by public services, and its form of distribution is more specific and more predictable than markets. The welfare state, for example, provides social security by giving people particular entitlements on the basis of 'right'. By contrast, market-based distribution is governed by uncertainty and risk thereby influencing people's behaviour in specific, albeit indirect, ways.

## MARKETS AND THE GOVERNANCE OF CONDUCT

Neoclassical economists argue that economic efficiency is promoted when markets are allowed to determine the distribution of income. This ensures prices produce incentives for people to act in particular ways. Markets can do this because they govern the exchange of important rights – property rights – that directly determine our income and wealth. The capacity of markets to facilitate choice and promote individual liberty and responsibility is also emphasised. Yet markets also constrain choice.

The price mechanism makes some actions costly and others more rewarding. However, while it does not specify what actions we must take it does provide a set of incentives that significantly influence our behaviour. This idea was taken up by Michel Foucault (1991, p. 97) using the concept of 'governmentality' to explain how markets regulate our conduct. He recognised that the exercise of power is not confined to the formal institutions of the state or the public regulations that directly restrict individual behaviour.

Following Adam Smith, Foucault (1997, p. 76) identified the economy as a place of 'privileged experience' where it was not necessary to directly govern the actions of individuals. Instead, power could be exercised *through* the economy where it 'consists in guiding the possibility of conduct' through the modification of freely chosen actions (Foucault 1982, p. 221). Conduct is shaped without the direct state regulation of individuals because markets act 'on the manner in which individuals regulate their own behaviour' (Hindess 1996, p. 106).

In modern market societies, governments can therefore exercise power 'at a distance' through a range of direct and indirect techniques and technologies that govern the conduct of 'autonomous' citizens (Rose & Miller 1992, p. 173). In other words, governments can influence our behaviour not only through prescriptive law, but also by changing incentives, such as changing the extent to which markets regulate our lives.

Our choices are also influenced by the resources we have available and our capacity to influence the choices of others. This draws attention to institutional actors like corporations, governments and trade unions. Institutional theorists emphasise that some economic agents have a greater capacity to exercise economic choices and to influence the choices of others because of the type and amount of resources they command.

Large corporations, for example, can influence consumer behaviour through advertising, or market prices through monopoly power. On this view, markets create incentives, but they do not operate according to the principles of 'perfect competition' or free and equal exchange. In practice, large institutions are better able to advance their interests relative to smaller, less organised and less wealthy actors.

Marxian theorists are also concerned with power. They emphasise the importance of property rights both in the operation of markets and the inequality of power between different market participants. They claim that the unequal distribution of rights effectively forces some people – those without property – to find employment in the labour market. This produces class relations where people have systematically different choices based on their access to economic resources.

From this perspective markets can be coercive because without access to market income, workers are unable to live. Marx claims that this means the apparent 'free exchange' of the wage labour contract is actually an unequal exercise of power between capitalist and worker. Thus, the more that markets become central to production and distribution – and alternative means of gaining subsistence are removed – the more exploitative the character of society.

### The role of risk

Market incentives produce uncertainty and risk, which is present whenever there is the chance of an adverse outcome (see Box 6.1). Human societies have always been subject to risks of one kind or another. In pre-capitalist societies risks were typically associated with the weather and other climatic conditions, war, violence and disease. To these perennial risks market societies added all the uncertainties associated with participating in and relying upon markets.

Market risk stems from the changing and unpredictable nature of the price mechanism where production for profit, rather than use, allows the forces of supply and demand to regulate the behaviour of market participants. Because of the centrality of markets to everyday life, individuals in market societies are subject to some kind of market-based

## Box 6.1 Probability and uncertainty

Economists distinguish between risk based on probability and risk based on uncertainty. Some risks can be calculated using probability theory. For example, the outcome of tossing a coin is subject to risk. We do not know if the coin will land heads or tails but this is a probabilistic risk because we know there is a 50 per cent chance of it being heads and a 50 per cent chance of it being tails.

In game theory, which has developed new tools for theorising this kind of probabilistic risk, rational actors are assumed to incorporate probabilities into their calculations. They do this by multiplying the potential outcome of an action by the probability of that outcome occurring. For example if an investment offers a 50 per cent chance of making $1000 and a 50 per cent chance of no return, then the investment would be valued at $500 ($1000 x 0.5 + $0 x 0.5).

However, it is less clear how the theory can deal with genuine uncertainty. Austrian and Keynesian economists criticise the neoclassical approach for failing to deal with 'radical uncertainty' where the relevant probabilities are not known. Indeed, the various potential outcomes may not even be known (see Chapter 3). Even on matters of probability experimental economists have shown that people systematically make errors in calculating risk (Hargreaves Heap et al 1994).

For example, many people are 'risk averse', meaning they give greater weight to a loss than an equivalent gain. This has informed the development of theories of 'bounded rationality' where people are assumed to follow 'rules of thumb', essentially acting in the same way in similar situations without fully calculating the best approach, partly to deal with the problems of an uncertain world (see Chapter 2).

---

risk. It might be the risk of one's work skills no longer being valued, or the risk that interest rates will rise, increasing a household's mortgage repayments.

In a market economy prices respond to movements in demand and supply and therefore continuously change. Human actions respond to those changed price signals. In turn, this may create new incentives and reward patterns. There are always risks involved in such processes of change. Neoclassical economists tend to emphasise the benefits of these kinds of risk. They see insecurity creating incentives by encouraging people to respond to price signals, arguing, for example, price movements force producers to respond to changes in consumer preferences.

Some economic sociologists argue that neoclassical models actually play an important role in shaping the economy itself. Michel Callon (1998) and Donald MacKenzie (2006) developed the notion of 'performativity' to capture the ways in which economic models of risk become embedded within new financial markets. They argue that as such models become adopted by market participants – traders and financial firms – financial markets come to resemble the markets depicted by the models. In this way, economic agents 'perform' the ideas of economists.

Policies that expand the role of markets have also made risk more prevalent. Neoliberal policies (discussed in Chapter 5), such as privatisation, deregulation and marketisation create greater scope for the price mechanism to adjust quickly through the interaction of buyers and sellers in markets. The process of globalisation, facilitated by changes to state regulation, has also increased the complexity of economic relationships and intensified risk. This has led some sociologists to claim we live in a 'risk society' (Beck 1992).

## MARKETS AND GLOBALISATION

Since the end of the post-World War II boom, the liberalisation of trade and finance as well as changes to the organisation of production (see Chapter 7) have helped to create a more globalised economy. National economies are more integrated with one another while investors have greater choice and more freedom to move their assets across borders. This phenomenon of 'globalisation' has greatly increased the level and complexity of risk, which has in turn driven the development of financial markets.

Such markets exert significant influence over the global economy at a time when the economic power of states has seemingly declined. Susan Strange (1996), for example, described globalisation as a 'retreat of the state', arguing that where 'states were once the masters of markets, now it is the markets which, on many crucial issues, are the masters over the governments of states'. Similarly, Thomas Friedman (1999, pp. 87–8) argues that '[g]overnments which deviate too far from the core rules [of global markets] will see their investors stampede away'.

This popular argument implies that for national economic prosperity, governments should avoid the risk of capital flight by implementing policies that financial markets and ratings agencies will reward. These include the lowering of tariff barriers to help trade liberalisation, privatising state-owned enterprises, reducing the size of state bureaucracies and balancing government budgets. Friedman (1999) suggested that adopting these and other familiar neoliberal policies was like putting on a 'golden straightjacket' because it generated growth but gave governments no room to move.

Against this perspective should be balanced the ongoing ability of states – particularly those in the largest national economies – to create, regulate and shape markets. An example is the responses by the major capitalist states to the Global Financial Crisis of 2007 when several large financial institutions were nationalised. Clearly, states are still able to exert enormous power and even contradict the accepted wisdom of financial markets and analysts when necessary.

It is also possible to overstate the novelty of globalisation. There is evidence that many of the trends evident from the 1980s had much earlier origins. For example, the flow of goods and services between national economic units is an old phenomenon (Hirst & Thompson 1996). Hence, John Maynard Keynes (1919) marvelled at the extent of international economic activity while others could argue that economic depression and world wars merely delayed an expansionary tendency that was part of capitalism from its very early days (Wheelwright 1999).

There is little doubt that the recent neoliberal decades have facilitated such expansionary tendencies. Since the collapse of the post-war boom, contemporary market societies have been profoundly shaped by major changes to the regulation and scope of markets. New distributions of market risk have been created with significant consequences for the everyday lives of many people.

### The demise of the post-war economic order

As discussed in Chapter 5, the post-war economic order was underpinned by a unique set of regulatory arrangements whereby states set limits on global financial markets. This was often called 'financial repression'. The cross-border flow of financial capital was restricted through taxation or quotas on international financial transactions. Furthermore, the Bretton Woods system of fixed exchange rates curtailed the ability of money markets to affect the value of currencies. Such arrangements sheltered societies somewhat from the fluctuations of global financial markets and restricted the choice of investors. In doing so, they mitigated market-based risk.

However, by the 1960s the institutional foundations of the post-war economic order were being challenged on a number of fronts. These stemmed from contradictions in the established institutional order whereby arrangements which supported economic growth in the short term had destructive effects in the long term (Kotz, McDonough & Reich 1994). The fixed exchange rate system, for example, was being eroded due to the growth of US dollars held internationally which exceeded the value of the public reserves of gold within the US (Wachtel 1986). In production, global competition was intensifying as the reconstruction of Europe and Japan, essential for resuscitating global markets after World War II, led to overproduction and falling profit rates for US manufacturing firms (Brenner 2002).

Furthermore, full employment regimes had strengthened the bargaining position of labour enabling a wave of strikes and spiralling inflation (Kotz, McDonough & Reich 1994). By the 1970s, many capitalist economies were experiencing 'stagflation' whereby rising inflation and unemployment occurred alongside low economic growth. This broke with the macroeconomic patterns of the post-war 'golden age' where strong growth had been buttressed by an inverse relationship between inflation and unemployment. The international situation was worsened when OPEC (Organisation of Petroleum Exporting Countries) cut the supply of oil into the global economy.

Faced with these pressures, the US government ended the convertibility of dollars into gold and moved to a 'floating' exchange rate system where, at least in theory, the value of the currency is determined by its supply and demand in international markets. This ushered in a market-based era of currency valuation as other national currencies were gradually floated. The capital controls that had accompanied fixed exchange rates in the post-war system were also wound back through financial 'deregulation'. The pressure to reduce capital controls also spread to developing countries through programs imposed and administered by the IMF.

Emergency loans were negotiated to manage the debt crises that had emerged in many of the developing economies of Latin America. However, the loans were conditional on Structural Adjustment Programs (SAPs). Governments were obliged to implement a series of policies known as the 'Washington Consensus' that included privatisation, deregulation and cuts to social spending. This reflected the common advice of US and international agencies that were based in Washington and is widely seen as forming the international component of neoliberalism (George 1999).

Structural Adjustment Programs were subsequently used in much of the developing world, highlighting how international financial institutions can exercise considerable power over less developed countries. They argued that by promoting competition, SAPs would aid growth and development. Yet, critics of the programs argued they undermined the sovereignty of poorer nations and increased inequality and poverty by reducing social protections (George 1999). International institutions have partly responded to this criticism by refocusing efforts on building social capital and governance (see Chapter 10).

Many of the communist nations of Europe and Asia were also moving into a period of profound change at this time (see Box 6.2). Just as the capitalist countries were exposing their citizens to greater market-based risk, so too most of the former communist countries dismantled their protective structures, making rapid transitions to market societies. Even those which remained nominally communist, such as China and Vietnam, increasingly shed their social protections and made markets more central to the operation of their economies.

### Box 6.2 Market 'shock therapy' in Russia

By the 1960s economic growth in Russia, as well as those of many of its communist allies, had begun to slow. In the 1980s, the new Russian leader Mikhail Gorbachev promised an era of political openness (glasnost) and economic restructuring (perestroika) to confront this situation. However, these reforms were too little too late, and in 1989 a popular movement swept communism from power across the 'eastern block' countries and by 1991 communism also fell in the USSR.

Perhaps no event highlights the changing exposure of citizens to market-based risk at the end of the twentieth century as the subsequent 'shock therapy' in Russia. This process of rapid privatisation and deregulation was first implemented in Bolivia in 1985, under the guidance of then Harvard economist Jeffrey Sachs, who later oversaw its implementation in the former communist states of Poland and Russia.

Prior to 1991, the Russian economy was controlled almost entirely by the communist state. Most production took place in state-controlled factories and farms and prices were tightly administered. While this began to change under president Gorbachev in the 1980s, when the USSR was dissolved in 1991 the new president Boris Yeltsin began a process of radical transformation.

Assuming dictatorial powers, and supported by successive US governments, Yeltsin embarked on a widespread and rapid program of selling the 225 000 state-owned companies and removing restrictions on prices. The immediate effects of 'shock therapy' are widely acknowledged to have been disastrous for much of Russian society while netting handsome profits for the few who were able to purchase formerly state-owned firms at bargain prices.

Suicide, alcoholism and poverty all increased significantly during this period as people were forced to adjust to (uncertain) market-determined provision of everyday services and commodities. While in some ways an extreme case, 'shock therapy' highlights a unique feature of market societies: that people become dependent for the necessities of everyday life on profit-oriented markets.

## THE NEW GLOBAL MARKET

Changes to the global economy in the 1970s effectively ended the post-war economic order based on the Bretton Woods system, ushering in the resurgence of international financial markets throughout the 1980s. The unique role of money in the capitalist economic system amplified these events, which ultimately reshaped market societies. The nature and scope of markets in national and international economies was transformed, as has come to be associated with the policy prescriptions of neoliberalism. A new global architecture for finance, production and trade emerged creating a system where citizens are exposed much more directly to market-based risk.

## MONEY AND TRUST

In Chapters 2 and 3 we argued that as markets expand in scope, money takes on a new importance, acting as a 'universal equivalent' exchangeable for all other commodities. Sociologists and political economists often point out that it is the 'social' character of money which allows it to play this role. Polanyi, for example, argued that money – a 'fictitious commodity' – is one of the central commodities, alongside land and labour, without which market society could not function. Yet, the production of money cannot be left to markets alone. Like labour and land, it requires social processes for its production and its maintenance as a commodity.

Economic agents need to be able to trust that money, a 'token of purchasing power', can act as a unit of exchange and a store of value. This trust is very often underpinned by political authority. When countries stopped using gold and silver as the primary unit of exchange they typically moved to using tokens, such as paper or polymers, which are next to worthless in their own right. The value of this 'fiat money' is sanctioned by state decree or authorisation. States also underpin trust in money by issuing currency and outlawing counterfeiting to prevent its private production.

However, while the decree of the state is central to underpinning trust in money, this creates problems when trade moves beyond a state's borders. As Wachtel (1986, p. 31) points out, money is 'defined in nation-state terms while trade [is]...conducted across national borders'. This raises the question of how one country's unit of exchange can be accepted in another. Mechanisms need to be developed to value different national currencies against each other and trust in the value of a currency also needs to be secured at an international level.

Social relations are also required for credit, a form of 'money' that has been central to the rapid expansion of capitalist commodity production. For the lender, advancing credit is an exchangeable promise of claim to future earnings of the borrower. For the borrower, credit is a promise that the debt will be paid back and that money will be accepted by the lender. However, there is always a risk that such promises will not be honoured. Risk arises because there is no objective way of knowing the future. There is uncertainty about whether a borrower *will* create future wealth and this was the catalyst for charging interest, effectively the price of a borrowers' promise to pay.

There is another dimension to the social relations of credit. These are also power relations. Credit money is not allocated through a 'free and equal' process of market exchange but is, rather, allocated on a discretionary basis. It is often determined by *personal* judgements about the borrower and their social networks thereby creating a cycle of advantage for those deemed to meet the appropriate criteria. Disadvantage is also cumulative for those unable to gain credit. Significant power therefore resides in setting the rules of credit creation and in determining who has access to credit money and for what purposes.

At the structural level, social relations organised through institutions including states and private sector banks work to minimise risk by fostering *impersonal* trust between borrowers and lenders, be they individuals, governments or businesses (Pixley 2004, p. 9). These considerations of trust or 'institutional confidence' are particularly pertinent in light of the growing prominence of finance and credit in the economy and in people's everyday lives. These ideas are closely related to Granovetter's (1973) 'network' approach which understands markets as a series of inter-personal networks (see Chapters 2, 4 and 10).

## The rise of finance

The expansion and growing importance of financial markets has been a striking phenomenon since the end of 'financial repression'. Indicative of this is the huge increase in the 'FIRE' (Finance, Insurance and Real Estate) industries' share of total production, which in the US has increased by more than 50 per cent since the 1960s (Bellamy Foster 2010). Alongside this has been the expansion of 'derivative' or 'futures' markets. Derivates are contracts that allow individuals or firms to trade exposure to risk, selling it to protect themselves against future changes. Derivatives are also used to take advantage of risk and uncertainty through speculating on such changes in order to make a profit (Bryan & Rafferty 2006, p. 1).

The derivative 'derives' its value from the expected performance or price movements in the 'underlying' asset to which it is attached (McDonald 2006). During 2010, the turnover in the world's derivative exchanges totalled more than four trillion US dollars (Bank of International Settlements 2010), more than tripling in 15 years. Transactions in derivative markets are many hundred times greater in value than global production of goods and services or levels of international trade, signalling that these markets involve very high rates of transaction.

As financial markets have expanded, so has their economic and social significance. Finance and insurance markets now play a much more important role in regulating investment in the global economy. International financial markets are used to set exchange rates, commodity prices and to signal future profitability through share and futures prices. This has been described as a process of 'financialisation' which Krippner (2005, p. 174) defines as a 'pattern of accumulation in which profit making occurs increasingly through financial channels rather than through trade and commodity production'.

The growth of financial markets has meant an increase in speculative activities drawing investment funds away from the production of non-financial commodities. In Australia during 2010, for example, the same value of Australian dollars was traded in currency markets every two days as was exchanged via exports and imports in the entire year (Bank of International Settlements 2010). Yet financialisation, with its new financial instruments and commodities, has also provided a new phase of wealth creation and job opportunities in the face of underlying stagnation in economic production since the end of the post-World War II boom (Bellamy Foster 2007). However, the reasons for financial expansion as well as its implications are controversial.

Neoclassical economists tend to see finance markets as similar to other markets, being subject to competition with participants receiving income proportionate to their marginal productivity. A private finance market is seen to add value to the economy by increasing the productivity of investment and more effectively channelling surplus funds into productive activities. The growth of finance markets might also be welcomed because of the role markets play in managing complexity, as suggested by Austrian economist Friedrich von Hayek (1967). They support the increasing scale of competition and production by coordinating investment flows between different firms, industries and countries.

However, the growth of the finance sector has also been associated with greater economic instability and inequality as well as the greater regulatory encroachment of financial markets into the activities of governments and households. Hence, a number of other traditions within the social sciences are critical of its expansion. Many classical political economists, too, were critical of the finance and real estate industries of their time. Based on the labour theory of value, they saw these sectors as 'unproductive', gaining income from their monopoly control of assets. Echoing these ideas, many current critics of finance view its expansion as undesirable when it comes at the expense of more 'productive' industries such as manufacturing.

The speculative nature of finance is also an object of concern for many economic and social theorists. Investments can produce an ongoing income such as dividends paid on shares or rent paid on land. They can also produce capital gains where the value of the investment increases. Investment focused on capital gain can be particularly volatile as it is often short term, speculative and based on expectations about price movements, rather than the long-term returns on capital. Speculation is also related to financial panics which certainly appear to have increased during the era of financialisation – financial crises in East Asia and Argentina, the dot-com bubble and the recent subprime crisis are some examples.

Drawing on the work of Hyman Minksy (1986), a number of post-Keynesian economists argue that the growth of the finance sector has increased economic instability because finance markets tend to exaggerate the business cycle by creating manias and panics. Kindleberger (1996), for example, showed how new investment opportunities with initially high returns led many more people to invest thereby increasing the price of the new investment further (like technology stocks in the dot-com bubble). However, as people begin to realise that the high price cannot be sustained by a flow of income to the asset, a panic would emerge and the price would suddenly plummet.

In focusing on the role of debt, Minsky (1986) explained how the finance sector could transmit this speculative panic into a broader economic crisis. Investors who borrowed money to make capital gains could be bankrupted by a panic. Banks would then respond by increasing interest rates and tightening borrowing conditions, leading many other borrowers to default and the credit system to seize up. The result could be a macroeconomic crisis where businesses are unable to access capital and investors lose confidence. Many argue this is what happened during the recent subprime crisis where bankruptcies and job losses occurred throughout the global economy (see Box 6.3).

### Box 6.3 Crisis and the burden of austerity

The consequences of financialisation are evident in the effects of the economic crisis following the collapse of the US sub-prime housing market in 2007. As people began to default on their loans a panic was triggered with institutional investors fearing they would lose money. Banks cut back on lending, which made it difficult for businesses to function. The crisis deepened as more people lost their jobs, more borrowers defaulted and more businesses went bankrupt.

The internationalisation of finance meant the crisis quickly spread beyond the US to the global economy. But these events signal broader lessons. The ways in which different individuals and groups experience the effects of economic crises provides insight into how market-based risk is distributed within a society at given times. How states respond to such crises also gives a picture of the distribution of power in market societies.

Prior to the crisis, many believed that the development of sophisticated pricing models and products such as credit default swaps had effectively dispersed the risks of finance, making a major crisis unlikely. The influential 'efficient markets hypothesis' also posited that financial markets allowed accurate pricing of risk by reflecting all relevant information. However, the extensive holdings of complex (and often linked) derivatives of various types meant that what began as a crisis in a small, localised market quickly spread throughout the global economy.

The effects of the crisis were also felt beyond financial markets *per se*. Two decades of privatisation and marketisation, combined with the spread of financialisation, meant that the viability of a range of social services and public institutions was also threatened. Throughout the advanced capitalist countries, local governments investing public funds in financial markets with the expectation of high returns saw their surpluses disappear. Private service providers whose business model was reliant upon complex financial instruments went bankrupt.

Many governments responded initially with a Keynesian-style fiscal rescue package designed to stimulate demand by pumping money into the economy. They also guaranteed the value of bank deposits and, in some cases, nationalised banks to prevent their collapse. New regulations were crafted for the global finance industry to minimise the exposure of major banks to risky speculative financial products. However, by 2010 it was clear that the flirtation with Keynesianism was short-lived as the neoliberal policies which characterised the pre-crisis years were the norm once again.

Governments sought to return their budgets to surplus by reducing expenditure. In Britain, the new Coalition government implemented extensive cuts to public services. Greece and Russia aimed to boost their budgets through widespread programs of privatisation. Such austerity measures led to demonstrations and the criticism that governments were forcing the burden of economic adjustment onto citizens, while corporations benefited from large government subsidies and bail-out packages. In the US, it was often said that the government was ignoring 'Main Street' in favour of 'Wall Street'. In the US this has been taken up by the Occup Wall Street movement, which spread internationally.

Marxian political economist John Bellamy Foster (2007) builds on these ideas. He argues that the dominance of large corporations since World War II changed the nature of capitalist economies by increasing productivity and profitability. However, consumer demand and new investment opportunities failed to keep pace. The result is a growing pool of surplus funds which, Bellamy Foster argues, drove the growth of financial markets. Finance creates new but often more speculative instruments and 'commodities' for investment which increasingly provide little new productive activity. Hence, while speculation temporarily causes a boom in the value of financial assets, it inevitably results in financial crisis, creating greater instability.

The expanded availability of credit associated with new financial commodities has also seen a dramatic increase in household debt. While some of this debt is associated with credit cards, the majority is mortgage debt used to buy housing. However, if the funds are used to buy existing assets, price inflation can leave people with large mortgages and vulnerable to interest rate increases. This is what happened during the sub-prime crisis in the US. New financial instruments were created which effectively allowed institutional investors to loan money to individual home buyers through 'sub-prime' mortgages. At the same time, rules for borrowing were relaxed, leading to an increase in household debt, inflated house prices and (temporarily) rising returns to investors.

Increasing inequality has also correlated with the growth of finance. Paul Krugman (2007) has shown that the rise of the finance sector is associated with dramatic increases in salaries and bonuses at the top of the income distribution. At the same time, the increasing cost of assets like insurance and housing has increased cost of living pressures for many people. Elizabeth Warren (2007) has calculated that middle-income families in the US now spend less on consumer products such as food and clothing but more on housing and health insurance as prices in these areas increase rapidly (see Chapter 8). In this context, the impact of the GFC was crippling for many US states and their citizens (see Box 6.3).

## TRADE AND INDUSTRY

Beyond the 'speculative economy' of finance, the collapse of the post-war order also brought about significant transformations in the 'real economy' with the creation of new institutions, agreements and regulations governing international trade and production (see Chapter 7). While there is a sense in which such labels capture the differences between these sectors, it is worth noting that the production of tangible ('real') goods and services in a capitalist economy is dependent upon access to finance. Hence, the 'real' and 'speculative' aspects of the economy are inextricably linked.

The national and international response to the crises of the post-World War II era went beyond the financial system to modifying the rules and regulations governing trade and industrial production. Together, deregulation in finance and trade triggered a significant restructuring in the advanced capitalist economies. Some of the greatest impacts of this were felt in the manufacturing industries which went into decline relative to the services sector in a process sometimes referred to as 'deindustrialisation'.

The General Agreement on Tariffs and Trade (GATT) that had been established as part of the Bretton Woods agreements was geared to facilitating trade liberalisation within a system that implicitly sanctioned national protections such as tariffs and subsidies. With the onset of economic crises in the 1970s national governments began to reduce tariffs in some of the highly protected manufacturing industries. In accordance with neoclassical theory (see Chapter 3) it was argued that the resulting exposure to international competition would improve efficiency and productivity within firms, stimulating innovation and economic growth.

However, the reality of competition for many manufacturing firms and their employees was bankruptcy. For those who could, production was located offshore often in developing economies where they were able to take advantage of lower labour costs. In either case, many workers found themselves in unemployment queues where their skill sets did not match those required by the bourgeoning services sector, itself growing substantially as a result of the rise of the FIRE industries. Long-term structural unemployment was the result (see Chapter 8).

The GATT was replaced in 1995 with a new institution – the World Trade Organisation (WTO) – which reflects the broader changes in ideology and practice away from 'protection' toward greater exposure to competition and risk. Its aim is the liberalising of international trade in goods and services through the continued removal of tariffs and subsidies. Like the World Bank and the International Monetary Fund, the WTO attracts widespread criticism for the neoliberal 'free market' model of development it promotes. Encouraging 'free trade' and export processing zones in developing countries has often resulted in poor working conditions and low environmental standards being the basis for attracting investors in what has been referred to as a 'race to the bottom' (see Chapter 5) (AFTINET n.d.).

Beyond the global focus of the WTO, there has been a growing incidence of 'free trade' agreements creating 'trading blocs' between different countries and regions (see Box 6.4). For example, the 1994 North American Free Trade Agreement (NAFTA) between the US, Canada and Mexico aimed to eliminate all trade protections between the three countries. However, NAFTA has been criticised for its negative impacts on the domestic economies of the participant countries. For example, Mexican farmers have struggled to maintain their livelihoods as local markets are flooded with cheap US agricultural imports. Similarly, US industrial workers have suffered as their industries have relocated in Mexico to take advantage of cheap labour.

The most integrated regional bloc for free trade and political cooperation is the European Union (EU). It has 27 member states and has attempted to create a 'single market' for labour, goods, services and capital. The EU has

### Box 6.4 Free trade to help the poor?

International, regional and bilateral trade negotiations are often characterised by differences in the interests of developed and developing countries. Under the rhetoric of 'free trade' developed countries have pursued 'market access' in developing economies through the removal of trade protections. Meanwhile, some developing countries have focused on the need to establish trade rules that promote development, including food security.

However, developed countries have been able to exploit loopholes emerging from unequal negotiating practices. This has effectively resulted in different global trade rules for agricultural and non-agricultural goods, services and intellectual property, whereby 'free trade' is not 'fair' trade. Developed countries exercise their power to maintain and reformulate trade protections, such as tariffs, subsidies and quotas. Concurrently, developing countries are forced to open their markets without the same protections enjoyed by the developed economies.

This has created significant opposition. Oxfam is one international development NGO which campaigns to change the imbalances in the global trading architecture in the interests of poor farming communities in developing countries. Their activities, part of the broader 'Make Trade Fair' campaign, target protectionist practices in the agricultural sectors of developed economies. The US has come under particular scrutiny for its 'Farm Bills', which provide substantial subsidies (over US$25 billion in 2003) including direct payments to selected industries and corporations (Oxfam 2008, 2009).

Oxfam works for the removal of trade protections such as these while at the same time seeking 'special and differentiated treatment' for vulnerable trade-exposed industries in developing countries. This aims to protect and promote the development interests of such countries by instituting a form of free trade that is 'one-way' (applying to developed countries). However, Oxfam's (n.d.) position highlights the complexity of international trade – it is highly critical of aspects of globalisation on the one hand, yet also argues in favour of extending free trade measures to many industries in the developed world.

a dedicated parliament and justice system and more than half its members are covered by a single currency (the Euro) managed by the European Central Bank. Within the European market, though, there are significant trade protections against non-European goods and services, particularly in agriculture. Indeed, protection of some domestic industries is an ongoing feature of many advanced capitalist states, even while they call for 'free trade' abroad.

These different examples of trading structures and the criticisms and resistance they provoke point to the contested nature of political, economic and social change as well as the contingent nature of institutional design and implementation. As we will see in the following section, although 'the market' has become a dominant policy paradigm penetrating areas not previously commodified or marketised, similar processes of contestation and resistance are evident.

## MARKETISING THE STATE

Beyond the international spheres of finance and trade states too have been transformed with the logic of markets being used to reshape their operations. The processes of privatisation and deregulation have increased the range of social services provided through markets as states have engaged private enterprise in areas formerly delivered by the public sector. Furthermore, many of the internal operations of states have become subject to market-like mechanisms. Both of these developments have profound implications for the relationship between states and their citizens and for people's exposure to market-based risk.

## SOCIAL PROTECTION AND THE MARKET

The state's role in providing social protections, as discussed in Chapters 4 and 5, has been the object of campaigns to 'wind back the state'. While these were partly ideological in nature they were also a response to the competitive pressures of globalisation. The advocates of neoliberalism promoted cuts to government spending and tax rates as well as the deregulation of labour markets. Tax rates on the highest income earners and corporations fell dramatically in many countries with the average company tax rate in the OECD falling from 44 per cent to 31 per cent between 1985 and 2004 (Kelly & Graziani 2004).

Neoliberals also had considerable success in reducing the direct role of the state in the production of many goods and services. In Britain, for example, many industries, including coal mines and steel works, were transferred from state ownership into private ownership. Similarly, in Australia public banks, airlines, airports and telecommunications were privatised. However, the most dramatic privatisations occurred in the developing world.

Neoliberalism also brought changes to the regulation of labour markets. In Australia, for example, the centralised award system (see Chapter 5) was gradually replaced with a system of decentralised wage bargaining. This was a radical institutional change with wages and conditions set at the enterprise (firm) level or with each individual employee, rather than at the industry level (Castles 2001; Mendes 2009). These changes generally reduced the role of organised labour in the regulation of wages and conditions and increased the role of market competition.

Forms of work that gave greater certainty to workers, such as permanent forms of tenure, declined compared with less secure, more flexible forms of employment, such as casual and contract labour (see Chapter 8). These flexible employment practices change the way that risk is managed in market society. Employers are better able to respond to changing market conditions by immediately changing the number of workers employed and the hours for which they are employed. This helps the firm manage risk, but adds to the risk experienced by workers as income and job security is undermined. These changes have resulted in increased income inequality and have also generated new inequalities based on the type of employment a person has.

Casual and contract employees have less access to benefits such as holiday, sick and parental leave, and often have less access to career progression. Some argue this creates a new type of 'precarious employment' and potentially a new class of precarious workers (see Chapter 8). Furthermore, the declining role of unions, falling union membership and less centralised wage setting has changed income distribution. In the United States real wages have stagnated since the 1970s even though productivity has increased significantly (Krugman 2007). Likewise, in Australia, economic restructuring is associated with a significant decline in the share of total income going to workers through wages and a rise in the proportion of national income going to capital through profit (see Pusey 2003, Appendix A).

The way people's everyday exposure to risk has changed over the last four decades is exemplified by changes to monetary policy which has downgraded the goal of full employment in favour of inflation targeting. During the post-World War II Bretton Woods era, monetary policy acted to shelter citizens from many market-based risks. International agreements made central banks responsible for maintaining the value of the national currency at an agreed rate, thereby shielding domestic economies from the fluctuations of global currency markets. Many central banks were effectively controlled by the government of the day (the US Federal Reserve being one notable exception).

Monetary authorities worked with governments to achieve full employment while the use of interest rate ceilings in many countries also sheltered mortgage holders from large increases in their repayments. However, with the crisis and breakdown of the post-war economic order from the 1970s these arrangements began to change. Rather than interest rates being effectively set by governments according to political goals (such as full employment) they were set by 'independent' central banks. Governments effectively lost one of their policy levers while the goal of monetary policy also shifted in many countries from securing full employment to ensuring price stability.

Interest rate adjustments created new uncertainties for mortgagees and businesses while potentially increasing employment insecurity for workers. Interest rates would rise and fall to control inflation while high unemployment returned as a persistent feature of economies. Market-based risks therefore grew for many citizens. In Europe these changes coincided with restrictions under the 1992 Maastricht Treaty, which bound member states to limit deficits to three per cent of GDP. These policy shifts were also accompanied by the application of market logic to many aspects of the state itself.

## MARKET LOGIC IN THE STATE

State institutions are organised differently to private firms and have traditionally been motivated by different goals. Internally, many public sector employees enjoyed the benefits of professionalism, retaining greater control over their work and over career progression. A public service ethos, particularly in Westminster systems, promoted an independent public service that could offer 'frank and fearless' advice to politicians because they did not have to rely directly on their employer (the Minister) for their wages and conditions. The state also provided services on the basis of rationing rather than consumer choice and competition. Health services, for example, were provided on the basis of need as assessed by professional medical staff, rather than ability or willingness to pay.

One influential strain of thought which underpinned changes to such arrangements was New Public Management (NPM) theory. It applied the management techniques of private business organisations to the public sector, arguing that public servants should be more responsive to, and regulated by, market imperatives. NPM reduced the control of the public service over promotions, subjected public servants to performance management and introduced performance bonuses to senior staff mirroring those of executives in the corporate world. Critics argued these changes undermined independence, encouraging public servants to tell politicians what they wanted to hear (McDermott 2007).

More broadly, NPM also advocated competition by allowing private firms to compete with the public sector in the provision of public services. In many countries governments began to outsource service provision either directly through the private sector or through new innovations like public–private partnerships (PPPs). These involved government jointly funding new infrastructure (such as a road or rail line) with a private firm which would operate the infrastructure according to principles set out in a contract. These projects created new opportunities for private profit but the financial risk ultimately rested with the state, which underwrites projects (see also Box 6.5). These changes meant that even while governments continued to spend large sums of money, such spending was increasingly subject to the imperatives of profit.

### Box 6.5 'Quasi-markets'

Within social services a variation of market logic became influential, particularly amongst 'Third Way' governments in Britain (Blair), Australia (Hawke, Keating) and Germany (Schroeder). Policy theorist Julian Le Grand (2003) argued that the traditional model of state service delivery placed too much faith in professionals to act selflessly and too little faith in those receiving services. Influenced both by the economic principle of rational self-interest and the principle of autonomy promoted by disability rights theorists, the new approach emphasised the use of internal incentive structures to encourage competition.

A key mechanism for achieving this was the introduction of what some call 'quasi-markets'. These were markets because they introduced aspects of competition but were 'quasi' because governments retained control over funding. For example, in education parents might be given more scope to select the school their child attends, creating competition between schools. Or services might be subject to tendering, with private providers able to win government contracts to provide services such as childcare.

Advocates claimed costs could be reduced and standards increased by making service sector workers subject to competitive pressures. However, critics argued that the incentives often encouraged providers to serve only the easiest or most profitable clients rather than those in most need (e.g. the long-term unemployed). This is known as 'creaming'. The changes were also associated with a move away from universalism so that government money could be focused on those in most need. But this could lead to a two-tiered system where poorer citizens were confined to public services, while richer citizens could opt out into better-funded private alternatives.

Governmentality theorists argue these changes could actually extend state power. By controlling funding and incentives states could effectively force citizens to behave in particular ways in order to access benefits or services. The new systems created more data, giving the state access to details about people's everyday lives. The focus on marginalised groups allowed more coercive strategies such as income management where those receiving benefits can only spend their money in ways approved by the state.

## CONCLUSION

The period since the 1970s has seen significant economic restructuring. Policy changes have expanded the scope of markets and reduced various forms of regulation designed to promote stability and predictability. As a result, new sources of uncertainty, insecurity and risk have developed. But alongside this, new mechanisms, like financial derivatives, have emerged for managing risks. Advocates argue these changes create efficiency by making producers more responsive to market conditions and consumer demands. Critics, however, point to financial instability and reduced social protections for workers and those on low incomes. One implication of the expanded role of markets has been increasingly globalised forms of competition. As we have seen, many theorists see this driving a shift in power from governments to market actors, especially corporations. Indeed, corporations have become increasingly important players in modern economies. Alongside states and markets, corporations directly and indirectly play a significant role in economic life and are therefore the subject of the final chapter in Part 2.

## Questions

1 How has the rise and evolution of market society generated new social risks?
2 How do different theorists explain the role of markets in regulating people's behaviour?
3 What is the relationship between money and trust in market societies?
4 How have financial markets and trade changed since the 1970s?
5 How have markets been used by the state to address social objectives?

# 7 Firms, corporations and competition

IN THE PREVIOUS two chapters we discussed how states and markets shape people's behaviour. We now turn to the business firm, which is the basic unit of production in capitalism but also an important vehicle of regulation. It occupies a privileged position in market societies because the resources needed to produce economic goods and services are privately owned. This means that private decisions taken by firms have social consequences. They regulate the flow of economic commodities available for purchase through their decisions about what, and how much, to produce. Firms also directly regulate the working life of their employees although workers' experience of such 'discipline' varies enormously. This is because the 'firm' itself comes in many shapes and sizes, including sole traders, partnerships and corporations. The incorporated firm is now the dominant form of business organisation and many have evolved into large-scale enterprises.

The large corporation has played a significant role in the growth of the global economy and the transformation of market societies. In this chapter we examine the historic character and evolution of the business firm and the mechanisms which enabled the rise of the corporation. This includes considering different theoretical perspectives that seek to understand the nature of the firm as a key economic institution and its role in social and economic life. We examine how the firm regulates the workplace 'internal' to itself as well as the broader economic, social and political environment. We therefore examine key organisational aspects of the business firm that stem from the contradictory nature of control and cooperation in the production process. In turn, we also consider the firm in its global context and the ways in which the corporation exercises power socially and politically.

## THE RISE OF THE CORPORATION

The separation of production from the household (discussed in Chapters 1 and 2) gave birth to the institution of the manufacturing firm. This is a legal entity providing goods or services for sale to consumers or other firms in order to make a profit. Today, there is a marked diversity in the size and character of business entities with small privately owned firms functioning alongside large publically listed companies, many of which operate across national borders. Yet the scale and complexity of these modern corporations should not be understood simply as the result of a natural evolution from small to large and local to global enterprise. The corporation is a 'legal fiction' initially created by the state for public purposes.

Different national contexts and cultures as well as the timing of industrial development shaped the evolution of the corporation – something not incorporated into the standard economic theory of the firm. Great Britain, for example, was the leading industrial nation through the eighteenth and nineteenth centuries, yet big business was a belated feature and the traditional 'family firm' persisted as a central part of economic production into the twentieth century. By contrast, big business, enabled by state support, was a key feature of the later industrialising countries such as the US, Germany and Japan in the second half of the nineteenth century.

## THE HISTORY OF THE CAPITALIST FIRM

The manufacturing firms that emerged with the industrial revolution in England during the late eighteenth century were centred on the textile industry. New technologies and the harnessing of steam power dramatically increased productivity. Production became less labour-intensive and more capital-intensive. A key turning point in establishing 'mass production in the factory system' (Tann 1979, p. 247) occurred when entreprenuer Richard Arkwright brought together new inventions in mills and factories with production organised on a 'continuous flow' basis. Many others followed Arkwright's example. As mechanisation improved through the industrial revolution and labour markets secured the necessary supply of workers, more mills and factories were built. These soon gave rise to wealthy business people who in turn built more factories, sometimes growing into quite large enterprises.

Large industrial firms were central to rising economic efficiency and industrial productivity in the UK, US and Germany from the 1880s. They drove increasing national incomes with the US overtaking Britain as the global leader in economic growth by World War I (Chandler, Amatori & Hikino 1997, p. 6). The rise of the large private corporation, especially in manufacturing industries, occurred along with the significant technological changes of the 'second industrial revolution'. The division of labour within firms and the pressures of competition from other firms were both sources of innovation and technological advance.

Steam power and electricity enabled recurrent waves of industrial innovation both in terms of production processes as well as the types of goods produced. Existing industries were transformed and new ones were created. Being much less labour-intensive than firms of the earlier industrialising phase, they required large investments in physical capital. The increased production this brought about was complemented by improved transport and communications such as railroads, steamships and telegraph networks. These enabled distribution of large quantities of goods. New forms of management and business organisation also developed to coordinate these new forms of production (Chandler, Amatori & Hikino 1997, p. 8).

Firms needed access to finance to mobilise the capital equipment as well as the workers and managers required for production and distribution. Those at the forefront of innovation who were able to gather the necessary resources enjoyed significant advantages. Capacity of firms to produce large volumes of product at lower prices created a barrier for other firms wishing to enter the sector, thereby reducing competition. A firm's market dominance, stemming from their economies of scale, was continuously reinforced by looking for ways to improve the productivity of existing technologies and developing new complementary technologies (Chandler, Amatori & Hikino 1997, p. 13). Ownership across industries became concentrated as a result.

### Creating the corporation

While technological advances were important in the growing size of business enterprises, the 'efficiency' associated with economies of scale is not a sufficient explanation for the rise of the industrial corporation (Roy 1997, p. 9). The corporation is a specific business form constituted as a legal entity separate from its owners. Such firms (or companies) are typically identified by the addition of 'Pty Ltd' to their business name, which signals that the liabilities of the business owners – the proprietors – are 'limited'. However, the incorporated firm was initially created for public purposes rather than private profit. An early example of this is the British East India Company which was established by royal charter in 1600 and eventually administered British interests in India for a century until the 1850s. At the beginning of the nineteenth century the privilege of incorporation was only given to companies undertaking special government projects such as the building of bridges or railways.

There were many restrictions associated with incorporation which granted the privilege of 'limited liability'. This means that private investors only risk the money they invest because they are not deemed liable for other costs incurred by the business they own. However, during the 1870s, the public or 'quasi-government' form of corporation was extended to private business and in the late 1880s US courts granted the status of legal personhood to corporations. This allowed corporations to conduct business as if they were a private 'individual'. They could own assets, raise capital, borrow money, enter into contracts and buy and sell securities.

Initially, the private corporate form was generally confined to infrastructural areas under government jurisdiction. There were very few manufacturing securities traded on the stock market. Indeed, the world of finance remained 'institutionally distinct' from manufacturing as its activities generally focused on lending money to governments and investing in railroads and communications (Roy 1997, p. 4). The ownership of most industrial firms tended to be personal and restricted to one or a few wealthy individuals who were able to finance their own activities. For example, the world's largest manufacturing operation at the time, Carnegie Steel Company, was an unincorporated limited partnership financed through the personal profits of Andrew Carnegie (Wall 1989).

However, with the extension of incorporation and all the benefits it conferred, there was a rapid increase in the number of incorporated manufacturing firms from the 1890s. A 'new corporate order in manufacturing' was ushered in as the aggregate value of manufacturing securities traded on major stock exchanges increased eightfold between 1898 and 1903 (Roy 1997, p. 5). Incorporation also dramatically changed the rights and obligations associated with ownership. Managers, rather than stockholders (the owners), became the key decision-makers overseeing the day-to-day activities of the business.

The US railroads provided a significant model for the private corporation, illustrating the politically *and* economically driven changes to the structure of the corporation. State and local governments had a major role in financing and planning railway networks, regulating their operation and then legislating for their privatisation in the new corporate form. This allowed for the concentration of ownership and formed the basis for the rise of the corporation as the dominant type of capitalist firm (Roy 1997). By the mid-1860s, the total privatisation of the US railway networks heralded a significant shift in the nature of corporations. They became large-scale private profit-making entities with accountability only to investors rather than governments.

Elsewhere, political and cultural factors were also evident in the creation of the corporation. In Germany, for example, many firms were 'born large' as part of state-supported industrialisation. These enterprises were initiated, financed or subsidised by government in a 'corporatist' model of economic cooperation reflecting 'explicit coordination' between government, big business and the powerful banking system (Kesselman et al 2004, p. 171). Similarly, Japan's process of industrial development featured large firms known as Zaibatsu. These were integrated financial and industrial conglomerates central to the Japanese economy from the 1860s until the end of World War II. Culturally, the Confucian tradition was important in the creation of close collaborative relations between finance and industry as well as between business and government (Wiarda 1997, p. 86).

## Organisational transformations

As industrial manufacturing significantly expanded its contribution to economic growth and employment, the corporation became the dominant mode of business organisation. This grew considerably throughout the twentieth century, transforming the character of the corporation. One of the most significant changes to the organisation of business was the development of the 'multi-divisional' structure (see Box 7.1). This permitted corporations to internalise many of the activities they had previously sourced through markets. In doing so, they considerably reduced the risks associated with their external environment. For example, by having their own transport division, corporations could exercise greater control over the supply of inputs as well as the distribution of finished goods.

## Box 7.1 The multi-divisional corporate form

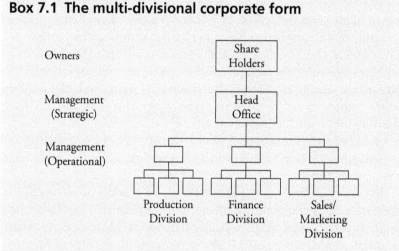

Figure 7.1 Multi-divisional business organisation

The 'multinational' corporation also became a more prevalent feature of the global economy. While gaining attention in the 1990s this trend was already evident after World War II. Corporate production dominated the post-World War II period and was assisted through foreign direct investment (FDI). This was facilitated by such mechanisms as the Marshall Plan for post-war reconstruction discussed in Chapter 5. Ushering in the age of corporate globalisation, multinational firms of the post-war era operated in many countries, allowing them to produce directly for each national market. For example, Ford was initially a US-based firm, but it established production plants in other locations – such as Ford Australia – to produce cars for those local markets.

Governments often provided special protections to these businesses because of their importance to employment in the regions where their plants were located. However, during the 1980s, many large firms began to 'downsize' and restructure their internal organisation in response to competitive pressures, partly brought about by the reduction or removal of state protections. Whereas the post-war 'giants' had brought ancillary services such as transport and accounting under the umbrella of the firm, they now began to shed such activities in order to focus on their 'core' business in the name of 'efficiency'. This process of hiring contractors to perform tasks previously undertaken by waged workers – 'outsourcing' – went along with widespread job losses and economic recessions.

More recently, the advent of the 'transnational' corporation reflects yet another change to the organisation of business. Such firms effectively break up their internal production processes to locate them in different parts of the world. For example, rather than producing a complete motor vehicle in a single plant, the manufacture of its component parts may take place in a number of different countries prior to assembly. The structure of these business entities is significant because they effectively 'transcend' national borders, taking advantage of laws, input costs and infrastructure in different locations for different aspects of their production process. This continues the pattern of 'externalising' costs but it also enhances the power of firms in relation to governments and communities seeking to attract investment.

The tendency to downsize or reorient production around smaller business units takes inspiration from counter-trends that existed in the shadow of mass production for much of the twentieth century. These trends have been described variously as 'post-Fordism', 'neo-Fordism' or 'flexible production'. Such labels attempt to signal a model of production which takes place across numerous firms through networks of producers instead of the mass production model of the Fordist assembly line (Trigilia 2002). Mass production persists, of course, but 'post-Fordist' production was seen as a response to the rise of niche markets that demanded differentiated products (see also Chapter 8).

## THEORETICAL PERSPECTIVES ON THE FIRM

Business firms have been an important part of market societies since the late 1800s, but their history and character is not generally reflected in economic theory. Firms have tended to receive less attention from economists than the process of market competition between them. The firm is often viewed as a 'black box' in which raw materials are transformed into finished commodities without a broader theoretical understanding of how this production takes place. Instead, firms are simply assumed to follow the same principles of profit maximisation as individual entrepreneurs.

### Firms and competition

Classical political economists, such as Adam Smith, argued that competition forced firms to lower their prices and produce efficiently. Thus, it was the context of competition rather than the behaviour of firms that was of most interest. They were particularly concerned about the social consequences of an absence of competition in markets. Classical, and also neoclassical, economists therefore developed theories of monopoly as well as oligopolistic and monopolistic competition (see also Box 7.2). These models sought to explain how firms would behave in various types of markets dominated by only one or a few firms.

**Box 7.2 The Australian banking sector and oligopolistic competition**

The banking sector in Australia is a classic case of an oligopolistic market. In 2010, Australia's four biggest banks – The Commonwealth Bank, National Australia Bank, Westpac and ANZ – held 75.3 per cent of deposits and controlled 74.6 per cent of the home loan market (Chessell 2011). Contrary to the idealist picture of 'perfect competition' in economic theory, the industry is dominated by a small number of large firms with smaller banks and other lending institutions competing for the remainder of the market.

Like many other countries, Australia went through a period of financial deregulation and privatisation during the 1980s and 1990s, designed to stimulate competition in the banking sector. While several new private sector banks were created, many of these were subsequently acquired by, or merged with, the larger banks. This led the Australian government to institute its 'Four Pillars' policy, which prevented the merger of any of the four largest banks.

The need for the 'Four Pillars' policy lends support to the Marxian argument that capitalism has a tendency towards the concentration of capital – for such a policy would not be required if the tendency did not exist. But is this tendency to oligopoly a negative development? Certainly some negative implications can be identified.

Australia's banking sector appears to have limited price competition. There have been allegations of collusion among them in the setting of interest rates. At the very least, the banks seem to engage in 'corespective' pricing (Schumpeter 1943, p. 90). This means they avoid destructive price competition and instead 'keep up with each other' by competing in other ways. For example, the major banks often 'compete' through advertising and promoting their 'superior' customer service.

Market concentration in the banking sector has also led to the major banks wielding significant political power and politicians seem unwilling to substantially restrict their market power. However, it has also been argued that Australia's highly concentrated banking sector helped the Australian economy avoid many of the worst effects of the 2008 global economic crisis.

For example, Ian MacFarlane, former Governor of the Reserve Bank (Australia's Central Bank), argued that competition led banks in other countries to take on excessive risk by lowering their credit standards for borrowers (Yates 2009). This was the origin of the 'sub-prime' crisis where home loans were made available to people without the capacity to repay the loans, or with little documentation to substantiate such capacity.

Defaults in this market triggered the crisis because these liabilities had been taken on by some of the world's largest banks and financial institutions. In Australia, by contrast, the relatively secure market share of the major banks meant that 'innovative' financial products such as 'low doc' loans and 'collateralised debt obligations' were not as widespread. For this reason, Australia's 'big four' did not suffer as greatly as other international banks.

Australia's oligopolisitc banking industry can therefore be seen to provide greater economic stability, but also reduce innovation and consumer choice. It also meant that the smaller banks and financial institutions felt the impact of the international financial crisis as many of them were unable to acquire funds to service their business clients and carry on their day-to-day activities.

The classical theorists argued that if competition was reduced because of the small number of firms in an industry there would be negative effects on the economy in the form of inflated prices and slowed growth. Without the force of competition to discipline them firms gained 'monopoly power' which allowed them to influence the price of the goods or services they sold. Competition, on the other hand, meant accepting prices determined by the market forces of supply and demand. However, for modern neoclassical economics the problem of 'monopoly' remains a marginal problem, or special case, rather than the general rule for the economy. The principle of 'perfect competition' remains a core assumption in its theoretical framework (see Chapters 2 and 3).

Karl Marx's critique of liberal political economy also assumed competition to be the normal state of affairs, at least in his modelling of the accumulation process. Marx, like Smith, acknowledged that competition would encourage a more advanced division of labour as firms sought to lower costs. However, he also suggested that over time this was likely to lead to larger firms that could gain economies of scale. In turn, this could potentially reduce competition and concentrate productive capital in the hands of fewer firms as smaller enterprises were forced out of the market. Marx saw this concentration and centralisation of capital as a normal outcome of the competitive process.

By the late nineteenth century the economic importance of large firms was growing. In the United States, a few powerful families came to control large parts of the economy through the companies they owned. People like Henry Ford, John D Rockerfeller and Andrew Carnege built companies that revolutionised production and often dominated whole markets, reflecting Marx's theory of capital concentration.

These wealthy industrialists often divided opinion. Some viewed them as 'robber barons', exploiting their power over workers and consumers, while others saw them as playing an important role in creating order in the 'anarchy' of competitive markets (Nevins 1940). However, the rise of corporations was also one of the catalysts for a new school of institutionalist analysis.

As we have seen, institutional analysis focuses attention on the historical development of market societies and in particular the different institutions and organisations that developed within them. Institutional economists view the large corporation as a response to the demands of industrialisation. As new technologies such as railways opened up new markets, the scale of production increased. This meant larger investments were required, along with greater standardisation and precision in the production process.

For institutional economists the corporation was central to understanding the 'second wave' of industrialisation during the late 1800s. Corporations became the engine room of the economy where new technologies and techniques in all areas (from engineering to finance) were developed. Business and management historian Alfred Chandler (1977) argued that this changed the nature of the economy from one governed by Smith's 'invisible hand' of competition to one governed by the 'visible hand' of corporate managers.

In a similar way, Thorstein Veblen (1904) had earlier argued that corporations led to a tension between the industrial impulse of engineers for innovative production and the business instinct of owners to maximise profits. This sometimes led managers to suppress new inventions that might require additional funding or to control the volume of output. Thus, instead of maximising production at the lowest price corporations could increase prices by reducing supply or inducing demand through 'competitive selling'.

JK Galbraith later developed this theme, arguing that the corporation constituted a new form of planning (1967). In earlier markets products were relatively simple requiring basic inputs and unskilled labour. The production process was short so there was little waiting time between investment and return through sales. These goods also satisfied more basic and stable demands such as the need for food. However, as markets expanded production became more complex with the result that, Galbraith argued, corporations developed to manage this complexity and the risks associated with it.

For example, corporations could ensure they had access to skilled workers by employing them directly and training them internally. They could also ensure access to specific materials by producing them through sub-units of the business. As societies became more generally affluent with improved standards of living new products were less essential and so demand was also more volatile. Thus, corporations developed marketing and advertising departments to generate new 'wants' and stimulate demand, ensuring a market for specific products when they were launched (see also Box 7.1).

Galbraith (1967) also argued that such developments produced two sectors in the economy. A competitive sector remained in some industries, such as agriculture, which were still characterised by a large number of small firms. Alongside this, a new planned sector of the economy developed in industries such as petroleum, steel manufacture and automobiles. Along with other institutionalists, Galbraith built a picture of an economy dominated by managers and engineers, rather than entrepreneurs, and by planning rather than competition. As he put it, '[a] firm must exercise control over what is sold. A firm must exercise control over what is supplied. It must replace the market with planning' (Galbraith 1967, p. 24).

Neoclassical economists have also acknowledged that market competition can be undermined by marketing and, more recently, the rise of branding. Branding can be used to differentiate products, leading consumers to see different brands (e.g. Coke and Pepsi) as different products, rather than versions of the same product. The result is 'non-price competition' where companies compete on other aspects of the product. This generates what economists call 'monopolistic competition', even in markets with numerous competing firms.

With large corporations dominating many markets by the 1950s, Marxian theorists also revisited their theories. Paul Baran and Paul Sweezy

(1966), for example, developed a theory of *Monopoly Capital* that built on Marx's ideas about the concentration and centralisation of productive assets. They updated his thesis for the new reality of large corporations, many of which contributed significantly to research and development and, consequently, productivity gains in the economy.

Baran and Sweezy focused on the implications of corporate forms of capitalism for the stability of the economy. They argued that large corporations were both more efficient and more powerful, and this allowed them to generate much larger profits. However, as production expanded, opportunities for new investment declined. This created a tension between the large profits of corporations and the limited opportunities for new productive investment, raising the possibility of stagnation.

However, other theorists have seen the rise of corporations as a more positive development. Austrian economist Joseph Schumpeter (1943) argued that the driving force of market society was innovation, rather than low prices. As a result, he saw competition playing a different role. Even if companies used their market power to increase prices, they were still vulnerable to the possibility of competitors creating new technologies that would radically change the nature of the market. As we discussed in Chapter 3, Schumpeter thought that new innovations resulted in a cycle of 'creative destruction', where the implicit competition from new breakthroughs provided discipline even in markets with a few dominant firms.

However, the principle of 'implicit competition' may be less valid in the contemporary context of large transnational corporations (TNCs). In 1975 Australian political economist EL (Ted) Wheelwright helped establish the Transnational Corporations Research Project to scrutinise foreign investment and the activities of transnational corporations in Australia. His work highlighted how large corporations can avoid competition and exert political power (see Crough & Wheelwright 1982).

These business organisations are more than merely large. Their ownership of resources straddles different industries with the result that they control a large proportion of global market share in production, services and finance. In planning and managing their own internal production and distribution processes across national boundaries, TNCs potentially evade market discipline and administer prices for a large proportion of global trade. Indeed, more than a third of global merchandise trade now occurs between TNCs and their subsidiaries (Stilwell 2006, p. 249).

## Firms and transaction costs

Initially, the internal dynamics of the firm were neglected by neoclassical economists who assumed businesses brought together 'factors of production' in line with prevailing market conditions. Exactly how this happened was given little attention. However, as firms grew in size and importance within the economy more economists began to look closely at their behaviours. The hierarchical nature of the firm posed an important conceptual challenge for neoclassical economists. Unlike market exchange, where both buyers and sellers are conceived as free agents exercising autonomy in negotiating transactions, managers and owners within the firm often direct workers on the basis of authority, rather than through explicit negotiation and agreement.

Confronted with this reality in the 1930s, economist Ronald Coase wanted to resolve the contradiction between the hierarchical nature of the firm and the neoclassical commitment to voluntary contract within the market. However, he wanted to do so without abandoning the core neoclassical assumption of the self-interested individual utility maximiser. Coase (1937) developed an explanation that subsequently became the basis of both the neoclassical theory of the firm and the growing discipline of new institutional economics (NIE).

The solution that Coase put forward was that firms were a rational way for individuals to overcome 'the cost of using the price mechanism', or what would later become known as 'transaction costs'. Coase argued that there are all kinds of direct and indirect costs involved in buying and selling goods including the cost of searching for information about market conditions or of negotiating contracts. Contracts were also inherently incomplete, being unable to specify every contingency in advance.

Firms, according to Coase, minimised these costs by internalising them. For example, by offering very broad, flexible and long-term employment contracts firms did not need to negotiate each service they required of staff separately, or negotiate separate contracts with suppliers. The same approach could also explain why in some cases firms would 'outsource', rather than internalise, parts of the production process.

Examples of outsourcing include the purchasing of components or hiring of independent contractors to complete certain tasks. The transaction cost approach claims firms do this when the cost of contracting through the market is lower than the cost of maintaining the capacity within the firm, such as employing permanent full-time workers. Essentially, the theory of transaction costs treats firms as rational actors seeking to maximise profit and minimise costs while using both markets and hierarchies to achieve their goals.

On the basis laid by Coase economists working in the NIE went further, arguing that we should look deeply within institutions like firms (and states) to understand how economic decisions are made (see Williamson 1987). Theorists of NIE argue that as people interact they develop shortcuts, or templates, for particular kinds of interaction. These templates become institutionalised over time. We get used to particular ways of doing things and tend to repeat them. Because of this, past actions influence current decisions through the institutional form that has been developed. The firm is one example where past legal and managerial decisions about how to organise production now shape the way current economic decisions are made.

However, some have criticised the NIE approach for being internally inconsistent. The assumption of methodological individualism, where individual action shapes institutions, sits uncomfortably with the NIE focus on institutions as an influence on individual action. Many NIE theorists have attempted to deal with this by assuming a 'state of nature' that exists before institutions. Williamson (1975, p. 21), for example, writes that 'in the beginning there were markets', but this is open to the criticism that it arbitrarily privileges markets, as well as being historically inaccurate. Nonetheless, by focusing attention on transaction costs, new institutional economics opens up a potentially valuable line of inquiry into the operations of firms.

## CORPORATIONS AND THE WORKPLACE

Just as firms try to control their external environment in order to minimise risk, they also try to control their internal environment. This is essential to ensure that the desired commodities and services are produced to the required standard, in the required numbers and in a timely manner to meet the perceived wishes of potential buyers. Economists and sociologists have put forward several theories to explain the dynamics of this internal environment.

### CONFLICT, COOPERATION AND CONTROL IN THE WORKPLACE

In contrast to the individualist tradition of neoclassical economics, the Marxian perspective, typically, has a focus on issues of power and conflict in their analyses of firms. The firm is particularly important for Marxian theorists because it is the institutional setting in which employers (capital) and employees (labour) directly interact. These relations of production are conceived as power relationships. Because employers hire workers, they dominate them, being able to direct workers to do things they might not otherwise do (Wright 2009, pp. 107–9).

Marx viewed the 'capital–labour' relationship as one of 'exploitation' because capitalists hire workers with the goal of having them produce more value than they are paid in wages. In this way, workers create the surplus value from which profit is derived. According to Marx, though, workers also have their own goals and interests, meaning that while they need to earn a wage to survive, they also resist attempts by capitalists to exploit them (Lebowitz 1992).

However, recent Marxian scholarship recognises that the relationship between employers and employees within firms today is more complex than this. Michael Burawoy (1985, pp. 123–8), for example, argues that Marx's focus upon coercion and control only captures the character of the 'despotic regimes' within workplaces during the early development of capitalism.

As capitalism evolved and the state began to institute minimum wages and other protections for workers, the owners of firms lost some of their coercive powers. As a result, consent, negotiation and persuasion took on greater importance in what Burawoy (1985, p. 126) calls new 'hegemonic regimes' of workplace regulation (see also Box 7.3). The picture of the firm which emerges from the Marxian perspective is one of ongoing internal conflict, alongside workplace protections and cooperation.

### Unions and the firm

We saw in Chapter 4 the ways in which unions developed as part of industrial capitalism to represent the interests of workers. Many accounts of unions quite rightly focus upon conflicts with company owners and management in pursuit of such interests. However, unions often also play a role in regulating the firm itself. Agreements between unions and the managers and owners of firms set down many of the conditions which regulate the conduct of employers and employees.

The levels of wages, occupational health and safety standards or the types of training provided to employees are just some examples of negotiated issues. Such agreements can provide stability and predictability for both workers and employers. By locking workers and managers into an agreed upon set of conditions such measures can function to lessen the incidence of workplace conflict. An example of this was the 1949 Treaty of Detroit made in the US between car manufacturing giant General Motors and the United Auto Workers (UAW) union (Krugman 2007, p. 138).

In this settlement, unions agreed to curtail their right to take industrial action and in return management agreed to give workers health insurance, pensions and wage rises linked to productivity. This set the parameters of industrial conduct between employers and employees in the US's large oligopolistic corporations for the subsequent two decades. It provided the basis for what has been called a 'capital–labor accord', whereby workers wages increased with productivity and relative industrial peace prevailed during the post-war boom years in the US (Gordon, Edwards & Reich 1994).

This is not to suggest, however, that the relationship between firms and unions is necessarily harmonious. There is a long history of firms using coercive tactics against unions and their membership. These include hiring strike breakers, vigilantes and private security contractors to physically confront striking workers or intimidate them with the threat of violence. For example, such tactics were used in Australia in 1998 when unionised stevedores were locked out of work and private security guards and police were used by the company to protect non-unionised workers, many of whom were ex-soldiers (Trinca & Davies 2000). Legal sanctions are also sometimes used by the owners of firms to prevent unions taking industrial action or to fine and imprison union leaders and activists.

## THE RISE OF MANAGEMENT

Alongside the growth of collective representation for workers, another noticeable trend within capitalist firms from the late nineteenth century was the growth of professional managers. This was related to the concurrent growth in the complexity of corporations, much of which stemmed from the imperative to control their external environment and monitor their internal environment. As companies became large, complex and vertically integrated, greater emphasis was placed upon managing the production and marketing of their products and brands (see Box 7.1 and Box 7.4). As they expanded geographically beyond a single location, the activities involved in running the corporation expanded further in volume and complexity.

Many scholars view the rise of management as a significant development in the internal dynamics of firms, even constituting a 'managerial revolution' (Chandler 1977). As firms became more complex the owners no longer had the time or expertise to take charge of day-to-day activities. A new class of professional managers took on this role and thereby accrued power over the long and short-term decisions and strategic directions of the firm.

Early capitalist firms were typically managed by their direct owners who were often a family or small group of shareholders. By contrast, large modern capitalist enterprises became characterised by a separation of the direct owners from management with boards typically having oversight of decisions made by salaried managers. Institutional theorists suggested this separation of ownership and control creates tensions and conflicts between managers and owners.

In their highly influential book, *The Modern Corporation and Private Property*, Adolf Berle and Gardiner Means (1932) argue that those who control the day-to-day decisions of the corporation are not tied to the interests of the owners – the shareholders – in generating profit. This is because their incomes are from salaries rather than share dividends. Game theorists have identified this as a classic example of the 'principal–agent' problem, whereby incentives need to be created to ensure that the person contracted to perform a service (the agent) does so according to the interests and wishes of those contracting them (the principal).

Several solutions have been put forward to ameliorate these problems, with varying degrees of success. For example, it is now common for high-level managers to have bonuses available in the form of large share options that create an incentive for them to maximise profits. However, such an incentive can have perverse outcomes. It may encourage managers to deliver a short-term spike in profits by, for example, shedding staff to cut costs. This delivers an immediate gain in terms of the 'bottom line', but may also leave the company vulnerable to longer-term developments. These tensions became apparent in the last decades of the twentieth century as managers were confronted with the uncertainties of globalistion and corporate profits seemed to take precedence over local workers and the broader population.

## CORPORATIONS AND THE GLOBAL ECONOMY

Previous chapters examined the process of 'globalisation' and debates surrounding it. In recent decades scholars have focused increasing attention on corporations for their role in this process. A recurring theme in debates about globalisation is the power of states versus the power of multinational corporations. Many theorists put forward various arguments for or against the process of globalisation. However, most believe the growth of multinational corporations and the collapse of various national and international regulatory systems put in place after World War II reflects the diminishing power of states and expanding power of corporations.

## THE RACE TO THE BOTTOM?

During the 1990s an emerging social movement expressed concerns about the implications of globalisation, particularly the role of multinational corporations. Protesters eventually shutdown a Ministerial meeting of the World Trade Organisation in Seattle in 1999. The movement claimed that globalisation undermined the power of democratic governments and transferred power to multinational corporations.

Globalisation effectively extended the competitive pressures of the market into international governance, forcing governments to compete for foreign investment and trade. Critics argued that this situation created a 'race to the bottom' (Brecher & Costello 2000). Corporations would play countries off against each other, moving their business to the countries with the lowest taxes, lowest wages and weakest environmental and labour conditions. This forced governments to make policies that were friendly to business, potentially ignoring the interests of workers, the broader community and the environment.

These concerns emerged in a context of declining employment in manufacturing and agricultural industries in the established industrial economies, with these industries experiencing competition from new emerging economies in Asia and Latin America. Orthodox economists argued this shift simply reflected comparative advantage (see Chapter 3). Emerging economies had a large supply of unskilled labour. It was therefore logical that labour-intensive industries would move to these countries. However, unions feared that globalisation was generating competition between workers in different countries with the result that wages were being forced down for all.

Many multinational corporations were at the forefront of the move into these new economies by setting up factories in the developing world. Some reorganised their production processes on a transnational basis by outsourcing to local companies before re-branding products to sell to first world consumers. Yet much of the shift to globalised production also reflected deliberate developmental policies by emerging economies in East Asia to build up domestic industries (see Chapter 5).

Likewise, while many governments used globalisation as a justification to follow neoliberal policies of privatisation and deregulation, diversity between countries continued. Indeed, in the first decade of the twenty-first century the World Economic Forum consistently ranked the high-taxing social democracies of Scandinavia amongst the most competitive (WEF 2010). One explanation of this comes from Hirst and Thompson (1996, p. 98) who suggest that the major powers, in particular, retain much of their autonomy over corporations and the economy more generally because the majority of business activities remain 'nationally embedded' in multinational, rather than transnational, corporate forms.

Indeed, most trade, foreign direct investment and corporate activity is concentrated within the territorial boundaries of the major capitalist nation-states. This stems in part from historical (institutional) factors but also because some conditions that are necessary for the successful conduct of business may not be present in developing economies. For example, a stable political environment, high-quality infrastructure and the availability of skilled rather than merely 'cheap' labour can impact on a firm's decisions to locate their production activities.

The need to access these conditions gives states the power to exert pressure over corporations and markets, and to shape them according to national priorities. This is similarly the case in developing economies where access to natural resources or cheap labour can be among the desired conditions. Hirst and Thompson (1996) warn the 'race to the bottom' thesis may be overstated. However, global business activities may still have negative consequences (see Box 7.3) for which, many argue, corporations ought to be made accountable.

### Box 7.3 Commodity chains

As capitalism has developed, the division of labour between workers and firms has become more complex. The production process for individual products is now routinely broken down into numerous separate components, each made in different plants, often in different parts of the world. Sociologists call this process of producing a commodity using components sourced from multiple locations a 'commodity chain' (see Hopkins & Wallerstein 1986).

The concept of a commodity chain helps us to see how the consumption that we experience as 'local' is really part of a 'global' economic system. It draws our attention to the role of corporations in coordinating these complex production processes. Sometimes corporations do this directly within subsidiaries of the one firm, something known as vertical integration.

At other times corporations outsource elements of the production process to other firms. Some activities take place in high-wage, affluent countries; others in low-wage developing countries. The commodity chain helps us understand who is doing what, who is getting what and who decides.

Commodity chains also highlight the enormous distances involved in producing individual products, as components are moved from one country to the next – and often back again. This travel has raised concerns from environmentalists about the sustainability of this global mode of production.

## Corporate social responsibility

Nigerian human rights activist Ken Saro-Wira was a prominent campaigner against the huge oil conglomerate Shell, whose environmentally destructive activities in Nigeria spawned a protest movement among the local Ogoni people. In 1995, Saro-Wira was hanged by the Nigerian government after being found guilty of murder in a trial that many around the world believed lacked credibility. It was alleged that Shell bribed witnesses in the trial to testify against Saro-Wira in an attempt to silence one of their main critics (Wiwa v Shell n.d.).

Shell is also alleged to have made payments to the Nigerian police which was involved in violent suppression of local protests against the company's actions (Wiwa v Shell n.d.). For some, this demonstrated the growing power of multinational corporations stemming from globalisation and an international solidarity movement developed to 'boycott Shell' and support the Ogoni people. Calls for 'corporate social responsibility' were one response to the actions of Shell and other corporations.

Corporate social responsibility (CSR) is where corporations recognise they have a responsibility to ensure the sustainability and reproduction of the society and environment in which they operate. It entails the recognition that corporations benefit from many unpriced inputs (clean air, educated workers, public transport) and can also produce many damaging, unpriced outputs (pollution). CSR is part of a broader idea of 'stakeholder capitalism' whereby firms are accountable not just to their shareholders but also to other stakeholders, such as the broader community (Banerjee 2007).

Despite some initial hostility, many companies have professed their commitment to the principles of corporate social responsibility in recent years. Large corporations are beginning to establish CSR divisions and report annually on their progress toward CSR goals. An example is the development of 'triple bottom line accounting' which is an attempt to recognise the economic, social and environmental costs of a firm's activities by representing these in their balance sheets.

CSR remains controversial. From one perspective, free market economist Milton Friedman (1970) rejects CSR, arguing that the forces of competition work most effectively when corporations focus only on maximising profits. If corporations try to satisfy other social goals this undermines the price mechanism. Other constitutional economists argue any social obligations should be codified in law, not through protests or the media (Vanberg 2007).

Alternatively, civil society scholars often criticise CSR as little more than spin, allowing companies to practice 'business as usual' while appearing responsible. Discussing BP's 'beyond petroleum campaign', Sharon Beder writes that:

> In the end, despite BP's rhetoric about social responsibility, triple bottom lines and enlightened self-interest, profits seem to count most. An oil company might invest in solar energy and admit that global warming should be prevented, but it will do all it can to ensure it can go on drilling for fossil fuels and expanding its markets for them.
>
> (Beder 2002)

## THE CHALLENGE FOR DEMOCRACY

Concerns about the relationship between business activities and social impacts are echoed in the political sphere, especially in debates over the meaning and practice of modern representative democracy. Parliamentary democracy has created some important opportunities for different groups and individuals to promote their interests in the political process. However, the importance of business activities to the economy and the influence of business over the political process have raised questions about the integrity and democratic nature of political decision-making.

The state creates the conditions for market society and business activity through private property law, contracts and the construction of markets. Governments also respond to competing interests through regulating the economy and placing social limits on the operation of markets to promote equity and other social goals. However, some theorists highlight ways in which business can have a disproportionate voice in democratic decision-making, undermining the principle of 'one vote, one value'. One of the most obvious ways this can happen is through political donations because of the control corporations have over money and other economic resources.

A recent scandal in India shows how destructive this can be. The Indian Communications Minister is alleged to have sold off rights to provide mobile phone services to his donors at cheap rates. Many then sold on these rights, making windfall gains. The '2G' scandal, as it is known, is estimated to have cost the Indian Government 38 billion US dollars (Bushell-Embling 2010). Such an obvious and crude example of the influence money has on politics is little more than corruption.

However, donations can also have a more subtle effect. Hacker and Pierson (2010, pp. 177–9) have discussed how business groups in the US donated to candidates from both major political parties, but only selected candidates that agreed with a pro-business agenda of lower taxes. This, they claim, had a strong influence on who won office because candidates with more funding had a better chance of winning. In this way, donations helped to build support for business policies in Congress. More recently, business groups have funded 'third party' advertising campaigns to oppose policies that affect their profits, such as the campaign by Australian mining companies against a mining tax during the 2010 election.

Situations like this have led many to argue for a ban on corporate donations in elections in order to limit the influence of money on political outcomes. Yet, parties and candidates continue to need funds to campaign. One solution is public funding of elections, such as the system in operation in Canada, where the vast majority of party funds come from the government itself. However, critics claim public funding removes the incentive for parties to build up large supporter bases to raise funds and volunteer. This can lead to parties that are overly professional and technocratic, rather than engaged with the people. In such cases, business may well maintain its privilege through the similarity of interests and 'culture' between party and corporate elites.

## CONCLUSION

The concentration of resources within the corporation gives it a special role in market societies. The scale of many corporations raises questions of market power and potential monopoly. However, many theorists go further than this, arguing that corporations exert considerable economic, social and political power through their control of supply chains, market share, advertising campaigns, investment decisions and even political donations. This power allows corporations some autonomy from both the competitive pressures of the market and regulatory controls of the state. Indeed, some theorists see corporations shaping markets and political decision-making rather than these influences working the other way around.

As a result, corporations can be seen as a source of regulation in their own right. Not only do they regulate economic activity through the decisions they make about production, distribution and consumption, corporations also shape our lived experience of capitalism. Corporations directly employ millions of people and through their influence in the labour market, and through their supply chains, impact the work of many more. Corporations also shape our experience of consumption, both through developing new products for us to consume, and through developing sophisticated marketing and branding campaigns. It is to this lived experience, starting with the world of work and consumption that we now turn.

## Questions

1 How have technological, organisational and political factors influenced the development of the corporation?
2 What explains the rise of management as a distinct component of the corporation?
3 What power relations exist within the firm? How do they impact on the regulation and steering of the corporation?
4 How has the rise of the corporation changed the nature of competition?
5 To what extent has globalisation privileged the interests of business and undermined the power of national democracies?

# Part 3
# Living market society

# 8 Work, consumption and quality of life

IT IS AS WORKERS and consumers that most of us directly experience the economy. Waged work is central to market society. It gives us meaning, provides income and fosters the division of labour that helps generate growth. This led many to see modern economies as 'work societies', while more recent changes to the nature of work have led others to argue that consumerism dominates our lives. Here we explore the development of the mass production model of Fordism, and the more flexible, diverse and precarious work arrangements that followed. We also look at the link between work, leisure and consumption and the growing role consumerism plays in our lives. Finally, we examine what this means for our quality of life.

## WORK AND SOCIETY

Many early theorists of capitalism argued that the nature of work defined the new economic system. An important issue was how changes in the world of work shaped both the economy and everyday life.

### THE IMPORTANCE OF WORK

One of the most significant theorists of the new division of labour was Emile Durkheim (1984 [1893]). He examined how the specialisation of work changed social processes, as well as the way individuals found their place within the social order. Feudalism, he argued, involved little differentiation in the economic roles people played. While there were distinctions between landowners and peasants, and between men and women, for most people feudalism involved a *simple* division of labour. This generated what Durkheim called mechanical solidarity. People felt a sense of shared identity based on their common experience of doing similar tasks and from having strong social obligations. A person's identity was closely connected to the group with little room for individualism.

By contrast, market society has much greater differentiation of tasks. Jobs became more specialised and this generated a *complex* division of labour. Durkheim argued this produced a different form of solidarity – organic solidarity. Our sense of common identity now comes from acknowledging the importance of all the different roles people play in society. Social bonds are increasingly based on work relationships rather than family, with our lives governed by law, rather than religious rules or family ties. This fits with Durkheim's structural functionalism, as the complex division of labour ensures everyone plays a role in securing the proper functioning of the social whole.

Another key figure in sociology, Max Weber, focused more attention on how people understand their own work. This is consistent with his interpretative sociology, which focuses on how people make sense of their own situation. He argued we can better understand how society operates by understanding why people act as they do (based on their own reasons).

Weber (2002 [1905]) argued an important part of the rise of market society was a change in the way people understood work. Work increasingly involved a sense of vocation, where people strongly identified with the sort of work they did, and this motivated them to work hard to do their job well. Weber claimed this reflected the rise of a 'Protestant work ethic' based on values of sobriety and restraint. This contributed to a savings culture, in which people saved and reinvested their money in expanding their business, rather than spending their money on ostentatious consumption.

Weber (1978 [1922]) also examined how the development of work reflected the broader processes of rationalisation. As we have seen, Weber saw rationalisation as central to capitalism, as people increasingly used the logic of rational calculation to make decisions. One element of this, he claimed, was the expansion of bureaucracy. For Weber, bureaucracy expressed the logic of rationalisation by ensuring that work was carried out according to objective and impersonal rules, rather than the whims of those in charge.

This was not uniquely positive. Bureaucracy did increase efficiency in Weber's mind, by making society more predictable, but it was also soulless, constituting what he called an 'iron cage'. Bureaucracy is now a part of most of our everyday lives, from paying phone bills to enrolling at university. It structures the internal operations of many state organisations and corporations (see Chapters 5 and 7).

Adam Smith also recognised contradictory tendencies within capitalism. While Smith (1904 [1776]) applauded the division of labour that powered economic growth, specialisation also made many jobs repetitive and dull, reducing workers to the role of machines. This may have produced greater wealth to enjoy through consumption, but it did little to recommend working life.

An even more critical view comes from Karl Marx. For Marx (1959 [1844]) our ability to use our minds and bodies to transform the world and shape it to our own imagination was an important part of our humanity, or 'species being'. Thus, he saw work as a defining feature of humanity. But in capitalism, he claimed, this capacity was subverted by the logic of wage labour.

Marx (1959 [1844]) argued that capitalism produced 'alienation'. Wage labour meant workers were not really in control of their own work but were directed by owners or managers. Moreover, workers did not control or often even have any connection to the end product of their labour. This left workers disconnected and disempowered.

Marx's focus on worker control is reflected in contemporary discussions of *autonomy*, or the ability of workers to control their own work, to make judgments about what tasks to do, how to do those tasks and even what the end goals of work should be. This is a central feature of post-Fordist debates, with differing views on how changes in work have influenced the autonomy of workers (discussed later in the chapter). Some argue paid work instills a sense of responsibility. For example Leslie Chang (2008) describes the freedom young women gain in Chinese factories away from their families.

For many social scientists, then, work is more than an input into production; it is a central part of identity and our experience. It shapes who we are and constitutes a large part of our everyday lives. Pay is an important part of work but so too is a sense of vocation and autonomy at work. Because work is so central to our experience of market society, many sociologists have argued that we live in 'work societies' (Beck 2000).

## THE WORK SOCIETY

The rise of wage labour meant the form of work people performed became central to their identity, income and position in the social hierarchy. The new pressures of market competition led employers to rationalise work. For example, much waged work became standardised and mechanised. This reduced the need for specialised craft skills, making the tasks involved in production relatively simple and repetitive so that most workers would be able to perform them with little training. Harry Braverman (1975) refers to this as the 'deskilling' of work.

Waged work also standardised time, changing how households organised their own time. The time at which people ate meals and socialised with family were now conditioned by the hours of the factory. New routines of everyday life evolved as the workplace became separated from the household.

As peasants left or lost access to their land, they moved to where paid employment could be found. This began a process of urbanisation, whereby people migrate from the countryside to cities. Recently, the world's urban population overtook the world's rural population as the process of urbanisation continues across the countries of the South (United Nations 2008). In some cities, work has failed to keep pace with migration, creating 'megaslums', where people find ingenious, and often dangerous, ways to survive (Davis 2006).

Changes to the nature of work also had implications for education. In peasant societies, formal education was confined to the wealthy. For most others, education took place primarily in the home, where children were socialised into their future roles within the household. In early capitalism children were pushed into waged work, leading to concerns about their health and welfare, and eventually prohibitions upon child labour (see Chapter 2). This coincided with the rise of compulsory state education for children. They were educated outside of the household and given skills to participate in the new world of waged work, representing the rationalisation of education and training.

### Fordism: the exemplar of the work society

While the rise of wage labour transformed everyday life during the early years of capitalism, the period most associated with the 'work society' is that known as 'Fordism' in advanced capitalist economies during the mid-twentieth century. During this period, waged work became the major form of social integration (Beck 2000) – the main way people found their place in (or were integrated into) society.

Fordism gets its name from the organisational practices of the Ford Motor Company and its owner Henry Ford, who pioneered the mass production of cars. Ford's system (discussed in Chapter 3) resembled the scientific management principles of 'Taylorism' (see Box 8.1).

## Box 8.1 Scientific management

Scientific management refers to techniques pioneered by US industrial engineer and manager Frederick Taylor from the late nineteenth century. Its practice is also known as 'Taylorism'. Taylor (1911) was concerned about the existence of widespread inefficiencies in industrialised economies. He believed these could be remedied through the 'systematic management' of work, informed by scientific laws, rules and principles.

Scientific knowledge of production methods would be developed through close analysis of the time taken and techniques used by workers in performing particular tasks. This information would allow managers to implement the most 'efficient' processes. However, there is disagreement about the impact of Taylorism on the relationship between workers and employers in the twentieth century.

A common argument acknowledges that Taylorist principles increased the planning power of managers and the mechanisation of production. It did so through increasing the division of labour and hierarchical organisation of firms while reducing the skills and autonomy of labour (Braverman 1975). Yet others contend that the work of Taylor and his associates was in cooperation with the labour movements of the time as part of a greater planning role for employees in the work process (Nyland 1996).

No matter the personal intent and ambitions of Taylor, his legacy is profound. Today, the concept of improving the 'efficiency' of workflows to increase productivity seems uncontroversial. Productivity improvement is a goal of firms and the idea appears commonly in the rhetoric of politicians and policy makers. Taylor's techniques are now used by managers in new sectors and industries, including services. Call centres, for example, are often closely monitored and tightly managed working environments which sometimes reflect the factory conditions of early twentieth century production lines (Hingst 2006, p. 7).

Ford was also involved in the lives of workers outside the workplace. In 1914 he doubled the pay of some of his workers in return for monitoring their private lives and encouraging them to adopt standards of 'moral' behaviour (Edgell 2006). The pay increase was designed to engender loyalty to his firm and to stimulate demand for Ford motor cars among his workforce. The enforcement of social norms was designed to mitigate the alienation, absenteeism and turnover of workers at Ford.

'Fordism' has since become synonymous with a broader set of institutions associated with the long boom. This was an era of broad economic stability and growth. Unemployment was at historic lows and most jobs were full time. Employment patterns were also more stable. Many people stayed in the one occupation, often with the same employer, for all or most of their lives.

Employment stability was underpinned by a series of 'compromises' based on implicit bargains between unions and firms. The nature of this compromise varied between countries, from formal agreements in corporatist countries like Germany, to the informal 'labour–capital accord' (Gordon, Edwards & Reich 1994) developed in the US and discussed in Chapter 7. These ensured workers received wage rises in line with productivity in return for accepting management decisions and forgoing industrial action, thus providing workers with steadily rising real wages.

Employment stability was often supported by industrial legislation that promoted collective bargaining, meaning unions were directly involved in negotiations over wages and conditions. This legal environment, combined with stable employment patterns, contributed to high union membership rates across the developed world. Industrial action did continue, but in many countries radical unions were harshly treated, including through direct state repression, which tended to reduce union militancy.

Technological developments enabled the more efficient production of a huge range of consumer items, from cars to white goods. This extended a consumerist lifestyle to a much broader section of the population. Stable employment also facilitated innovations in credit markets. Where previously credit had largely been confined to businesses and those with significant means, new forms of credit, such as mortgages and 'hire purchase' made credit available to a wider demographic, enabling greater consumption.

Job stability also fostered a widespread self-identification of workers with their occupation and workplace. Sharon Beder (2000) demonstrates how employers made deliberate efforts to encourage workers to identify with their company (rather than with their class) through in-house company magazines and pamphlets. Employers believed this would diminish conflict in the workplace. Beder suggests these measures were intended to foster values similar to Weber's 'Protestant work ethic'.

Fordism also rested upon a welfare state targeted at workers and their families. In many countries health insurance, pensions and unemployment benefits were linked to employment. This is what Richard Titmuss (1958) called 'occupational welfare'. Conversely, those outside the labour market only received a minimal 'safety net' level of support from the state.

However, Fordism was not a system of equality, but a 'segmented' labour system (Gordon, Edwards & Reich 1982). As the so-called 'blue collar' manual labouring workforce expanded, so did the 'white collar' and managerial workforce, creating a new bureaucratic layer within large firms, as discussed in Chapter 7. The Fordist workforce was also divided into 'primary' and 'secondary' labour markets. Primary labour markets contained jobs with relatively high pay, some stability of employment and opportunities for promotion (called 'internal labour markets'). Secondary labour markets generally offered lower pay, less job security and fewer opportunities for career advancement.

White, male workers in the large oligopolistic industries typically enjoyed the benefits of Fordism. Women and non-white workers were often disadvantaged by labour market segmentation that left them confined to less secure and lower paid jobs. This was the result of formal discrimination (such as policies preventing married women from being employed) and processes of informal discrimination discussed in Chapter 4. While new social movements have successfully campaigned to remove most formal discrimination, inequalities in the labour market persist.

## CHANGES IN THE WORK SOCIETY

From the 1970s the organisation of work in capitalist economies began to change. The term 'post-Fordism' is used to describe a movement away from the mass industrial production systems, strong working class and large managerial bureaucracies of Fordism. 'Flexibility' and 'decentralisation' are the guiding principles of work organisation and production in post-Fordism.

## POST-FORDISM

Theorists of post-Fordism make both positive and normative claims. That is, they argue about how the economy has changed and whether or not these changes are to be welcomed. Some argue that the flexibility of post-Fordism is felt across the economy, while others argue it is confined to particular sectors. Supporters of post-Fordism see flexibility promoting competition and even increasing the skill and autonomy of workers. Critics argue that flexibility increases inequality and undermines working conditions.

A series of economic and social changes are associated with this transition. Social movements challenged some of the social foundations of Fordism. Since the 1960s, women have entered the workforce in greater numbers, while many ethnic minorities demanded greater political and industrial rights. Rising education levels and new technologies helped to decentralise some forms of production. The economic crisis of the 1970s (see Chapter 6) raised broader economic questions that led some to advocate radical market reforms that undermined the stability of Fordist employment.

Advocates of post-Fordist production, Michael Piore and Charles Sabel (1984) argue that post-Fordism allows for 'flexible specialisation'. This is where firms are able to respond quickly to changing market conditions by altering the quantities and types of goods produced. The central component of this is the use of production teams, which include a number of multi-skilled workers who collaborate on producing whole commodities rather than each worker focusing on a discrete activity.

Piore and Sable claim team-based models enable less centralised, less hierarchical decision-making and greater integration between management and production teams. Workers are then able to collaborate in the operation of the firm (Amin 1994, pp. 20–1), reducing worker alienation and boredom. Post-Fordist theorists also argue multi-skilled teams are more efficient. They are better able to respond to changing conditions quickly through 'just-in-time' production. This has the advantage of reducing the time lag between investment and sale and can allow firms to respond more quickly to changing technologies or consumer tastes.

Many economic sociologists have argued that this model facilitates the rise of smaller firms, thus breaking down the bureaucratic control of large oligopolistic corporations (Trigilia 2002). Here production teams are effectively organised into a series of smaller firms rather than as units within a single larger firm. The smaller firms are connected through contractual networks, allowing them to achieve advantages of scale in areas like marketing and training skilled workers by pooling resources. This is seen as particularly successful in high-tech manufacturing where craft skills have become more important and demand changes rapidly. Examples are the new industrial districts of the 'Third Italy' producing high-end fashion or glassware (see Goodman & Bamford 1989), or the wine industry in Australia (Smith & Marsh 2007).

The development of new technologies is central to the emergence of post-Fordism. New technologies can aid flexibility, reducing the need for labour and enhancing productivity (Amin 1994, p. 17). Also important has been information technology based around new methods of communication for overcoming time and space constraints. This has facilitated 'work from home' which offers employees flexibility in organising their work time.

### Flexibility and fragmentation

However, critics of this ideal type point toward a number of negative aspects associated with 'flexibility'. The autonomy of workers in team-based production can be stressful and exploitative as workers are expected to meet very high targets. Flexibility can allow a better integration of work with other commitments or it can see work invade the rest of life, as the distinction between 'work' and 'home' is blurred, such as when workers check their email from a work phone on weekends.

New technologies have also led to job losses in some manufacturing industries as well as a kind of 'industrialisation of the service sector' (Amin 1994, p. 18). For example, large call centres use new telecommunications technologies to develop a form of mass production in the service sector, potentially raising issues of deskilling and alienation once associated with factory work.

Alongside technological innovations, post-Fordism has also developed out of political changes, such as labour market deregulation. Labour market deregulation replaced a partly centralised system for setting wages, where conditions for workers across entire industries were largely standardised. The reforms made it easier to set wages and conditions at the level of the firm (sometimes called enterprise bargaining) or even allowed conditions to vary between workers in the same firm (through individual contracts).

Some economists argue this level of flexibility aids productivity. It can allow employers to tailor employment conditions to their needs, and potentially to the needs of their employees. Such a view reflects a neoclassical understanding of the labour market as a bargain between formally equal partners – workers and employers – who both benefit through exchange.

Other social scientists see most employers having greater bargaining power than most workers. This inequality leads them to advocate for regulation to protect vulnerable workers by ensuring minimum standards.

This reduces the scope for diversity in employment conditions between firms.

Theorists also disagree about the effect of flexibility on employment. Critics claim it allows workers to be sacked more easily, creating insecurity. David Harvey (1990) uses the term 'flexible accumulation' (see also Chapter 3) to conceptualise these 'post-Fordist' transformations, arguing flexibility shifts power from workers to employers. Alternatively, neo-classical economists often welcome flexibitility, arguing employers are more likely to hire unemployed workers if they know they can sack them if times get tough.

These different understandings of the labour market, and of the nature of post-Fordist changes to work, have produced controversy over the impact of post-Fordism on the skills of workers. The uneven nature of post-Fordism means that there has been both de-skilling and re-skilling in different occupations, industries and regions. According to Atkinson (2003), this has produced a 'U' shaped labour market. Many middle-income jobs, such as manufacturing, have declined. The growth in service sector employment has been both at the top end, such as finance, and bottom end, such as hospitality (see Box 8.2.)

Those like Piore and Sabel focused on 'flexible specialisation' emphasise the re-skilling potential of post-Fordism. They point to the constant training required by technological innovation. (Amin 1994, p. 21). Many sociologists and political economists, however, emphasise how new tasks can increase the intensity of work, without granting greater autonomy (Braverman 1975).

### Box 8.2 The 'McDonaldisation' of work

George Ritzer (1983) coined the term 'McDonalidisation' to describe how the principles of the fast food industry are applied to broader capitalist society. These principles include rationality, speed, efficiency, standardisation, homogenisation and alienation, and are most clearly represented in the employment model of fast food chains such as McDonald's.

McDonald's tends to employ very young workers and the production of food is highly standardised, reducing the skill needed. Ritzer claims this model of employment is used throughout the services sector.

The rapid extension of 'McJobs', as Ritzer describes them, includes both the creation of new unskilled employment but, most significantly, the deskilling of previously skilled jobs, such as those in the banking industry. There are five characteristics to the McDonaldisation of work:

jobs involve a series of simple tasks, tasks are monitored and efficiency levels calculated, the work is predictable and repetitive, machines are used to replace human labour and restrict the autonomy of workers and there is high staff turnover.

For Ritzer (1983, p. 100), the McDonaldisation of society is '[a] wide ranging process of rationalization' where the fast food industry, rather than the bureaucracy (as Weber argued) is the model. This rationalisation can be seen more broadly in food production and distribution systems such as factory farming, packaged holiday tours, in education through its focus on quantifiable outcomes and in the use of genetic engineering to alter natural organisms. Ritzer (1983, p. 100) argues that the rationality of McDonaldisation is unreasonable, and ultimately irrational, because efficiency becomes the end rather than the means of an activity and the impersonal nature of such a society leads to dehumanisation and widespread disenchantment.

A more distinctive trend is the 'fragmentation' of work. Working hours have changed, moving away from the standard model of full-time employment to include a range of 'non-standard' employment forms. Across the OECD there has been an increase in part-time employment (dominated by women workers in all countries), as well as many countries experiencing significant overtime (work beyond normal full-time hours), which is dominated by male workers (OECD 2005).

Employment is also now less likely to be permanent and more likely to be on either a casual or contract basis (OECD 2008). Casual workers have less job security, effectively being employed hour-to-hour or shift-to-shift. They receive fewer benefits, such as leave entitlements, but tend to have higher hourly pay rates. Contract workers are effectively small businesses. The worker is paid based on outputs rather than by hours worked and is often responsible for their own insurance and benefits.

Jobs are also less stable under post-Fordism. People are more likely to move between jobs and careers more frequently, creating a more individualised career history and producing greater individualisation. Zygmunt Bauman (2000) describes this new reality as a 'liquid modernity' whereby people move between short-term projects and cultural identities, in ways that vary for each person, rather than finding certainty in long-term employment and prescribed social roles.

However, casual and temporary employees are often low paid and are subject to working hours which can vary significantly or end in the short term. Similarly, while employment based on individual contracts or self-employment as a franchisee can generate a reasonable income, there is a lack of job security. This means workers are more exposed to the volatility of markets, something reinforced by much higher unemployment rates in recent decades than during the period of Fordism.

Finally, at the bottom of the labour market, flexibility has become associated with income insecurity. Casualisation and rising underemployment – where people have work but for fewer hours than they wish – are associated with the growth of the 'working poor', particularly in the United States (Ehrenreich 2001). Such workers are often in 'precarious employment' (see 'quality of life' later in the chapter) having little savings or social protections.

### 'Workfare' and post-fordism

Changes in the structure of employment are often accompanied by changes in social welfare. Since the 1990s, new practices known as 'workfare' have emerged, particularly in the liberal welfare regimes of the English-speaking world. 'Workfare' refers to 'a range of compulsory programs and mandatory requirements for welfare recipients with a view to enforcing work and residualising welfare' (Peck 2001, p. 10). Workfare is part of the broader neoliberal shift in policy-making discussed throughout this book.

The linking of welfare assistance to work and the labour market is not new. For example, under the poor laws in England the unemployed were only able to access unemployment assistance by going to workhouses, where they were forced to labour under brutal conditions (Fox-Piven & Cloward 1971).

However, 'workfare' marks a shift from a Fordist welfare system which extended subsistence payments to workers outside of the labour market, with minimum compliance requirements. This system reflected the implicit assumption that unemployment was largely due to structural problems, such as insufficient demand, that meant workers were unable to find work.

The new approach, in which the unemployed have greater compliance requirements, reflects a belief that unemployment is largely the result of poor incentives or poor work ethic rather than macroeconomic conditions, with workers effectively 'choosing' not to work. Compliance activities are increasingly monitored by the state, with recipients forced to perform various types of low or unpaid work to qualify for payments.

An important example of workfare is the *Personal Responsibility and Work Opportunity Reconciliation Act* passed under the Clinton administration in the US in 1996. The bill placed a five-year lifetime limit on individual unemployment payments and mandated that unemployed workers had to move into work within two years of losing their jobs (US GPO 1996).

One variation of workfare, associated with Third Way policy-making (discussed in Chapter 10) is to combine compliance tests with changes to the tax and welfare systems. This identifies a potential problem in the interaction of taxation and welfare systems that sees recipients lose payments while also paying tax, and potentially gaining little income from work. It reflects a neoclassical understanding of unemployment as linked to incentives but seeks to both increase the rewards of work as well as increasing the costs of unemployment. The low-income in-work tax credit is an example of this, reducing taxes for those moving into low paid jobs.

Critics see workfare as reinforcing post-Fordist changes to work. Workfare can make unemployment a harsh existence, encouraging people to accept precarious work. Third Way reforms can allow those with low labour market incomes to survive by increasing government payments (such as family assistance) to those in precarious employment.

## A POST-INDUSTRIAL SOCIETY?

Some theorists, such as Daniel Bell (1999), claimed that the changes associated with post-Fordism constitute a larger shift in the nature of market society. Bell suggested we live in a 'post-industrial society'. He argued that advanced capitalist societies underwent a process of major transformation moving from an industrial-based economy, to one where economic success is based on data, information and knowledge services.

The driver of post-industrial societies is innovation stemming from the organisation of information. Post-industrial society has significant implications for the organisation of work because, according to Bell, value is created primarily through knowledge work rather than manual labour. Therefore, the importance, and prevalence, of blue-collar jobs, such as factory work, is replaced by white-collar jobs, such as consultants, information technology specialists and managers.

The post-industrial thesis is closely linked to the idea of post-materialist values developed within political science. Ronald Inglehart argued that these changes in the economy are linked to changing values, which no longer emphasise the politics of class, but rather focus obstensibly on non-economic issues, such as the environment and human rights (see Chapter 10). Inglehart's thesis is associated with growing numbers of tertiary educated professional and technical workers, sometimes called the 'new class' (Inglehart 1990), 'knowledge workers' (Drucker 1999) or the 'creative class' (Florida 2002).

Critics of this thesis, however, contend that market societies continue to be based on industrial production. Soja (2000) and Scott (1988) argue that while there has been some deindustrialisation, particularly in the inner cities of advanced capitalist countries, industries have largely moved to the edges of cities. These new industrial spaces offer more flexibility in industrial production systems as well as cheaper labour for jobs that have been deskilled through post-Fordism, but remain necessary.

Secondly, as the term 'newly industrialised country' suggests, much of the deindustrialisation that has taken place in the developed world over the past four decades has been accompanied by a rapid rise in industrialisation in developing countries such as China, India, South Africa, Mexico and Brazil. Much manufacturing production has been 'exported' from developed countries to developing countries in search of cheap and unorganised labour, lower taxation and lax environmental regulation. This has resulted in an international division of labour, where many of the goods that continue to be consumed in developed countries are produced in the developing world, linked through processes of globalisation such as world trade and foreign direct investment.

Advocates of globalisation emphasise how the new factory jobs can bring higher wages than previously available (e.g. Sachs 1998). However, wages are much lower than in developed countries, benefiting Northern consumers as well as multinational corporations. These countries also have much poorer working conditions and are often denied the right to form independent trade unions.

Conversely, the growth in services-based employment in developed countries is assisted by international migration. The countries in North America, Western Europe and Australasia are the destination for workers from developing countries in Africa, the Pacific, the Middle East, Asia, Eastern Europe and Latin America. Developed countries 'import' services from developing countries in response to short or long-term labour shortages in occupations of all skill levels.

Highly educated professionals, like doctors and engineers, are encouraged by government policy and higher wages to migrate from developing to developed countries. This can cause a 'brain drain', where developing countries lose 'human capital' and labour for essential services, often after considerable funding of education and training by the state.

Concurrently, low-skilled workers migrate for service jobs in cleaning and construction (also see 'care chains' discussion in Chapter 9). This is often encouraged by government policies but can result in more precarious situations for migrant workers because of temporary working visas, low pay and dirty and dangerous working conditions. However, both forms of service importing have become important sources of income for developing countries through remittances (Castles 2000; 2001).

## CONSUMPTION AND BEYOND

Consumption is the other main way most of us engage with markets. A defining feature of market societies is that markets become 'compulsory' – the only way to access the goods and services we need is through markets. Over time, more and more of what we rely on has been commodified. Home production has been replaced by capitalist production and the structure of contemporary societies requires new types of goods and services – such as cars, mobile phones and bank accounts – that were previously unnecessary.

Just as the rise of market society entailed an increasing importance for waged work, it also required increased market consumption. Some theorists claim affluence has produced 'consumerism', where our consumption goes beyond what we need and instead starts to shape our identities and life goals (Stearns 2001, p. ix). In this section we take up such issues through an examination of consumption and consumerism in market societies.

## APPROACHES TO CONSUMPTION

For neoclassical economists, consumption lies at the heart of the benefits of market society. Markets produce economic growth that increases the commodities available to consumers and thus increases living standards. Markets also offer consumers choice, allowing us to decide what will best suit our needs and desires, rather than having this decided for us, particularly by governments. In this sense, the neoclassical viewpoint takes the side of the consumer, as expressed through the theory of consumer sovereignty (see Chapter 2). Markets may make us work harder, and push down producer incomes through competition, but this is all to ensure we, as consumers, get what we want.

On this neoclassical view, a person's utility is largely equated with their consumption. Because we choose to consume, economists reason that this consumption must bring us satisfaction. But this view is not universal. We have already seen some criticisms of this account. Marxists argue that capitalism is a system of social relations, not merely a way of satisfying material desires. They cite the problems of alienation and 'commodity fetishism', arguing that while capitalism increases the production of commodities it does so in ways that damage our relationships and deny our humanity.

Many sociologists and institutional theorists also claim that numerous motivations drive our consumption, and not all result in higher utility. Consumption serves social purposes, such as signalling our status or our membership of a group. Indeed, many sociologists argue that in contemporary societies our identity is more deeply marked by our consumption than by our role as workers. They claim we now live in a 'consumer society' rather than a work society.

Political economists and sociologists also draw attention to the role of advertising and marketing in shaping our desires. This brings into question the claim of consumer sovereignty. If consumers are not really sovereign, and producers, social norms and expectations shape our desires, then consumption may not make us happier, particularly in the already affluent North.

More recently, another source of concern has been the growing use of information to track our behaviour. Nigel Thrift (2005) calls this 'knowing capitalism'. Electronic tracking of spending habits can be combined with website hits to allow specialist marketers to target consumers with new products.

## Consumption or leisure?

Some luxury consumption existed before capitalism became dominant. Werner Sombart, for example, identifies its roots as far back as 14th century Europe (Sassatelli 2007, p. 20). As trade spread beyond Europe and European powers began to exploit the natural resources of their growing overseas colonies, more precious metals began to circulate as commodities and new luxury goods entered European markets. Fashion and taste rather than simply material necessity became a motivation for the consumption of luxury goods such as clothes and jewellery (Slater 1997, p. 17).

Much of this consumption was concentrated among the wealthier sections of European society. It was not until the expansion of capitalism that consumerism became a central feature of the lives of the less well off. In part, this developed out of the basic survival needs of waged workers. As people began to rely more upon waged work and less upon producing for themselves, they had to rely increasingly upon markets for their means of survival. This led to the development of a host of consumer markets: for food, clothing and household items.

Higher living standards produced by economic growth raised tensions with the norms of pre-capitalist society. This posed an important social question: what should be done with productivity gains? Workers could be paid higher wages, or they could do less work and enjoy more leisure time. Conflict over the increased productivity of machine production became a key factor in the evolution of capitalism.

Some thought that capitalism would reach a 'stationary state' of needs satisfaction, allowing free time and the pursuit of self-development. John Stuart Mill in the nineteenth century and John Maynard Keynes in the twentieth century, for example, both thought the emphasis on economic growth for material needs would be short term. As basic needs were met, they believed society's resources could be channelled into the pursuit of 'higher' goals.

Unions also campaigned for shorter working hours, while maintaining real wages. The push for an eight-hour day reflects this goal of a 'balanced life'. However, many conservatives and employers feared social disorder might result without the positive values of work (Cross 1993). Without sufficient work, some believed workers would develop anti-social behaviours, or radical political views, making the campaign for shorter working hours a 'moral crisis'.

However, unions made some gradual gains in the early twentieth century as 'compensations' emerged in the form of slowly increasing wage rates and paid holidays. Leisure, in the form of the annual holiday, was viewed as reward for hard work. But the conflict over regulating workers, both in and out of work, continued, especially in the period between the two world wars (Cross 1993).

Economic growth also opened the gateway to modern consumer society. Henry Ford predicted that the production line and the car would revolutionise American society. However, the Great Depression, with its high levels of unemployment, marginalised the push for leisure and a balanced life as people became concerned with having a job *per se*. It was not until the end of World War II that Ford's prediction came to fruition with the post-war era of full employment and stable growth.

The flipside of mass production was the need for mass consumption. Machines were invented to facilitate increased production, but at the same time consumers were encouraged to increase consumption. During the long boom consumerism increased and working hours declined. However, more recently working hours have stabilised while consumption continues to expand.

## The rise of consumerism

Developments in technology made mass production possible. However, without changes in consumption patterns, the resulting increased capacity could generate problems. Economists influenced by Keynes began to see the Great Depression and other economic instability as the result of a mismatch between the productive capabilities of firms and the consumption patterns of households. Keynes identified the importance of demand, arguing that without growing demand, economic growth and employment would be compromised.

Later theorists developed Keynes's ideas, arguing that as capitalist economies became more affluent, stimulating demand has become more central to economic management. Institutionalists such as Galbraith (1967), and Marxists such as Baran & Sweezey (1966) argued that the 'sales effort' had become more central to the operation of corporations needing to sell a growing output (see Chapter 7).

Smart (2010, p. 62) argues advertising is premised upon the 'notion that customers or consumers could be persuaded or encouraged in various ways to buy particular goods and services'. We saw in Chapter 3 that scholars are divided as to the effects of advertising. Some take the view that consumers are manipulated by advertising, while others argue that consumers have a significant degree of autonomy. Still others recognise that both approaches speak to aspects of consumer behaviour – 'consumers are active and they do exercise choice and make decisions, but they do so under a range of influences and not under conditions of their own making' (Smart 2010, p. 63).

The proliferation of the sales effort can be seen in the expansion of marketing aimed at children. Juliet Schor (2004, p. 15) has examined this phenomenon in the US, arguing that 'the sheer extent of children's immersion in consumer culture today is unprecedented... Now, marketed leisure has replaced unstructured socializing, and most of what kids do revolves around commodities'. Schor (2004, p. 13) demonstrates how consumerism has reshaped the identities of children in the US, many of whom are now 'bonded to brands'.

Some scholars point to 'planned obsolescence' as crucial in perpetuating consumer culture (Packard 1978). This refers both to the construction of commodities whose parts quickly break down and to a broader process whereby new desires for new products must be constantly manufactured, thus rendering older products unfashionable. Examples include the release of slightly modified versions of the iPod and iPhone, each with a distinct look to ensure people will know if others have the latest model, encouraging consumers to upgrade more quickly.

Sociologists have focused attention on the link between individual identities and consumerism. An early expression of this came in the work of Herbert Marcuse (1991 [1964]). Consumerism, he argued, became a form of social control. Instead of seeking true freedom, choice was confined to purchasing decisions, producing a 'one-dimensional man'. However, he was equally critical of the bureaucracy of Soviet economies, arguing this also limited freedom.

The short-term nature of the satisfaction brought by some forms of consumption has led some sociologists and cultural theorists to identify a paradox whereby the 'emptiness' of consumption creates a cycle of desire that generates ever more novel ways of enticing and satisfying the consumer habit, no matter how short-lived. Beyond the consumption of tangible commodities, 'experience' too, has been commodified, such as adventure holidays advertised to destinations like New Zealand. More importantly, consumption, rather than production, has been identified as the key element defining the character of contemporary societies. The 'aesthetic of consumption' is seen to have replaced the 'work ethic' as people have been mobilised as consumers (Baudrillard 1998, p. 144).

Acts of consumption send information about one's status and identity. Hence, sociologists argue 'people increasingly define themselves, their culture, their world by means of commodities' (Carrier & Heyman 1997, p. 356). Bauman (2007, p. 6) goes even further, arguing that our 'identity' itself becomes a commodity to 'market, promote and sell'. It is in this sense that Baudrillard highlights commodities as 'signifiers'. Rather than consuming the 'substance' of a commodity, what is important is the image, symbol or sign that is conveyed. The consumption of signs is, according to Baudrillard (1973, p. 121), *the* defining characteristic of 'postmodern' consumer culture.

Various social movements have arisen to contest consumerism. In the 1960s, consumer rights movements grew in many advanced capitalist countries. They campaigned for legislated consumer protections including truth in advertising and product safety disclosures. One of the best-known figures of this movement is Ralph Nader (1965) whose bestselling book *Unsafe at Any Speed* was a critique of the safety record of the car industry. Nader established numerous consumer rights organisations, with their employees nicknamed 'Nader's raiders'.

Radical and anticonsumerist movements have become incorporated into consumer culture. One example of this is the Sydney Gay and Lesbian Mardi Gras. Begun in 1978 when a march for gay rights in Sydney was violently broken up by police, it has been transformed into one of the world's largest events celebrating gay and lesbian culture. However, some critics from within the gay and lesbian community argue its original radical ideals of human liberation have been compromised by the desire to make the event commercially attractive (see Kates 2003).

## QUALITY OF LIFE

Orthodox economists acknowledge that material living standards are only one component of our overall wellbeing and that other factors such as health, relationships and self-esteem are also important. However, the neoclassical focus on subjective value and consumer choice tends to privilege rising consumption as a measure of rising material standards of living. This view has increasingly come under question.

### Consumerism and happiness

There is growing evidence that despite rapidly rising incomes many people continue to feel poor (Hamilton & Denniss 2005). This seems to present a contradiction. If rising consumption is responsible for increasing our quality of life, how is it that people in the richest societies to have ever existed feel like they do not have enough?

One response is a growing body of literature on the relationship between consumption and happiness, which argues that affluence reduces the importance of consumption to wellbeing. Robert Frank (2000) describes increased consumerism as a form of 'luxury fever'. Others argue market societies suffer from 'affluenza' (de Graff et al 2001; Hamilton & Denniss 2005) as people borrow money and work long hours to buy more, without it making them happier. To the extent that new wants are generated by making people feel inadequate or insecure, as some feminists claim is true of the beauty industry (Wolf 1992), then the cycle of consumption can leave us feeling worse.

Another criticism is based on the social meaning of consumption. Veblen (1899), for example, argued that consumption was a way of displaying status, showing our place in the social hierarchy, rather than a way of satisfying our personal desires. Thus, we might buy a luxury car, or a large house, as a way of showing our social success. Bourdieu (1984) builds on this theme, describing how different social groups tend to eat different foods and wear different clothes, reflecting structural inequalities through consumption patterns.

Economists call goods purchased for their social impact 'positional goods'. Unlike the production of normal 'private' goods, increasing the production of positional goods may do little to increase utility, or quality of life. This is because the goods are desired precisely because others cannot afford them; as a good becomes more widely available, so new goods take on the attributes of social status. This produces an endless process of consumerism as people attempt to 'keep up with the Joneses'. However, the extent of 'affluenza' is disputed (see Box 8.3).

### Box 8.3 Consumerism and debt

Elizabeth Warren (2007) is interested in what is driving growing consumer debt. In 1970 the average middle-income worker in the US saved about 11 per cent of their income, by 2006 the equivalent saving rate was negative, despite most middle-income families having two paid workers rather than one. Some linked rising consumer debt to 'affluenza'.

Yet Warren discovered the pattern of consumer spending did not quite match this theory. In the 2000s, the average family of four people spent less money on things associated with consumerism – clothing, food and appliances – than did a similar family in the 1970s.

The reasons are partly cultural and partly economic. Our tastes have changed to more casual clothes and less meaty foods. The global economy has also become massively more productive, reducing prices. But these savings have been more than offset by increases in other areas. Average US families now spend much more on education, childcare, health insurance and housing.

While the average family house is now five per cent larger, mortgage costs are 75 per cent higher. Health insurance has increased by the same margin. Having two incomes also comes with costs. It has meant families often have to fund two cars, childcare and pay higher taxes.

She argues the failure of public policy to provide affordable social services, not consumer greed, is the main driver of household debt. Recent evidence suggests that many people are working longer hours to service their debts, eating into time they would prefer to spend with their families, or on leisure activities (Drago, Wooden & Black 2009; Schor 1992, 1998).

### Measuring quality of life

If consumption can have negative effects, then how are we to assess economic progress and wellbeing? In Chapter 3 we discussed a number of alternative measures to economic growth, such as the Genuine Progress Indicator and the Human Development Index (see Chapter 3).

These are objective measures of progress, in that they seek to measure observable aspects of life – such as environmental destruction, literacy levels and life expectancy. But increasingly, economists have become interested in subjective measures of wellbeing, measures that tap into how we feel about our lives and whether we think we are better off.

Subjective measures fit more comfortably with traditional neoclassical approaches that are based on a subjective theory of welfare and value (see Chapter 2), but they go further. Where economists traditionally argued that we cannot know how much utility a person enjoys, subjective measures attempt to measure wellbeing. They do so more directly through methods used in cognitive psychology including questionnaires.

This has produced some interesting results. It is clear that rising incomes are associated with higher subjective wellbeing, but the relationship is much weaker than many imagined. It is strongest for those on low incomes and is weakest for those on the highest incomes, suggesting that after basic needs are met, income is less effective in increasing our quality of life.

A number of other factors prove more significant to quality of life: health, family relationships and secure, fulfilling work. This does not suggest that efforts to raise incomes should be abandoned. But, consistent with the affluenza thesis, if higher incomes come at the cost of our relationships or our ability to control our work and economic circumstances, this may actually diminish quality of life. The importance of relationships to our wellbeing echoes other research that shows inequality (how much we have relative to others) is more important in rich countries than income (how much we have as individuals) (see Chapter 4).

## Work–life balance

Concerns over quality of life, and an end to the long-term trend for shorter working hours, has led some social scientists to question working patterns, and raise the need for a better 'work–life balance'. This refers to people's ability to balance the demands of paid work alongside the other demands of their lives – such as family responsibilities, education and leisure.

Barbara Pocock (2003) highlights a particular tension between the demands of paid work and those of care work. The ways we perform these tasks are changing – more women are in the paid workforce, many caring tasks (such as childcare) are now accessed through markets rather than the home, and we are less able to call on unpaid family and social ties for support.

Pocock argues that our institutions are not keeping up with these changes. Women are increasingly pulled in many different directions. Paid work does not properly accommodate their care responsibilities. Full-time mothers are often more isolated because other carers are in paid work. Social norms about the appropriate role of men and women as carers are only changing slowly. As a result, many people, particularly women, feel guilt about their decisions either to place children in paid care or to withdraw from paid work themselves.

The rise of non-standard forms of work raises further issues. While advocates see flexibility allowing employees to choose working hours that suit their needs, critics argue flexibility decreases security. Casual employees may find it more difficult to borrow money for a home. They are less likely to have access to parental leave to help manage the birth of children. And casual jobs often have poorly defined career paths, making it difficult to gain promotion. Some sociologists claim the growth in this type of employment is creating a new pool of 'precarious workers' who face greater uncertainties and risks than others in society (see Box 8.4).

### Box 8.4 The precariat

The 'precariat' (see Standing 2009) describes workers with insecure employment. It mimics the language of Marx's 'proletariat', arguing that the problems of exploitation in market societies are now primarily expressed through workplace insecurity.

There is significant international evidence that the proportion of workers experiencing work insecurity is growing. A report by the International Labour Organization (ILO 2004) found that 85 per cent of the world's workers experience economic insecurity, and that insecurity corresponds to lower levels of happiness. This is not simply a function of income – Asian workers tend to have greater economic security compared to their incomes than Latin American workers (see ILO 2004).

This is not only confined to traditional service work. Some professions in the 'knowledge' industries have also seen an increase in short-term contracts, such as casual academics, sound engineers and photographers in the fashion industry (Hesmondhalgh & Baker 2009).

> One innovative response to this situation comes from Europe. Union organisers have begun to use the image of the fictitious San Precario – the patron saint of the precariat – in their campaigns for more secure work. Young people, dressed in religious attire, hand out information about San Precario at shopping centres and other workplaces with poor employment security. (Rossi 2006; Tari & Vanni 2005).

## CONCLUSION

As market societies have developed, waged work and the consumption of commodities through markets have become more widespread and have come to constitute two of the most obvious ways by which people experience the economy. Nonetheless, these developments have brought with them changes to the very nature of both work and consumption. This has prompted theorists to debate the relative importance of work and consumption as modes of social integration, with some arguing capitalism has moved from a 'work society' to a 'consumer society'.

However, the continuing importance of both waged work and market-based consumption is indicated by debates about their impacts upon quality of life. Such debates concern the effects of economic processes on the social world of families as well as the natural world of the environment. While these have often been considered to lie outside of the formal economy, as we discuss in the next chapter, they are central to the reproduction of economic processes and deserving of close scrutiny.

### Questions

1 Why do some sociologists call modern market societies 'work societies'?
2 How did Fordism change the nature of working life?
3 In what ways does 'post-Fordism' promote flexibility?
4 What factors explain the rise of 'consumerism'?
5 How have changes to the balance between work, leisure and consumption affected quality of life?

# 9 | Family, environment and sustainability

THE PREVIOUS CHAPTER focused on work and consumption as two aspects of life most clearly identified with the economy. Traditionally, the study of economics evolved around the notion of the economy as a closed and discrete system with little attention paid to the broader social and ecological systems in which production for the market takes place. The natural environment was seen as a relatively limitless source of raw materials and an equally limitless destination for waste products. Non-market production occurring within the household was largely ignored as were the broader affective and reproductive functions of the family which raised, socialised and supported the workforce of (largely male) paid workers. In recent decades this neglect has begun to change due, in part, to real changes in the economy.

The limits of natural resources, the damaging effects of pollution and the large-scale entry of women into the workforce have all challenged the assumptions supporting Fordist production. This has prompted examination of issues like environmental behaviours, childcare, working hours and volunteer work. Such preoccupations also stem from social movements which have questioned our understanding of the environment and the family and raised important questions about the sustainability of our economic system. In this chapter we consider how economists have sought to incorporate these concerns into existing frameworks of economic analysis. We also consider an alternative *reproductive* framework in which market-based commodity production is located in the broader social and environmental systems that constitute a large part of our everyday experience.

## THE FAMILY AND THE HOUSEHOLD

Chapter 1 discussed how the rise of market society was associated with significant changes in the organisation of economic life. The household production in pre-capitalist feudal systems gave way to an increasingly complex social division of labour. Consumption and reproduction remained in the household while production gradually moved into separate workplaces thereby creating the distinctions that marked off 'work' from 'home'. Reflecting the processes of commodification and rationalisation, tasks once associated with the home gradually moved into market-based production. Activities such as growing and preparing food, making and mending clothing and educating children are now increasingly 'outsourced' while final commodities continue to be consumed in the household.

## ECONOMISING THE FAMILY

In neoclassical economic theory the household is seen as a supplier of factors of production – labour, land and capital – for which it receives income in the form of wages, rent or profit (see Box 9.1). This income is used to purchase goods and services for immediate consumption, or to save for future consumption. However, as feminist theorists have pointed out, the household and the family play many other significant roles.

### Box 9.1 Household income flows

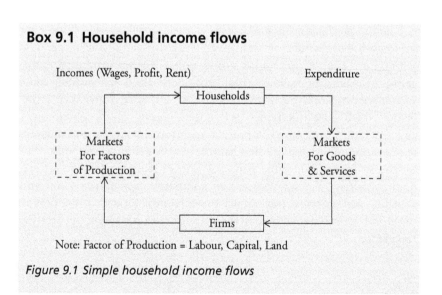

*Figure 9.1 Simple household income flows*

FAMILY, ENVIRONMENT AND SUSTAINABILITY 191

Families produce unpaid equivalents of many goods and services produced in the market, such as cooking, cleaning and childcare. There appears little justification for excluding these forms of production from economic analysis when they are critical to reproduction of the market system. Indeed, some welfare economists argue this production should not only be analysed, but the imputed (or implied) income it generates should be taxed (see Chancellor 1988)!

However, analysing household production is more challenging than analysing production in the market. Household labour is not sold and without a price it has no 'economic' value, as Waring (1988) points out. It is also difficult to observe household production because of its 'private' nature. The most common method for doing so is time use surveys. Surveys ask people how they divide their time between paid work, unpaid work and leisure. Time on unpaid work is then valued by comparing it to similar work in the paid market. An Australian survey from 1997 estimated the value of unpaid labour to be over 260 billion dollars, which is equivalent to half the total market economy (ABS 1997).

The onset of 'mass consumption' changed the way household work is performed, rationalising household labour in ways that are similar to paid work. Many consumer durables, such as washing machines, ovens and vacuum cleaners are designed to aid household production. However, it is difficult to estimate the effect of labour-saving devices on household productivity. This is because the time spent on household labour has been falling (see ABS 2006) at a time when women have been entering the paid labour market in greater numbers. Further, the surveys used record the time spent on tasks but not the output of such tasks.

Another important aspect of household labour is the *affective* relationships between family members (see Box 9.2). Unlike the 'impersonal' market, where we do not know the identities of the people who produce the goods we buy or sell, people within families know each other intimately. The difficulty in capturing the personal nature of relationships in the family through markets raises issues in the area of paid care work (discussed later in this chapter).

**Box 9.2 Economics of the family**

From the 1960s a number of economists began to apply the 'economic method' to a broad range of social phenomena. This involved making the same assumptions as neoclassical economics – of individual, self-interested, rational agents – in other contexts. Economist Gary Becker

(1981) used this method in a famous and controversial analysis of the family.

Becker argued that many family decisions could be explained on the basis of rational economic action. For example, he suggested that the likelihood of divorce was influenced by its relative costs and benefits with wealthier couples less likely to divorce because they faced higher costs. He also argued that the division of paid and unpaid work between men and women was the result of rational calculation. Women spend at least some time out of the workforce for child rearing and this reduces the returns on their investment in skills and education. However, the economic returns to education increase over time, leading more women into the workforce, creating a decline in fertility rates.

Many found Becker's approach offensive because it suggested that affective relationships – love for a partner or the desire to have children – could be reduced to rational self-interest. Feminists also objected to Becker's highly individualistic methodology. They claimed it did not properly account for the gendered social norms that usher men and women into different roles, or the structural discrimination of the labour market (Bergmann 1995). Despite such controversy, Becker subsequently won the Nobel Prize in economics and his broader approach has proven widely influential.

## THE FAMILY AND SOCIAL REPRODUCTION

Beyond economic theory, the family can be understood as constituting part of the broader set of social relationships that make up market society. On this account, households are responsible for *social* reproduction (see Laslett & Brenner 1989). This includes the biological reproduction involved in having children and also the broader processes of socialising children and caring for the physical, emotional and mental health of the members of the household. It also includes production and provisioning within the family.

Social reproduction is essential for the operation of the economy and it satisfies many of the needs we have as social beings that are not directly addressed by market production. This perspective is also implicit in Polanyi's argument that labour is a 'fictitious commodity' (see Chapter 2) produced outside of markets, in families and the education system. However, households also embody power relations that reflect a 'gendered' division of labour.

Carol Pateman (1988) developed this theme in her concept of the 'sexual contract'. Mirroring the 'social contract' concept used by earlier political philosophers, Pateman's 'sexual contract' represented the separation of production from reproduction. This allowed men to act as independent and autonomous individuals in the marketplace because women performed the home-based care work required for social reproduction.

Yet, in Fraser and Gordon's (1994) study of 'dependence', they argue the complex social division of labour in market society creates interdependence. Hence, the separation of family and 'economy' created a false sense of independence for men. It also denied women the market income necessary to exercise autonomy, relegating them to the status of 'dependence'. The family not only reproduces people, but it does so according to the norms and relationships sanctioned by society and which structure the broader economy.

### The development of the family in market society

The organisation of reproductive work changed significantly after feudalism, where the household often included the extended family. According to Friedrich Engels (1942 [1884]), the modern nuclear family first developed amongst the emerging capitalist 'bourgeoisie' as a way to manage property relationships. Monogamous marriage established the basis for passing on inheritance to children and meant that, for the middle class, marriage was always partly related to concerns for property rather than love alone. Only the property-less working class, he argued, could marry solely for love.

Weber (1978 [1922]) also discussed the connections between the family and capitalism. He argued the combination of family structure and private property law, along with Protestant cultural values, contributed to the development of capitalism. Yet the culture and experience of families was, as suggested by Engels, somewhat different according to gender and class. The 'idleness' of middle-class women was used as a signal of the family's status (Phillips 1987, p. 34) whereas the gender division of labour was initially less pronounced among workers.

Women and children worked alongside men in factories to earn sufficient family income to buy the commodities they needed to survive. However, this changed with the *Factory Acts* (see Chapter 2) that outlawed forms of child labour and placed restrictions on women's paid work. Thereafter, laws and economic institutions supported the emerging nuclear family with different wages for men and women reflecting a social expectation that men were required to support their family. Formal restrictions also made it difficult for women to work once they were married.

Work was structured in a way that presumed children would be cared for by a stay-at-home partner, with little provision of childcare facilities. This remained confined to the nanny services used by better off families. Education was also gender segregated to prepare boys for paid employment and girls for homemaking. Divorce laws made it difficult for women to leave relationships and, later, welfare payments were designed for families with both a full-time male worker and a stay-at-home female carer.

These economic structures reinforced the 'gender norms' that feminist scholars argue encourage men and women to take on different roles. Whereas 'sex' is a biological category, gender is a social category referring to the way society makes sense of sex by valuing, rewarding and punishing certain activities and behaviours. In defining gender, sociologist RW Connell (2002, p. 10) argues it 'is the structure of social relations that centres on the reproductive arena and the set of practices (governed by this structure) that brings reproductive distinctions between bodies into social processes'.

Gender norms emerge as 'taken for granted' ways of understanding the social significance of biological sex – the 'housewife' or the 'male breadwinner', for example. Feminist economist Nancy Folbre (1994, p. 54) argues that gender acts as a 'structure of constraint', defining 'choice' and imposing sanctions on 'nonconformity'. This affects women *and* men. As Connell (2002, p. 6) notes, '[t]hough men in general benefit from the inequalities of the gender order, they do not benefit equally'.

However, gender norms can, and do, change. During World War II governments actively encouraged women into the paid workforce to replace men leaving for the armed forces. This was supported by women's magazines publishing quick and easy meals for those combining work and family. At the end of the war governments encouraged women back into the home to make way for returning soldiers at work which was supported culturally by glorification of the 'homemaker' (Honey 1995; Kossoudji & Dresser 1992).

Family structures and gender norms continue to change over time and between countries. In some Asian cultures there is a strong tradition of older generations raising children while both mothers and fathers enter the paid labour force (Maurer-Fazio et al 2009). In the West, new legal and economic institutions have accompanied the increased workforce participation of women. Divorce laws have been relaxed, women's pay has been increased and new welfare measures such as paid parental leave and childcare have been introduced in most developed countries.

However, despite economic and legal change, a gender wages gap persists with much 'women's work' remaining relatively poorly paid and concentrated in part-time and casual jobs. Women also continue to be responsible for the bulk of unpaid care work, bringing about the 'feminisation of poverty'. Their care responsibilities often restrict access to market income leaving women vulnerable to poverty as they try to balance unpaid care for family with limited paid employment (Northrop 1990; Chant 2008).

### Services and the care economy

The care work of social reproduction has become more visible with changes to the family and the workplace. Much care work – education, childcare and aged care – is now part of the formal economy, although often organised as part of the government-controlled public sector rather than through markets. However, care work is increasingly evident in the for-profit economy too, because of the growth in service sector jobs.

Sociologist Arlie Hochschild (1983) uses the term 'emotional labour' to describe how many service workers, particularly women, are required to display particular emotions as part of their work. For example, beyond carrying out the tasks of their job, female flight attendants are required to be pleasant and attentive to their passengers. Unlike markets for physical commodities, services often involve a direct relationship between the producer and consumer. This relationship creates a tension between the exchange relationship of markets and the emotional relationship of human interaction where people like to feel a sense of appreciation and connection that goes beyond payment.

Emotional labour is an important aspect in the care work of social reproduction but it has substantial implications for the 'economics of care'. It is difficult to fully commodify such work because part of its value is the relationship of care that would be devalued if monetised and commodified. It also presents challenges to the concept of a 'perfect market' because consumer decisions are not only based on price but also on personal connections which might serve as a barrier to entry for new producers. Regulating care through the price mechanism can also be problematic for our sense of justice when people are prevented from accessing care – health or aged care – on the basis of an inability to pay.

The gendered nature of care also affects the structure of the labour market. Many care workers are women reflecting gender roles that continue to define who performs care work even once care is incorporated into the market. The norms around care – both gender norms and distributional norms that promote equal access – influence the way care is delivered and explain why much care work is poorly paid, despite the activities being seen as socially valuable. These norms can discourage workers from taking industrial action that might harm the recipients of care, or from seeing their work in terms of maximising income.

Alongside this, other changes have made unpaid care work more visible and highlighted tensions between the obligations of unpaid care and paid work. Family care for disabled children, partners and parents has increased with medical advances, extended life expectancy and changing social values towards institutional care. Where this was somewhat mitigated by the nuclear family, which redistributes care work and market income between husband and wife, there is now a greater prevalence of single-parent families. There is also greater household inequality with more single person and dual income households with significant market incomes and more households with substantial care responsibilities and very limited market income.

Ageing populations reinforce these trends, presenting policy makers with the conflicting priorities of increasing women's paid labour market participation *and* increasing fertility rates and care work in the unpaid labour market. In the social democracies of Scandinavia the regulatory functions of the welfare state have been extended to better account for care (see Korpi 2000). Work has been regulated to allow family-friendly hours, better promotion opportunities for part-time staff, generous parental leave and childcare provisions. These measures attempt to ensure the care work of social reproduction is recognised in the formal market economy.

This also raises tensions around productivity and future economic growth. Care services are labour intensive and less readily produce the high productivity growth of capital-intensive industries such as manufacturing (Iversen & Wren 1998). Yet, as populations grow older and richer and the relative price of manufactured goods falls due to past productivity gains, demand for services such as education, health and care increases. These are also more likely to be funded by the state than private firms, increasing the size of the public sector relative to the private sector and putting pressure on government spending in a context of generalised slowed growth. It is unsurprising that international bodies such as the World Bank (1994) have advocated greater *private* provision of pensions and social services.

However, a growing international market in care services is attracting concern. The international movement of people looking for work is generating international systems of care that sociologists call 'global care chains' (see Hochschild & Ehrenreich 2002). As women enter the workforce in the affluent world, more care work is performed by paid workers who are increasingly migrants from poorer countries. In turn, these migrant women rely on female relatives to provide care to members of their own families. Thus, a chain of care work is produced across the world, with women from different countries and stages of life providing different links in the chain but with each receiving very different rewards that reflect inequalities of gender and race (see Chapter 4).

## THE ENVIRONMENT AND MARKET SOCIETY

In addition to the household, the natural environment is also a crucial element in the reproductive systems underpinning market societies. However, concern about the integrity of ecological reproduction has grown significantly since the middle of the twentieth century. This has led to a range of theoretical responses aimed at informing policy development. Neoclassical economists have sought to incorporate the environment into the market system. Others have seen the environment posing a more radical challenge that requires new approaches to analysing and governing human interactions with nature. Some of these alternatives have drawn on existing economic traditions, like Keynesian, feminist and Marxist economics, while others have developed distinctly ecological perspectives.

## PERSPECTIVES ON ENVIRONMENTAL DEGRADATION

The environment has rarely been the central focus of economic thought. However, the early classical political economists raised many of the themes that now confront contemporary environmental economists and sociologists concerned with climate change and the 'risk society'. Thus, problems of unlimited growth, intensified use of the environment and limits to the supply of natural resources have long been the objects of specific theoretical attention.

### Malthus and the population debate

One of the most famous early discussions of the environment comes from the work of the Reverend Thomas Malthus. In 1798, Malthus (1992) wrote his *Essay on the Principle of Population*, arguing that population growth outpaces growth in food production which inevitably and continually results in strains on the ability of a society to provide the means of subsistence. In contrast to his contemporaries, Malthus was pessimistic about the progress that could be achieved through economic growth because of the unavoidable but socially damaging checks on population growth such as war and famine.

Critics of Malthus point to the use of technology in market societies to overcome population pressures through increased agricultural productivity. Yet, Malthusian arguments continue to influence today's debates about the relationship between environmental degradation and rising population levels. Paul Ehrlich (1969), for example, argued in *The Population Bomb* that increases in the global human population lie at the heart of environmental problems. This claim remains controversial, though, even amongst environmentalists.

It has underpinned the advocacy of radical policies to reduce population growth, particularly in the developing world, but also by limiting immigration to richer countries. Yet, on most measures it is the richest countries, where population growth is slowest, that generate the greatest environmental impact. This is because their *per capita* consumption is much higher. Hence, critics argue the population debate merely refocuses attention away from unsustainable first-world consumption patterns towards the higher population growth of the poor (Monbiot 2008).

The 'Green Revolution' was thought by many to demonstrate the potential for technology to overcome the environmental problems generated by population growth and poverty (Gaud 1968). It significantly increased global food production through the application of scientific and industrial techniques to agriculture. However, the environment movement has identified negative ecological and social consequences from such intensive forms of agriculture. These include the effects of pollution from chemicals used in production, threats to biodiversity as monocultures are introduced and the risk of catastrophic outbreaks such as foot-and-mouth disease.

Some have also argued that intensive food production has had negative effects for developing countries. Vandava Shiva (1991) demonstrates how the Green Revolution undermined local ecologies while concentrating power in the hands of political elites and large corporations. Others have argued that integrating local food production into the global market has exposed developing countries to price instability and redirected resources away from meeting basic nutrition needs to the less immediate desires of Northern consumers and businesses (Bello 2009).

## Polanyi and commodification of the environment

Another important component of the environmental debate centres on the intensive use of environmental resources. This reflects the dynamics of capitalist production which rationalises the use of inputs to continuously expand output. However, the natural environment undertakes its own process of reproduction which is not necessarily consistent with the intensive production processes of the economic system. One early conception of this tension comes from Karl Polanyi's theory of 'fictitious commodities'. Just as the intensive use of labour produces social feedbacks, so the intensive use of land can also have negative effects.

In *The Great Transformation*, Polanyi (1944) pointed to the problems of integrating land into the self-regulating market 'experiment' of the nineteenth century. Prefiguring the concerns of contemporary environmentalism, he (1944, p. 73) argued that '[n]ature would be reduced to its elements, neighbourhoods and landscapes defiled, rivers polluted... the power to produce food and raw materials destroyed'. In effect, Polanyi cast doubt over whether the regulation of land through the price mechanism was sustainable. His analysis suggests that the process of commodifying land creates tensions between the demands of ecology and economy.

As discussed in Chapter 1, a critical factor preceding the commodification and regulation of land in the creation of market society was the process of 'enclosing' common lands. Revisiting this process is useful for understanding the in-built pressures that a system of commodity production has on the environment. Enclosure created conditions of competition over access to fertile land (Wood 1999, p. 83). This competition, and the growing trend of production for markets rather than personal needs, encouraged the application of scientific principles to farming practices.

These were critical steps in the growth of English capitalism because they encouraged the development of highly productive large-scale farms. With the commons turned into privately owned enterprises the land was cultivated and harvested more intensively and more extensively than ever before. In turn, the growth of agricultural production, especially sheep and cotton, supported expansion in important new manufacturing industries such as textiles.

By the eighteenth century, ongoing competition and technological innovations had given birth to the first phase of industrialisation, creating pressures for more land enclosures to facilitate expansion of factory production. This aided an increasing scale and concentration of production that made the impositions on the environment more intense, threatening its ecological integrity (Altvater 1994, p. 77).

### The Jevons paradox and non-renewable resources

One of the nineteenth century pioneers of neoclassical marginalism, William Stanley Jevons, also put forward a theory about society–nature relations with continued relevance to policy makers and green movements today. In his book, *The Coal Question*, Jevons (1865) argued that the depletion of finite coal supplies, a key driver of British industrialisation, would not be slowed by technological gains in the efficiency of its use. This was because efficiency gains would lower the cost of energy, thereby increasing demand for energy and raising the rate of coal consumption (Alcott 2005, p. 12).

Jevons was concerned about the impact on British imperial power stemming from the depletion of British coal reserves. However, his theory remains important today. The Jevons Paradox suggests that technological improvements alone are not able to deal effectively with the problem of resource depletion. This is reflected in contemporary energy debates where technological innovation has both increased energy efficiency – the output produced by a given input of oil or coal – and has led to the discovery and extraction of new sources of energy. However, these innovations have also led to low energy prices and to considerable expansion in total energy use.

This situation raises two concerns. First, while energy efficiency has improved since 1975, *per capita* greenhouse gas emissions continued to grow in advanced capitalist countries (Matthews et al 2000 in Clark & York 2005, p. 512). This suggests efficiency alone is unlikely to address the increasingly urgent concerns about climate change. Second, there is growing acceptance of the idea that we are approaching (or have reached) the point of 'peak oil' where global oil production can no longer expand. Given the importance of energy to the global economy, large increases in energy prices due to oil scarcity may also have wider economic implications.

### Contemporary environmentalism and the limits to growth

Concern over environmental degradation, population levels and resource use were given widespread attention through *The Limits to Growth*

(Meadows et al 1972) report. This publication argued an environmental 'crisis' was inevitable if developed economies continued on their growth paths. World industrial output had grown fifty times in the century from 1890 to 1990 (Ponting 1991, p. 325). Between 1950 and 1970, gross world product more than doubled as did the consumption of fossil fuels which underpinned the immense increase in industrial production (Brenton 1994, p. 20).

In subsequent decades, the growing environment movement raised concerns about both the limits to non-renewable resources as well as the unsustainable use of renewable resources such as forests or fish stocks. By the 1980s, concern about 'sustainability' was widespread prompting policy action on 'sustainable development' by national governments and international institutions like the United Nations. More recently, with insights from complex systems theory, pollution and over-use threats to whole biophysical systems, such as the atmosphere, oceans and weather patterns have also been highlighted.

In 2006 *The Stern Review* in the UK, and *Garnaut Review* (2008) in Australia, put some of these problems on the international political agenda. The concerns raised about climate change have also given a renewed sense of urgency about sustainability. This has lead to a vigorous debate, not only about climate change, but also about the nature of economic development. Stern and Garnaut use relatively conventional economic analysis in proposing solutions to these complex problems which have generated significant opposition. Critics from the environment movement, developing countries and other academic disciplines have argued that much more radical change is needed in addressing the environmental impacts of economic activity.

## ECONOMIC RESPONSES TO ENVIRONMENTAL CHALLENGES

Drawing on neoclassical economics, environmental economists use the concept of 'externalities' to explain both the existence of environmental degradation such as pollution as well as resource depletion through overuse. As discussed in Chapter 5 economists generally agree that the market mechanism is the most efficient way of allocating resources. The claim of 'efficiency' assumes 'perfect competition' and that all costs and benefits associated with the production of a good are captured in its price. Externalities are a category of 'market failure' arising when aspects of the production process are *not* captured in the market price for goods.

The presence of pollution, for example, is a cost borne by society, either through 'clean-up' or loss of amenities, rather than by the firm producing the good that gave rise to it. Economists argue that when the full costs of production are not reflected in the price of the commodity, markets cannot achieve an 'optimal' allocation of resources (Pearce 1976, p. 24). It is for this reason that environmental economists place such an emphasis on 'getting the price right'. According to the logic of 'supply and demand', when the price of a commodity does not include the costs of its pollution effects, its price will be artificially low and demand for the product higher than it would otherwise be.

In turn, the distorted price-signal attracts additional investment to the polluting industry (because of increased demand for the product) with the result that society will have available more product than it may want relative to clean(ish) air or water (Sagoff 1994, p. 289). The distorted price is said to deny consumers the ability to make optimal tradeoffs between the commodity they wish to purchase and the level of pollution created by its production. It is presumed that with full-cost pricing the demand for the polluting product will fall thereby giving rise to a new (somewhat less polluting) market equilibrium, as well as providing incentive for the development of greener production techniques.

This theory of 'environmental economics' thus constructs the depletion and degradation of the environment as a problem of inefficient market allocation due to inadequate pricing (see also Box 9.3). It continues to assert that the market mechanism is *generally* the most efficient means of allocating scarce resources, but that in some instances the market may fail to provide socially optimal outcomes. In this circumstance, correct pricing can prevent market failure and the presence of externalities. Policy prescriptions therefore revolve around the creation of markets and extension of pricing as reflected in the Stern and Garnaut investigations into climate change.

### Box 9.3 The tragedy of the commons

One of the most influential ideas in liberal thinking about the causes of and responses to environmental problems is the notion of the 'tragedy of the commons'. This is the title of an article published in *Science* by Garrett Hardin (1968). He argues that natural resources held in common will inevitably be destroyed because the self-interested actions of each individual, such as individual cattle farmers, will lead to overexploitation of the commons.

This overexploitation occurs because individual farmers will expand their herds based on the reasoning that while the environmental cost of each additional cow is shared throughout the commons, the benefit from the sale of that cow will accrue to the individual. When these individual actions are multiplied across those using the commons, the result is the destruction of the natural resource through overexploitation.

In response to the problem of the tragedy of the commons, Hardin and his followers advocate the extension of private property rights over natural resources. This is said to create an incentive for the sustainable management of resources. These ideas have gained considerable currency among policy makers, but they are also the focus of numerous critiques. The argument that individuals using commons will seek to expand their herds is based on the assumption of rationality. But this is understood in the narrow sense of utility maximisation within a competitive capitalist economy rather than farmers in pre or non-capitalist communities (Angus 2008).

Furthermore, Hardin provided no empirical evidence of instances representing the tragedy of the commons, or instances of successful environmental outcomes of privatisation. However, others, such as economic Nobel laureate Elinor Ostrom (1990), have documented instances of the sustainable self-management of commons by communities in the presence of social institutions such as community-sanctioned rules which are monitored and enforced. Ostrom's analysis draws on the social capital literature (which views the tragedy of the commons as similar to a 'prisoner's dilemma') to show how social norms can overcome what appear to be economic problems (see Chapter 10).

### Optimal use

Economists do not necessarily moralise or try to minimise pollution. Rather, they promote the 'optimal use' of resources. Consistent with the methods of neoclassical economics, environmental economics uses a subjective notion of value based on market supply and demand. Thus, it does not necessarily view all pollution as bad, but rather attempts to balance costs (of polluting production) against benefits (of increased consumption) based on people's willingness, or ability, to pay.

Different forms of cost-benefit analysis are employed in order to determine the level of resource use and pollution that is 'economically optimal'. This optimal use is calculated based on the point at which the marginal economic benefit from a particular form of production or consumption is equal to the marginal economic cost of the pollution or resource depletion necessary for that particular economic activity (Pearce 1976, p. 24). From a policy perspective, price-based environmental policies (such as green taxes) aim to achieve the optimal rate of resource use by altering marginal costs (see later in this chapter).

This form of reasoning has been used to determine the optimal use of fossil fuels and other greenhouse gas-producing resources in response to the global environmental problem of climate change. For example, William Nordhaus (1994) has used cost-benefit analysis to argue that only very minimal reductions in greenhouse gas emissions over the next century represent the economically optimal use of resources in responding to global warming. However, there are inherent problems in calculations of optimal use.

First, because these calculations are based on future costs and benefits, the calculations can be altered and manipulated using different 'discount rates' (where individuals are judged to value the present more than the future). Second, a number of uncertainties make the calculations on which to judge optimality extremely imprecise. These uncertainties include the probabilities and costs of pollution, of resource use and future economic conditions as affected by the impacts of climate change themselves. Third, it is not possible to value distributive justice or determine the intrinsic value of a clean environment, both of which are important ethical considerations.

In neoclassical economics, value is derived from market exchange (see Chapter 2). This would seem to restrict the application of such theory to items which can be traded in markets; that is, commodities with property rights attached. Clearly, much of the environment does not (as yet!) conform to these criteria. However, economists nevertheless extend the logic of economic value to commons and other environmental resources that cannot be 'fenced off' as property. They use the method of contingent valuation in the consumption of environmental 'assets' such as the existence of wilderness or unpolluted views.

These methods, often based on surveys or questionnaires, treat the environment or its services 'as if' they are a commodity. They do so in order to use consumers' 'willingness to pay' as a proxy for value (Edwards 1987, p. 79). This provides a basis for rationing access according to rights when 'assets' (like clean air) cannot be broken up into individual pieces of property. The same method can also be used to determine how much compensation would be required to cover the loss of such environmental goods. However, because such methods seek to optimise consumption rather than reduce environmental problems, their usefulness in sustaining ecological systems is limited.

## THE QUESTION OF SUSTAINABILITY

The proposition that mid-twentieth century patterns of economic growth were unsustainable served to challenge the legitimacy of how market societies are organised. Concern with biodiversity loss and human survival in the context of demand for ongoing 'development' prompted the United Nations to establish a World Commission on Environment and Development (WCED). The ideas about sustainability in its report, *Our Common Future* (WCED 1987), were enthusiastically embraced with the concept of 'sustainable development' becoming a key goal of national and international governance. Yet, environmental degradation persists and a new wave of environmental concern has emerged around climate change. These circumstances point to the unresolved issue of 'sustainability' which requires ongoing efforts in both theory and practice to bring about social and economic transformations.

## ALTERNATIVE APPROACHES TO THE ENVIRONMENT

Conventional economic approaches see environmental damage as the result of the failure to incorporate the environment into the market system. In contrast, a number of critical perspectives see environmental damage as related directly to its interaction with market-based economic processes. These approaches extend Marxist, feminist and other social science critiques of capitalism to the environment. Similarly, developments in the natural sciences have also underpinned ideas that provide alternatives to the method of 'economic science'.

### Uncertainty and the precautionary principle

Developments in complex systems theory have had significant implications for our understanding of the environment. These approaches differ from traditional neoclassical economics, and much early physics, by focusing on how entire systems work, rather than on individual components. Such holistic analysis reveals complex systems can change behaviour in unpredictable ways due to non-linear dynamics. This produces 'tipping points' where at some levels a change in one part of the system has little overall effect but at other levels small changes have large effects, as in the saying the 'straw that broke the camel's back' (see Waldrop 1992).

As well as the macro dynamics of environment and economy, systems theory draws attention to uncertainty, a key concept in Keynesian and Austrian economics. We have limited understanding of ecological systems, and because relatively small changes can have large effects, the relationship between economic and ecological systems can be unpredictable. Given this uncertainty, many ecological economists argue that the risks arising from negative externalities are fundamentally unknowable and therefore cannot be adequately modelled by standard economic methods. They recommend using the 'precautionary principle' to guide policy in the face of uncertainty and this proposition is now broadly embraced across much of the environment movement.

The precautionary principle suggests, for example, that states should take action to curb activities of corporations where they suspect they may be harmful to humans or the natural environment (Holt, Pressman & Spash 2009). It is also important to arguments about intergenerational equity. Unlike many economic models, which discount future consumption on the basis that the present is worth more than the future, the precautionary principle acknowledges we have a moral obligation to protect the environment for future generations. Many argue the precautionary principle is important for environmental challenges as well as for negotiating the uncertainties of the 'risk society' more broadly (Giddens 1998). (See Chapter 8.)

### Economic contradictions and environmental exploitation

Although economy–environment relations were not the primary focus of Marx's work, he offers a theorisation of the environmental impact of capitalist agricultural and industrial practices. This is expressed through the idea of an 'irreparable rift in the interdependent process of social metabolism' (Marx 1894). For Marx, the metabolism is the complex set of relationships between society and nature. John Bellamy Foster (1999) has recently popularised the concept of 'metabolic rift' which refers to the separation or 'rift' that capitalism creates between the natural and social systems because of the disruption, or unequal exchange, between such systems.

Marx viewed the imperative for economic growth, urbanisation, world trade and technological developments such as the invention of synthetic fertilisers, as having caused a rift in the natural systems on which society depends (Bellamy Foster 1999, p. 373). Traditional agriculture was a more local affair, often based on a metabolic system where nutrients were returned to the soil in cycles. However, capitalism transformed agricultural processes with products transported from country to city, rupturing the cycle of returning nutrients to the soil and instead created urban waste problems.

In turn, Marx argued, declining soil fertility created the need for synthetic fertilisers which only intensified the metabolic rift by increasing the degradation of the land (Clark & York 2005, p. 397–8). The idea that industrial systems operate according to a different set of principles to environmental systems, creating different industrial and ecological 'metabolisms', has been discussed by a number of other theorists. It suggests that sustainability requires a rethinking of the very organisation and operation of industrial processes, rather than simply extending the logic of industry further into the environment (Huber 2000).

James O'Connor (1998) has also drawn on Marx's work to develop a different set of ideas about economy–environment interactions. He argues that capitalism impairs its own 'conditions of production' (labour power and the natural environment) by exploiting ecosystems and threatening the health of workers. This potentially leads to crises of underproduction when the costs of capitalist production increase as the state acts to make capitalist firms accountable in the face of demands from new social movements. O'Connor's (1998) 'second contradiction of capitalism' mirrors the potential crises of underconsumption Marx identified in the contradiction arising from the capitalist's need to keep wage costs low while maintaining high demand for their product.

Ecofeminists also link the treatment of nature with the treatment of humans. Some argue that the exploitation of nature mirrors the exploitation of women. They point out that nature is historically described in western societies as female ('mother nature') and the destruction of nature often described in terms of rape and desecration, thus paralleling violence of men against women (Merchant 1992). Others highlight the particular ways in which women are affected by environmental pollution such as the damage caused to their reproductive capacities through environmental toxicity. In many developing countries women are more exposed to environmental damage through their gendered responsibilities to gather food and water and care for their families (Shiva 1988).

## The intrinsic value of nature

Consistent with the view that gender discrimination is partly based on a failure to acknowledge and value the perspectives of women, ecological feminists argue that nature should be valued on its own terms, rather than through the instrumental terms of industrial production. Similarly, deep ecologists argue that nature has intrinsic value and therefore should be valued in itself rather than because it is necessary for human survival. Deep ecologists call for a new ethic, based on these values, to guide a new eco-centric society (Merchant 1992). These approaches challenge both market-based perspectives as well as Marxist and Keynesian theories which are concerned about preserving the environment only because it is central to the reproduction of human society.

A similar perspective comes from indigenous peoples who have become part of environmental debates, challenging traditional western modes of thought. Indigenous peoples have been at the forefront of many campaigns for environmental protection. Often such campaigns have been necessary to protect their livelihoods and way of life against the actions of corporations and states. The campaigns by indigenous people against logging in the Amazon forests, for example, have helped to give wider recognition to indigenous worldviews and practices.

For many indigenous communities the environment holds sacred values, which should not be compromised for short-term economic purposes. Indigenous economic practices are usually less rationalised than those in market societies. Many have noted, for example, that indigenous worldviews are more holistic in nature than dominant western philosophies (Knudtson & Suzuki 1992). This often means indigenous practices are more sustainable, placing greater emphasis on non-economic values and reflecting subsistence principles that seek to maintain living standards rather than achieving continuous growth.

Some ecological economists have also critiqued the 'growth paradigm' at the heart of most economic traditions. Nicholas Georgescu-Roegen (1971) drew upon physics and the laws of thermodynamics to reconceptualise the economy as a series of energy stocks and flows. Industrial economies tend to rely on earth-based (rather than solar) flows of energy which creates large stocks of entropy (energy which is not useful for production). Because matter cannot be created within this system, the result of economic production in advanced economies is a gradual depletion of the limited stocks which sustain it.

## ADDRESSING ENVIRONMENTAL DAMAGE

Alternative views on how the problems of unsustainable environmental practices might be addressed reflect the varied views on the nature of the environmental problem. Neoclassical economists advocate a range of solutions that price the environment and subject it to market regulation. Other approaches associated with Keynesian and social democratic perspectives seek a greater role for explicit state intervention. This would use political regulation (rather than market regulation) to effectively decommodify aspects of the environment, mirroring the way welfare state provisions decommodify social life. Finally, radical approaches reject capitalist production and suggest a reorganisation of market society in ways that make ecological systems more central to the economic system.

### Pricing nature

Neoclassical analysis has tended to focus on market mechanisms for addressing environmental problems. Part of this work directly centres on turning the environment into a commodity by extending property rights over it. Ronald Coase (1972) argued that this was the most efficient solution to problems like pollution, which appeared as social, rather than individual, costs. Coase's work has since inspired a number of others, including many Austrian economists who see private property rights as preserving freedom as well as promoting social efficiency through the process of 'voluntary' exchange.

Coase did not have a strong view on how rights should be allocated, or to whom, but in practice the state is involved in allocating new rights. More recent work has favoured auctioning systems that see the government gain revenue from the initial sale when 'privatising nature', thus compensating the community for the loss of the asset (Cramton & Kerr 2002). Even this does not provide a concrete policy guide, though, as there are numerous auctioning systems and the rights themselves can be defined in many different ways. Legal scholars have highlighted these contingencies, arguing that even property rights systems involve extensive state regulation and decision-making (Driessen 1998).

An alternative neoclassical perspective favours taxes rather than rights-based mechanisms. This derives from the work of Pigou (1938 [1920]) on market failures (see Chapter 5). The aim is to set taxes at a rate equivalent to the social harm caused by the undesirable activity, thus ensuring producer costs are the same as the real costs to society. Proposals for a carbon tax to reduce emissions causing climate change are an example of this approach. Taxes also provide an ongoing revenue stream for governments and so may be favoured for other reasons.

Finally, the complexity of environmental challenges has led to numerous hybrid schemes. The most notable are trading schemes based on government-issued permits. Emissions trading schemes are an example of this. They involve the state setting the overall level of production by issuing a certain number of permits, while market competition is used to allocate the permits between industries and firms. By contrast, pure property rights schemes allocate full rights to the environment and allow market competition to determine the level of pollution.

While often advocated as 'market-based' solutions, many economists acknowledge that taxes and trading schemes both combine elements of state regulation and market competition. Taxes allow governments to set prices, but not to set total output, while trading schemes allow government to determine total output, while market competition sets the price (Garnaut 2008). Many economists favour trading schemes because they allow 'science' to set total production levels (Garnaut 2008). Alternatively, taxes allow greater predictability for business and reduce problems like speculation, which can affect trading systems.

## Regulation and decommodification

Until the recent rise of market-based instruments, policy responses to environmental damage were based on direct forms of government intervention such as limiting market access to the environment through direct prohibitions on use. Establishing national parks or placing bans on the killing of threatened species are examples of this. Other measures have been used to influence production (Driesen 1998). These include rules setting minimum size and maximum catch limits on fishing, or international agreements that ban the use of ozone depleting hydroflurocarbons.

Such policies reflected direct responses to environmental problems because of both the moral imperative of environmental arguments and scepticism about market solutions for sustainability within the environment movement. Recently, debate has focused on the complex problems of climate change, generating alternative proposals that seek to reconstruct the economic system more thoroughly. Two of the most influential ideas in this context have been proposals for a 'Green New Deal' and the 'steady state' economic model. Both require greater substantial state intervention to change economic dynamics.

The 'Green New Deal' (Barbier 2010) reflects the influence of Keynesian thought. It is a reference to the 'New Deal' policies of the Roosevelt administration in the US during the depression of the 1930s. At that time, government took a strong role in providing infrastructure and services and sheltering citizens from markets. In a 'Green New Deal' the state would take an active role in stimulating new environmentally friendly industries, such as alternative energy technology. They would facilitate employment *and* equitable access to environmental resources, allowing for a 'just transition' to an environmentally sustainable economy.

These proposals reflect Keynes's interest in 'socialising investment'. This allows markets to allocate finished commodities between consumers but gives a much greater role for the state in making investment decisions. Keynes argued that private markets would often produce recession because of under-investment in the face of low demand. Likewise, some environmentalists argue markets, even when prices are adjusted, fail to provide adequate capital to environmentally sustainable industry, thus creating a second argument for social control of investment.

Finally, a growing number of economists have argued that the growth model of economics itself needs to change. Herman Daly (1996, p. 31) proposes a 'steady-state economy' based upon the re-use of production inputs. Steady-state economists argue that in their vision the 'economy can develop', through innovation and new techniques of production, 'but cannot grow' in terms of its use of energy and matter (Daly 1996, p. 31). The emphasis is on qualitative rather than quantitative growth. More recently Tim Jackson (2009) has outlined how this might work in practice, incorporating ideas from the Green New Deal, in *Prosperity without Growth*.

### Radical alternatives

Radical critics of the environmental costs of economic activity have posited more substantial transformations. Because these critics see capitalism as inherently contradictory and exploitative of both the environment and of people, solutions that simply modify the operation of the market are seen as unlikely to substantially address environmental degradation. However, the radical nature of the solutions proposed means that these ideas tend to be less concrete, but they sometimes do focus attention on how change might be achieved.

Many radical theorists extend the logic of Marxist thought by identifying how the tensions within capitalism might give rise to social groups that can act to promote change. For example, O'Connor (1998), departs from classical Marxism with its focus upon the working class and communist parties as agents of social change. Instead, he focuses on the rise of new social movements, including the environment movement. O'Connor suggests that such movements have the capacity to call for greater government coordination of the economy thereby opening up the possibility for a transition to socialism.

Anarchist theorist and activist Murray Bookchin's 'social ecology' approach also views capitalism as inherently environmentally destructive. But, he is also wary of the new forms of domination in state socialist economies that continued to promote large-scale industrial production and engage in highly centralised and bureaucratic economic and political decision-making (1971). Bookchin, instead, advocates a radically decentralised, non-hierarchical society that exists in harmony with the natural environment.

This anarchist sentiment is also reflected in some eco-feminist thought and in much of the environment movement in the developing world, as evident in the structure and practices of the World Social Forum (see Chapter 10). Eco-feminist Ariel Salleh (2009) calls for a radical reconstitution of economy and society to ensure the sustainable reproduction of both humans and nature. Women, Salleh argues, are in a unique position to lead such a change because they are already involved in reproductive activities from childbirth and child rearing through to sustainable agricultural practices in peasant societies.

## CONCLUSION

Our experience of economic life is not confined to the spheres of market production and consumption. Changing values and circumstances have increasingly highlighted the important roles played by unpaid labour and care work in the household and the ecological productivity of the environment. This provides a different understanding of the market economy as a system dependent on social and natural reproduction and, therefore, social and ecological sustainability. But exactly how we understand the interplay between market, family and nature is contested, as are the appropriate responses. In the final chapter we turn our attention to civil society, the sphere of life where we most actively engage in the debates about how we shape economic and social life. It is here that we build community, shape social norms and create alternative futures.

## Questions

1 How has conventional economics understood the role of the household?
2 In what ways is the household a site of social and economic reproduction?
3 How is care work related to the gender division of labour?
4 How has environmental economics interpreted the relationship between the economy and environmental degradation? What are the criticisms of this conception?
5 Compare market-based solutions that price nature to proposals for a green 'new deal'. What other approaches might be needed to address environmental problems?

# 10 | Civil society, community and participation

IN THIS THIRD part of the book we have discussed how market society is experienced. We examined the world of work and consumption and areas of life that are often seen as 'outside' the economy, even though they support its reproduction. In this chapter we focus on civil society. Unlike families, work and the natural environment, which existed in various forms prior to the development of capitalism, many view civil society as a uniquely modern development – but one that provides a space outside the bureaucratic imperatives of the state and the profit motive of the market. It is a space where values are formed, debated and contested and, therefore, where the very operation of market society itself is shaped.

However, the nature and significance of civil society and its relationship to the capitalist economy is contested. In this chapter we explore three different understandings of civil society and how such ideas can be applied to different contemporary debates: first, the classical liberal perspective oriented around free exchange between individuals; second, the model built by social liberals and communitarians which focuses on social cohesion and building community; and, third, a perspective developed by critical theorists which views civil society as a place of conflict and struggle over the values and organisation of society. We also consider the role of social movements, the changing nature of participation and the relatively recent trend of transferring welfare responsibilities from the state to civil society.

## UNDERSTANDING CIVIL SOCIETY

The basis of modern civil society developed during the transition from feudalism to capitalism and reflects the social changes evident in the emerging market society. The separation of work from home led to a new social division of labour, as discussed by Durkheim (1984 [1893]). At the same time, liberal political reforms gradually saw a separation of powers within the state, creating the conditions for limited and representative government and protection of individual rights. These democratic reforms opened up space for public participation in law making and for voluntary organisations to mediate the growing roles of the state and the market stemming from the reorganisation of production and reproduction.

Both political and economic transformations opened up new spaces where people could meet in public, outside the home and their place of work. In these places they could cooperate, discuss and debate, free from direct state control. Furthermore, new technologies, such as book printing, played an important part in fostering a space in which debate and discussion could be extended by helping to disseminate new social and political ideas more widely. Access to information and political participation grew with the extension of education and social protections by the state to the poor and women. This continues to grow and evolve with new technologies, such as the internet and mobile phones.

Other social developments had similar effects. The rise of capitalism promoted urbanisation, breaking down old communal ties, but also creating spaces for new forms of community based on shared interests and values rather than common ancestry. However, capitalism also brought new social problems of poverty, homelessness and crime (see Chapter 4) which produced a number of different responses. Alongside calls for greater state regulation, other alternatives developed based on mutuality. Some employers acted directly while workers also created collective responses.

For example, George Cadbury established a 'model village' for his factory workers in Birmingham, designed to alleviate the problems caused by poor living conditions. His actions were inspired by his commitment to religious principles as a Quaker, rather than attempts to maximise profit as a businessman (Cadbury n.d.). Workers also responded to the social challenges of capitalism with their own mutual aid or friendly societies. These often grew out of craft associations and early trade unions. They allowed workers to collectively share the risks of market society – such as the loss of income from illness or temporary unemployment – by making contributions in good times and receiving support in bad times.

Market society fostered civil society, both by creating new social spaces and through generating social tensions. Access to these spaces expanded as social movements demanded greater economic and political rights on behalf of workers, women and other social groups. Civil society also plays important economic roles. It is directly responsible for significant economic production. It also acts to support and facilitate economic activity, by providing the trust, social cohesion and 'glue' that enable states and markets to operate effectively. Yet it is also where we contest the operation of states and markets, make claims for the redistribution of resources and different forms of economic organisation, or simply organise economic activity ourselves in new and different ways.

## THREE CONCEPTIONS OF CIVIL SOCIETY

The complexity and diversity of activities and relationships associated with civil society has, understandably, led to a number of competing, but not necessarily mutually exclusive conceptions. The processes of market exchange prioritised by classical liberals are necessarily embedded in the social relationships and communities at the centre of less 'individualistic' perspectives. The co-existence of individual *and* social imperatives in market societies means tensions inevitably arise. But it is through civil society, critical theorists suggest, that such tensions can lead to the reshaping, for better or worse, of the social world.

### Classical liberalism

Pre-liberal theorists developed the modern meaning of 'civil society' in the 16th century. As early as 1583, Thomas Smith declared that the breakdown of feudal bonds in England had created 'a multitude of free men collected together' in 'common wealth' or 'civill societie' (in Wood & Wood 1997, pp. 42–9). The key concern of political theorists at this time was how to limit political authority in a context where 'free' individuals were nevertheless dependent on one another for their livelihoods and must therefore live together collectively.

Reflecting the growth in commercial contracts, the idea emerged that civil society functioned according to agreements and covenants among individuals with certain rights. These were not yet democratic rights, but in the early seventeenth century people began to accept that 'free men' possessed certain legal rights and liberties that gave them protections and claims against the state. John Locke (1967 [1689]) built on these ideas by refuting the feudal idea that the political authority of monarchs came from 'divine right' and outlining the principles of a 'civil society' in which political authority stemmed from the people (see also Box 10.1).

At the centre of Locke's schema was property, indeed he claimed that 'the chief end... of [civil society] is the preservation of property' (1967 [1689]). Hence, civil society is said to come about because individuals voluntarily entered into a 'social contract' for political authority to be exercised impartially for the 'common good' whereby that 'good' was conceived as the protection of private property.

For the early liberal thinkers, civil society was more or less equivalent to the growing commercial society of their day. It was an arena of freedom 'distinct from the political state' (Polanyi 2001 [1944], p. 120). Yet the complex social division of labour that arose as production moved out of the household meant that people were also dependent on each other. Hence civil society was seen as the 'fulcrum where individual and collective energies come together in a market economy based on the legal recognition of private property as the root of freedom' (Chandhoke 2005).

According to Adam Smith, freedom in economic endeavours had intrinsic value because it represents emancipation from feudal forms of dependency, thereby fostering individual self-reliance. However, he also saw economic freedom facilitating a growth in income that made 'the good life possible' by furthering progress in learning and the arts, social and political relations and the moral quality of a society (Grampp 1965, p. 15). For Smith, these advances make a society 'civil'.

However, Smith also had concerns about the negative effects of greed on people's sociability and condemned what Veblen (1899) would later call 'conspicuous consumption'. Smith feared the rich might pursue the acquisition of wealth while neglecting to develop the 'moral and intellectual excellence' of civil society that was its end (Grampp 1965, p. 17). These fears were echoed by later liberals who tried to reconcile the tension between individualism and civil society (see Communitarian Responses later in this chapter).

John Stuart Mill (1975 [1859]) had similar concerns about the individual and collective life in a civil society. For Mill, people should be free to do as they please except when their actions harm others. It is only on this basis that there is a justification for political authority to 'interfere' with a person's liberty. This is what Isaiah Berlin (1969) would later call 'negative liberty', as discussed in Chapter 4.

More recently, neoliberals have returned to these ideas of civil society. Like neoclassical economists, they conceive of individuals as autonomous, and civil society as a space where individuals can choose to come together. Neoliberals argue we should foster civil society by reducing the role of the state, allowing voluntary organisations to replace its welfare functions (see Green 1993).

### Box 10.1 The French and English Revolutions

The French Revolution was a period of social, political and economic conflict between progressive republicans and conservative monarchists in France and across Europe between 1789 and 1799. The Revolution, known for its extreme violence, was marked by various political uprisings and declarations, and civil and external wars. But it was also important in the development of ideas and movements which have shaped the development of civil society since.

The French revolutionaries sought to replace the *ancien regime* ('old regime'). This was an order in which absolute power was vested in the monarchy and the political organisation of the state was controlled by those of noble hereditary descent. Instead, the revolutionaries worked to extend the ideals of liberty and equality to the greater public.

Aside from its practical and historical demonstration of both the possibilities and costs of collective social change, the French Revolution resulted in significant reforms, especially the primacy of a secular and representative state (the French republic) over both the monarchy and church. It also ushered in reforms to citizenship, the rule of law and human rights, as enshrined in the Declaration of the Rights of Man and of the Citizen of 1789 (although the document did not extend rights to women and slaves).

A century before, and in many ways the basis of inspiration for French progressives, England underwent its own political revolution in 1688 (Porter 2000). After decades of civil war, the English Revolution established a constitutional monarchy which ended the absolute power of the monarch.

This established English parliamentary democracy. However, old ideas about hierarchy and tradition nevertheless persisted (c.f. Edmund Burke 1790). These found their way into new political structures that emphasised citizenship and individual rights. The result was the modern political institutions (parliamentary rule and separation of powers) which linked political participation with property ownership. There was no universal vote for parliamentary representation, with women and the poor excluded from voting, and Catholics excluded from the new parliament and royal family.

By challenging the institutions and customs of tradition with ideas of liberty and equality, the French and the English Revolutions were important events in marking out civil society (although with sometimes 'uncivil' means). They were also catalysts for the two great humanist movements of the nineteenth century – liberalism and socialism – both of which have deep roots in civil society.

### Communitarian responses

In contrast to the classical liberal approach to civil society, communitarians are critical of the representation of humans as atomistic individuals. They focus on how civil society helps form us as individuals, rather than simply being a space in which already developed individuals interact. This account has a stronger emphasis on history and tradition. Civil society is often equated with community and the combination of inherited values, traditions and beliefs that are held by a group.

The *agency* of civil society is of critical importance to communitarians who favour non-governmental and community organisations in furthering their goals. These include fostering democratic checks on government and political authority in addition to strengthening the bonds of community. Although 'communitarianism' is a relatively recent invention, ideas about the importance of community and communitarian values have a long history. They were particularly important among the 'social liberals' and social reformers of the 19th century (see also Chapter 5).

Social liberals drew on the renewed interest in social bonds and community growing out of the contradictions of industrial capitalism. The decline of custom, growth of consumerism, moral and religious scepticism, urbanisation and persistent poverty were interpreted as a weakening of the traditional social fabric. This stimulated a desire for the 'ethical bonds which unite... citizens' and help them overcome the 'uncertainty of... individual lives' (Caird 1907 in den Otter 1997, p. 67).

However, such 'ethical bonds' did not ignore the individual. Instead, social liberals argued that strong individual rights and pursuit of the common good could be compatible. Hence, they promoted rights in a positive sense (see Chapter 4) as a means for giving all citizens the opportunity to develop and prosper because the 'good citizen' made a positive contribution to society, which in turn facilitated progress (Sawer 2003, p. 8). The notion of positive rights and active citizenship within civil society were very different emphases to that suggested in the *laissez-faire* 'night watchman' state (see Chapter 5).

Social liberals rejected the neoclassical position that an individual's values and rights originate within themselves and instead acknowledged that the individual was a product of society and that community was central to the 'genesis of the moral self' (Alexander 1898 in den Otter 1997, p. 70). Thus, civil society and community provide an 'ethical frame' that shapes the common good (den Otter 1997, p. 70). As discussed in Chapter 5, the theoretical and policy innovations of social liberals reflected a strengthening social democracy and paved the way for the modern welfare state.

However, the ascendency of neoliberalism in the late twentieth century (discussed in Chapters 5 and 6) again provoked renewed interest in community and civil society. The kind of theorising commonly drawn upon by neoliberals is reminiscent of classical *laissez-faire*. Communitarians argue that liberalism generally is individualistic and rights-oriented and therefore unable to take account of social relationships and communities (Sandel 1982). Some critics claim that neoliberal economic reforms undermine social bonds that are central to civil society, creating a more individualised society (Cox 1995). Others point to reduced political participation, arguing this individualism ironically reduces civil society's ability to restrain the state.

Contemporary communitarians, by contrast, refocus attention on aspects of the 'common good' and the ways in which citizens can make a meaningful contribution to civil society and politics. Hence, they seek to bolster social capital and the institutions of civil society. These goals are clearly reflected in the manifesto of The Communitarian Network founded by Amitai Etzioni in 1993:

> A communitarian perspective recognizes that the preservation of individual liberty depends on the active maintenance of the institutions of civil society where citizens learn respect for others as well as self-respect; where we acquire a lively sense of our personal and civic responsibilities, along with an appreciation of our own rights and the rights of others; where we develop the skills of self-government as well as the habit of governing ourselves, and learn to serve others – not just self.
>
> (Communitarian Network n.d.)

Underpinning such ideas is a notion of positive rights. Without society, individuals would not have rights; they therefore share the responsibility of contributing to collective life. Hence, communitarians generally support tax-funded policies like state-subsidised education and housing, universal healthcare, unemployment support and environmental protection. These help create the 'good citizen' as well as the 'good life'.

However, many communitarians also concur with some elements of the neoliberal approach to the state. Communitarians emphasise a grassroots 'bottom up' approach to policy delivery, rather than the 'top down' delivery of centralised state bureaucracies. The state may fund 'services' but these should be delivered by the family or community wherever possible. These sorts of ideas are evident in many of the policies and practices of 'Third Way' governments, discussed later in this chapter.

### Critical theory and civil society

Critical social theorists have taken an approach that reflects some communitarian concerns for social connection but places less emphasis on the importance of tradition and more emphasis on power, conflict and struggle. Two influential conceptions come from the work of Italian Marxist Antonio Gramsci and German sociologist Juergen Habermas, who was more optimistic than Gramsci about civil society. Gramsci (1971) focused on the relationships between the different spheres of market society, such as law, culture and economy. In doing so he addressed the criticism that Marxist scholarship placed too much emphasis on economic structures, ignoring social agency.

Gramsci wrote some of his most influential work while imprisoned by Benito Mussolini's fascist dictatorship. His central concept of 'hegemony' means power exercised through both coercion and consent. Civil society was where the consensual aspect of power resided. It is where people's 'common sense' views of the world and their place within it are formed. According to Gramsci, dominant social groups (such as the capitalist class) and institutions (such as the state) can achieve hegemony by shaping these common sense views, so that the status quo appears normal and legitimate. For example, consumerism is normalised through the proliferation of advertising in the mass media (see Box 10.2).

**Box 10.2 Cultural norms**

In Part 2 of the book we discussed how regulation maintains social stability and economic order. Cultural norms of everyday life also 'regulate', but they are less tangible than the regulations of the state, market and corporation. We may be free to formulate our own beliefs, but that freedom is expressed within cultural constraints that we may not always be aware of.

> Cultural norms are important because they serve as the 'social glue' holding together the diversity of peoples and practices that make up any given society. But they are potentially always open to challenge in a way that pre-enlightenment belief was not because people accepted the word of the King as the word of God. In modern society, certain behaviours and beliefs are 'normalised' – when you are accustomed to something it goes unquestioned – and this is how social norms engender stability and cohesion in market society.
>
> Cultural norms are similar to what Bourdieu calls 'fields' and 'habitus' (Bourdieu 1990). These are essentially the social relations that shape our behaviour. People in similar social or economic positions will be shaped by a similar habitus, such as a masculine habitus, or a working-class habitus. They constrain our behaviour, they shape our goals (what we want) and our strategies for achieving them (how we get them). Yet they are also actively reconstructed, as individual behaviour feeds back to, and affects, broader social norms.
>
> Common norms and values are central to social stability, yet their form varies across space and over time. They are neither 'natural' nor permanent, but are strategically constructed and reconstructed. This evolution is evident in the battles for peoples' 'hearts and minds' at times of economic crisis and social distress, during which social norms are often reconstructed, creating new social 'cement'. For example, the social reforms responding to the post-World War II period were underpinned by the normalisation of consumption habits that conflicted with the mentality of thrift dominant during the depression and war years.

However, hegemony can also be challenged. This requires subordinate groups, movements or parties to win their own hegemony in civil society – to convert 'common sense' into 'good sense' – as a precursor to taking over the state. In this sense, civil society is the meeting place between the power of the state and the market, and people's common sense understanding of market society. It is where we come to understand what is 'normal' and 'expected' and, like the communitarian account, it is a place where we gain values. However, unlike the communitarian view, Gramsci emphasises how our values reflect underlying power relationships, and so views civil society as a place of conflict between different accounts of the world.

Juergen Habermas sees greater potential than did Gramsci for civil society to serve as a space for constructive debate. For Habermas, civil society is closely linked to his concept of the 'public sphere', a realm of social life where private individuals come together and form a public body. It is independent of other roles they may have as business people, workers or members of the state. This body exists in countless situations and is evident wherever the freedoms of assembly, of association and of expression are present. These freedoms are critical because they are the source of public opinions about matters of public interest (Habermas 1989 [1964], p. 49).

Habermas (1989 [1964]) argues that the public sphere was a historically specific development that emerged in the late eighteenth century. It grew out of the long breakdown of feudal authority and the cementing of capitalist familial relations. This allowed recognition of private individuals with identities separate and distinct from the state. In places such as coffee houses, public squares and playhouses, the public sphere developed as a space where people with new class, familial and political identities came together for rational and critical discussion about public matters (Calhoun 1993, p. 397).

For Habermas, it was the sphere of the newly emergent 'bourgeoisie' within the rising liberal order that separated the social world into public and private realms (see also Chapter 9). The public sphere allows values and practices to be debated. It is through meaningful debate, which Habermas (1987) describes as communicative action, that we are able to challenge current practices and make claims for a more just social order. Habermas argued that this communicative action is challenged by both the state and the market.

These institutions involve what Weber called instrumental rationality, which follows a rationalised 'systemic' logic, rather than a broader rationality based on reasoned debate of what constitutes a good life. Habermas claimed that when this happened the 'lifeworld' of everyday experience is colonised by the 'systems' of instrumental rationality (1987). For example, the commercial media, especially television, is a central component of everyday life in all advanced capitalist countries. Media is also a business, which generates profits based on advertising. This extends the values of the profit system into the realm of public debate and discussion, impinging upon the lifeworld.

Habermas therefore problematises the concept of civil society, recognising that it is not simply autonomous from markets and states, but deeply intertwined with them. This does not necessarily mean that civil society lacks its own unique values and logic or that civil society cannot influence the nature of states and markets (as discussed later in the section on social movements). But the relationship is not a straightforward one.

Somewhat less optimistic about the prospects of change, but also influential, is the work of the Frankfurt School (with whom Habermas was initially associated), including Theodore Adorno and Herbert Marcuse. Adorno (1991 [1964]) rejected the term 'popular culture' in favour of 'mass culture' – and later, the 'culture industry' – to argue that the cultures which pervaded everyday life did not emerge from the people, but were part of the profit system. Borrowing from the concepts of rationalisation and commodification, Adorno argued culture was standardised and mass produced, offering few avenues for truly critical expression. Marcuse (1991 [1964]) argued that capitalist society had become 'one dimensional' as politics, media and culture more generally closed off avenues for dissent.

The influence of the state and corporate interests within civil society has, however, been challenged. For example, the labour movement developed its own media (particularly newspapers) as well as educational institutions (such as working men's colleges) and leisure organisations (such as working men's clubs). Some historians claim these institutions constitute an 'alternative public sphere' (Scalmer & Irving 2005) because they enabled workers to articulate their own interests and concerns outside the official discourses of the state and corporate media.

While the labour press developed separately to commercial cultural forms, more recent challenges use commercial culture itself. 'Culture jammers', for instance, modify popular media images to change their content to a subversive one. One example is the defacement of tobacco and alcohol billboard advertisements in Australia during the 1970s and 1980s by the group BUGA UP (Billboard Artists Utilising Graffiti Against Unhealthy Promotions), or the contemporary magazine *Ad Busters*, which alters popular commercials to expose the anti-social interests they promote (see also Box 10.3). This process of 'détournement' is inspired by the Situationist International, a radical European movement from the 1960s which used culture to critique capitalist society (DeBord 1956).

### Box 10.3 WikiLeaks – civil society versus the state

*WikiLeaks* is a website which makes classified government information freely available to the public. It shot to international prominence in 2010 following its publication of a secret US military video showing US aircraft killing journalists and Iraqi civilians. The title *WikiLeaks* gave to this video, 'Collateral Murder', was a reference to the phrase 'collateral damage', used by the US Government since the first Gulf War in 1990 to describe civilian deaths caused by the US military (WikiLeaks 2010).

The phrase 'collateral damage' is an example of the way governments frame information to shape media reporting and, ultimately, public opinion. It does not refer directly to human beings and frames civilian deaths simply as the side-effects of advanced technology, much as a building might suffer incidental damage from a nearby explosion.

While democratic governments no longer have official propaganda departments, some scholars argue they still perform a propaganda function. According to Edward Herman and Noam Chomsky (1988), phrases like 'collateral damage' attempt to desensitise civil society to the human cost of US wars. It is part of the way in which the US Government and mass media 'manufacture consent' for US foreign policy, by glossing over the deaths of enemy civilians, thus casting them as 'unworthy victims' while disproportionately highlighting the deaths of US and allied civilians who are deemed 'worthy victims'.

In bringing to light the practices of the US military through 'Collateral Murder' and the leaking of thousands of other classified documents, *WikiLeaks* can be seen as an example of a civil society organisation asserting the importance of the public sphere in which rational discourse can occur based on access to accurate information.

## CIVIL SOCIETY IN PRACTICE

The different conceptions of civil society are central to a number of ongoing political debates about the appropriate roles of states and markets. Civil society is usually viewed as a positive sphere that helps us gain control and autonomy. But different theorists see this working in different ways, reflecting different conceptions of civil society, and indeed of market society. Social movements are seen by many as the central actors in civil society, but individuals and their levels of 'social capital' and civic participation are also important to debates about the economy and welfare states, as is the increasingly prominent role of non-government organisations in providing public services.

## ACTIVISM, SOCIAL MOVEMENTS AND ECONOMIC CHANGE

As we have discussed, civil society is partly a product of social activism. Revolutions, like those in France and Britain, facilitated individual rights and a separation of powers in the state. Over time social movements, from the early chartists to more recent civil rights and independence movements, called for these rights to be extended to other groups initially excluded. This was crucial in establishing what Habermas calls the 'public sphere'. As we saw in earlier chapters, the struggles of social movements also included claims for economic redistribution and the reorganisation of the economy, and so have deeply shaped our economic lives.

Movements usually involved non-elites, such as manual workers, peasant farmers or the unemployed coming together to press for change. Rather than using conventional methods that are an accepted part of politics (such as voting is today), they used 'contentious' methods, such as refusing to work, destroying machinery or civil disobedience. Thus, within sociology, social movements were initially seen as somewhat chaotic and irrational. Sociologists explained people participating in social movements as expressions of the social strains caused by rapid industrialisation and urbanisation (see Jenkins 1983, p. 528).

Within economics, Mancur Olson's (1965) work on collective action has been highly influential. He argued that large groups created little incentive for individuals to commit time and resources. An individual's actions made little difference to the overall outcome and even if movements were successful, non-members often enjoyed the benefits. His argument has been compared to the Prisoner's Dilemma (see Box 10.6). Because of this, he argued, movements like the labour movement would use selective benefits, such as access to pension schemes, or restraints, such as union or closed shops, to ensure individuals' participation.

By contrast, the Marxist tradition focused less on why people were involved and more on the role social movements play in shaping society. For Marx, the development of mass resistance to changes in capitalist society was not irrational but an expected consequence of the exploitative and alienating nature of capitalism. Marx saw trade unions and radical political parties as natural developments in capitalism. Yet, over time, trade unions have become institutionalised rather than radicalised. Indeed, it was a smaller, more elite group of professional revolutionaries (Lenin's Bolsheviks) that ultimately led the Russian revolution in 1917.

## Social movement theory

Ranging from civil and indigenous rights protestors to environmentalists and feminists, movement activism increased from the 1960s and the growing radicalism exposed more people to social movements (see also Box 10.4). Political sociologist Sidney Tarrow (1998) argued that the ability of social movements to overcome Olson's 'dilemma of collective action' was not as surprising as it first appeared. Movements, he argued, were social, in the sense that they drew on social resources, such as a shared identity, common cultural understandings and social networks. Similarly Charles Tilly (2004) argued movements emerged because new forms of social organisation gave rise to new identities and interests.

Movement theorists identified three broad factors that influenced the development of movements (McAdam, McCarthy & Zald 1996). One was the broader political context – called the political opportunity structure. When elite groups were unified, movements were less likely to form or succeed, as in some totalitarian regimes. But tensions within the ruling group could open opportunities and as movements grew, further opportunities developed. For example, achieving democratic reforms opened new avenues for action. However, movement success was also dependent on the internal resources available.

Movements needed to be organised, both internally and through networks to other actors. This allowed them to mobilise resources, such as people, specialist knowledge and finance. Movement success is also influenced by 'framing', or the way an issue is presented and understood. Frames give people the story about why a situation is unjust and what can be done to fix it. This perspective emphasises that social movements are not just the result of structures, but also the clash of ideas. George Lakoff (2004) has developed this in a modern context, explaining how political parties attempt to win support by influencing the way we understand (or frame) problems.

## Box 10.4 Non-violent direct action

Non-violent direct action has long been a feature of social movements and political thought. It is most often associated with the movement against British rule in India led by Mohandas Gandhi in the 1920s–1940s.

Gandhi advocated the use of civil disobedience and non-cooperation to confront British power.

In 1930 he led the 'salt march' – a month-long march through the countryside and seaside, to take salt from the sea. This violated the British monopoly on the production of salt, from which it also derived tax revenue. It induced a violent reaction from the state (Martin 2005). The use of violence against peaceful protesters helped to undermine the moral legitimacy of the British occupation. But the protests also helped to undermine the ability of Britain to govern India by attacking its revenue sources.

This highlights two important principles of non-violent direct action. First, 'a movement (using non-violent direct action) can expose and dramatise the will to violence that underpins oppression, severing the regime from its remaining popular support' (Ackerman & DuVall 2000, p. 500). As long as this violence can be communicated to the broader population, it can undermine support for oppressive regimes. Second, civil disobedience and non-cooperation, when used strategically, can disrupt the ability of oppressive systems to function.

Non-violent direct action recognises that the power of the state is partly based on a monopoly on the means of violence, meaning that opposing state oppression through violence rarely succeeds. However, states also rely upon the cooperation of their citizens, which gives the oppressed their power. When such cooperation is withdrawn, the ability of states to govern is threatened.

Other prominent examples of struggles using non-violent direct action include the US civil rights movement of the 1950s and 1960s, the Polish Solidarity movement of the 1980s, the movement against eastern European communism in 1989–1990 and, more recently, some of the events of the 'Arab Spring', particularly in Egypt and Tunisia in 2011.

### Movements and society

Alongside the operation of movements, many theorists focused more attention on the changing nature of market society and how this gave rise to different types of movements and claims. Many of these theorists thought the older social movements, particularly the labour movement, reflected the class structure of industrial capitalism.

Habermas, for example, argued that these older movements resulted from the unequal distribution of work and rewards, and workers' desire to claim a fairer share of economic resources. These were struggles for redistribution and, Habermas (1987) argued, such struggles led directly to the formation of the welfare state as a way of reducing inequality and the risks of market society.

However, he argued the radicalism of the 1960s and 1970s reflected different dynamics. The 'new middle class' of educated professionals drove the new social movements. Instead of claims for economic redistribution, these movements sought control over meaning and identity. Habermas (1987) saw these movements as a reaction to the rationalising forces of market society, both the discipline of market competition and of state bureaucracy, which he thought were impinging on the 'lifeworld' of civil society.

Axel Honneth (1996) took up Habermas's argument that new social movements expressed different types of claims. He argued that many struggles could be understood as claims for recognition – the claim to be understood on our own terms rather than economic claims for resources. Nancy Fraser, a fellow critical theorist and feminist philosopher, has since criticised Honneth for placing too much emphasis on recognition (see Fraser & Honneth 2003).

Fraser (1997) argues that most social movements reflect a mixture of claims for both redistribution *and* recognition. She acknowledges that even the labour movement has always combined claims for economic redistribution with claims for dignity and control at work. New social movements, such as feminism, combine a focus on recognition claims around sexuality and identity, with claims for more equitable distribution of work and income.

All these theorists connect developments in market society – the changing nature of work, social class and politics – with developments within social movements. Movements thus respond to tensions within market society while also influencing how market society develops.

## From hierarchy to network

Studies of new social movements have focused more on the different ways that movements organise and frame their actions (see Norris 2002; Mertes 2004). For example, workers' movements tend to develop centralised and hierarchical organisations (such as unions and political parties) with official spokespeople, policies and processes. New social movements tend to be more anarchic, based on networks of actors that develop and dissipate relatively quickly, although in practice there are elements of both forms in all movements.

This reflects the nature of the claims made by different movements. For example, strong organisational structures and hierarchies sit comfortably alongside attempts to unify and build solidarity within a class-based movement. Alternatively, networks more readily accommodate the different claims of new social movements and the philosophy of decentralising power. The network structure of new social movements also reflects changing technologies, such as the importance of the internet and the pressures of globalisation.

Networks have become an effective mode of resistance, enabling numerous small-scale but powerful protests, such as the release of embarrassing information through WikiLeaks, while still allowing different 'affinity groups' to work together on specific issues through events like the World Social Forum (see Box 10.5). Hardt and Negri (2004) argue networked movements provide the basis for the 'multitude', describing diffuse and decentralised resistance to commodification and exploitation (see Chapter 4).

### Box 10.5 Fórum Social Mundial (or World Social Forum)

The Fórum Social Mundial began in Porto Alegre in Brazil in 2001. It has since held annual meetings in a number of continents and spawned local social forums across the world. Attendance is international and can exceed 75 000 people.

The forums are part of the broader 'global justice movement', which opposes neoliberal forms of globalisation. As with many new social movements, it functions more like a network than a strong centralised organisation. Its charter aims to provide a space for activists to come together, debate and organise, allowing local campaigns to connect globally.

The movement has been particularly influential in Latin America, where some of the most extreme neoliberal policies have been implemented. Most global forums are held in the south, or majority world, reflecting a commitment to global equality. The Forum played an important role in organising the largest global demonstrations in history, against the Second Gulf War in 2004.

## SOCIAL CAPITAL, COMMUNITY AND PARTICIPATION

The 1980s and 1990s were periods of renewed interest in civil society. Many attributed the fall of communism in the Soviet Block to civil society movements that challenged communist rule. But as research into civil society increased, concerns emerged that civil society was weakening. Interest centred on work by political scientist Robert Putnam, which focused on what he termed 'social capital', a resource developed in civil society, but which helped sustain a healthy economy and democracy.

## Social capital

Putnam's (1993) work was based on extensive research in Italy, where he examined the health of civic, political and economic institutions. He found that the north of Italy fared better on all his indicators than the relatively poorer south. This Putnam attributed to differences in civil society, arguing that 'social capital' explained stronger economic and political outcomes.

Putnam's concept built on work by economic sociologists, such as James Coleman and Mark Granovetter. Coleman worked closely with a number of prominent rational choice economists, including Gary Becker, at Chicago University. He applied this economic method to his sociological analysis, using tools such as game theory.

Part of Coleman's (1990) work focused on how societies overcame the problem of collective action, which suggested it was sometimes difficult for people to cooperate for a common good. He (1990) argued that many situations look like a 'Prisoner's Dilemma', where individual incentives hinder cooperation, even though cooperation leads to better outcomes for all (see Box 10.6).

Coleman argued that in some situations people were able to overcome this dilemma by building strong social norms that led people to make more collectively rational decisions. These norms, which he called social capital, facilitated trust and allowed people to work together for common purpose without having to invest in expensive monitoring or enforcement costs.

Alternatively, Granovetter (1973) analysed how different types of social networks facilitate different sorts of actions. For example, many of us develop strong ties to a small group of people that are quite like us – such as our family and close friends. These strong ties facilitate high cost actions – such as making soup for a sick friend.

By contrast, we make weaker connections to many other people – through work and social clubs. These weak ties tend to be to people less like ourselves – in terms of ethnicity, religion and upbringing, and are not as good at facilitating high cost action – we do not regularly cook for, or lend large sums to, work colleagues. But they do facilitate access to new resources that might not be in our immediate family networks (such as access to a new job).

Putnam (1993) built on this theory to explain how different types of social ties produce different sorts of social capital that could either bind us together (strong ties) or create bridges between different communities (weak ties). Social capital, he argued, consisted of both social norms and social networks that facilitated action. The two reinforced each other. As citizens engaged in civic institutions, like sporting clubs and Meals on Wheels, they developed more social networks and built trust with others. These resources would then allow them to work together for common purposes more easily.

Putnam's ideas were taken up by the World Bank after it was criticised for policies that focused entirely on building large infrastructure – leaving developing countries with large debts that were difficult to pay (see Chapters 5 and 6). The Bank saw social capital as an alternative basis for development policy. It looked to build strong institutions and governance arrangements in developing countries, rather than simply focusing on physical assets such as dams or roads (for example Dasgupta & Serageldin 2000).

However, critics like political economist Ben Fine (2010) argued this failed to take account of power and inequality, both within communities and within broader international trading systems. Thus, the World Bank would focus attention on building trust within a community without properly acknowledging that a lack of trust might be the result of genuinely unequal power – or the poverty caused by unfair trade.

The World Bank's use of social capital is also quite different to that of Pierre Bourdieu (1986). He saw social capital as an individual resource (rather than a resource for a society) that came from having connections to rich or powerful people. It is similar to his concept of cultural capital (see chapter 4), where he identifies social and cultural mechanisms for maintaining privilege and inequality. On this account, it makes little sense to see social capital as a resource primarily of the poor.

### Box 10.6 Game theory and the Prisoner's Dilemma

Game theory (Varoufakis 2001) applies rational choice principles, showing how people will act strategically to gain the greatest payoff. But it also highlights some situations where individual rationality can lead to a collectively irrational outcome. This has implications for civil society and social capital.

The classic example of this is the Prisoner's Dilemma. It is modelled on the story of two prisoners, caught and interviewed by police. The police offer each a deal: rat on the other and you will get off while your colleague will get life. If you both rat, you get a moderate penalty, a few years in prison. But because of lack of evidence, if both remained silent they would only face a lesser charge and get a fine.

One would think they both hold out. But game theory says otherwise. Take the perspective of prisoner one: you know that if your friend rats, you are better off ratting too – getting a few years rather than life. You also know that if your friend holds out, you are still better off ratting (you get off rather than paying the fine). So no matter what your friend does, you should always rat. The game predicts both rat, and both serve several years in prison, when a little trust (or social capital) would have allowed them to only pay the fine.

Game theorists have since applied the same logic to many other situations, such as looking after environmental resources or volunteering in the community. But the example also highlights how social capital can have a 'dark side' by assisting bad actions, not just good ones.

### Community and participation

Putnam later applied the concept of social capital to the United States, where he found a significant decline in civic participation. He (2000) coined the term 'bowling alone', to highlight how the institutions of social participation, such as bowling leagues, were dying out.

He cited a number of potential culprits. Part of the explanation, he suggested, was generational. Those living through depression and war developed a stronger sense of community than those growing up in more prosperous and individualistic times. Social changes, such as women entering the workforce, may have reduced people's time for engaging in social clubs. But most importantly, he claimed, television was robbing us of time and making us less social.

The decline in participation was also associated with growing cynicism towards the institutions of government. International surveys showed declining trust in government and politicians. Party memberships fell and people failed to turn out to vote. Putnam saw these trends as linked to declining social capital.

Alternatively, Pippa Norris (2002) argued that citizens were simply changing the way they engaged in civil society. Instead of joining mass-member organisations, they were more likely to attend street rallies, boycott products for ethical or environmental reasons or sign petitions. Norris suggests political participation has changed in similar ways to the organisation of new social movements.

## CIVIL SOCIETY AND THE WELFARE STATE

Neoliberalism has also influenced debates around civil society. Neoliberalism argues the state's role in the economy should be limited. But some free market theorists also suggested that by removing state support (like public healthcare), people would be encouraged to build mutuals and friendly societies to help themselves. On this account, the welfare state replaced these earlier mutuals and in the process weakened civil society and self-reliance (Green 1993).

In the late 1990s communitarian concerns over the loss of community combined with neoliberal efforts to reduce the role of the state in the economy. Even many traditional opponents of market reform, such as trade unions and social democratic political parties, accepted the analysis that globalisation made it difficult for the state to play an active role in the economy. However, many of these traditional critics disagreed with the neoliberal attack on the welfare state arguing that neoliberalism could undermine social cohesion by promoting individualism.

The Third Way emerged as an influential response to these forces, incorporating elements of the neoliberal critique and more conventional welfare state politics. Developing first in Australia, where a Labor Government had worked closely with the trade unions to implement market reforms in the 1980s (Frankel 1997) it spread to Britain, the US and parts of continental Europe. Its most prominent advocate was British sociologist Anthony Giddens (1998).

While Giddens was critical of *laissez-faire* economics, he wanted to strengthen communities while also accepting a greater role for markets in public policy. The Third Way represented a compromise between radical neoliberalism and the ideals of an older form of social democracy.

Key to this approach was to accept a more limited role for the state in directly regulating economic outcomes. Instead, the state had a key role in helping citizens compete in the new global marketplace and to help strengthen communities at a local level. For example, by investing in education workers would be better able to compete for high wage jobs.

At a local level, the Third Way advocated devolving many government functions to the non-government sector, potentially strengthening community and civil society. Community organisations were also seen to be more flexible and responsive to local concerns than large bureaucracies.

The Third Way emphasised social inclusion. This usually involved encouraging people into the labour market. Third Way theorists were particularly concerned at the number of households where no one did paid work and the potential for this to breed a cycle of poverty and exclusion for children raised in this environment (see Powell 2000). As a result, programs were established to encourage (or even force) single parents, the long-term unemployed and those with a disability into the workforce.

This partly reflected the growing influence of communitarian ideas, but it was often consistent with neoliberal reform. Indeed, some have labelled the Third Way as a neoliberal 'Trojan horse' (Green & Wilson 1999). Both schools of thought saw involvement in the labour market as important: neoliberals because it promoted efficiency and productivity, communitarians because it promoted social cohesion and integration into community values. Both neoliberals and communitarians favoured using non-government organisations to provide welfare services.

## WHO RULES?

One example of this process of devolving welfare state programs to non-government organisations comes from early reforms in Australia. One element was the creation of new 'managed' or 'quasi' markets (see Chapter 6) in which non-government organisations receive funding to provide services on behalf of the state.

In his book *Who Rules?* Michael Keating (2004) argues that such managed markets allow governments to control important aspects of service delivery without having to directly run the services. They do this by setting the rules (such as minimum standards for a childcare centre) and by providing most of the funding. Thus, services operate according to rules set by government but benefit from private and non-profit provision.

While Keating welcomes the use of 'managed markets' as an efficient way for states to get the outcomes they want, other theorists have expressed concern. Interestingly, this has come from theorists with quite different approaches to civil society. For example, Vern Hughes (2011), Director of the Centre for Civil Society, who has worked with neoliberal think tanks, argues that government control of funding has undermined the spirit of volunteerism in many non-government organisations. Because these organisations are now funded by the state to provide services, they use paid workers and rules set by the state rather than the principles of mutuality.

Alternatively, John Falzon (ABC 2006), the CEO of St Vincent de Paul in Australia, reflected a view consistent with critical theory, emphasising the structural causes of poverty and the need for strong social supports. He is also critical of the model, arguing that it forces church agencies to be complicit in state policies that stigmatise the recipients of welfare services, by imposing fines and penalties on those who do not comply with state rules.

This range of criticisms, as well as Keating's defence of outsourcing welfare services to community agencies, suggests we need to look closely at the detail of policy. How is civil society involved in providing services? Who sets the rules? And who benefits most from the arrangements?

## CONCLUSION

Civil society is most clearly the realm in which the operation of both the state and the market are challenged and debated. While there are different understandings of civil society, there is consensus that it is a place where people are able to build the social relations they want – whether as free individuals, as members of a community or as participants in movements that challenge the status quo. Indeed these understandings are not always inconsistent. Like the family and the environment, civil society is often conceived as being 'outside' the economy. Yet it is in civil society that the movements that gave rise to the welfare state and to forms of state regulation arose.

Civil society is where new economic experiments, from friendly societies to the wiki internet movements are born. And it is increasingly where many social services are delivered by non-profit providers funded by the state. In this sense, civil society does represent our experience of how states and markets come together. It is where the lived experience of market society – the lifeworld – engages with the rationalised systems that regulate our lives. It is also where we contest and remake how we live in market society.

### Questions

1 How does the emergence of civil society relate to the development of market society?

2 What explains the similarities and differences in the major conceptions of civil society?
3 How have social movements responded to and changed market society?
4 Is the trend towards devolving state provision of services to civil society to be welcomed?
5 What role should civil society play in reshaping market society?

# Concluding remarks

IN THIS BOOK we set out to understand market society by linking a range of conceptual lenses to the historical experience of capitalism in practice. We have sought to demonstrate how the economy is both embedded in social life while also shaping social life. In the first part of the book we examined key elements constituting the capitalist economic system and the way these have been understood. We discussed how commodity-based production expands, generating wealth but also periodic crises. These, in turn, exacerbate the inherent inequalities and conflict upon which market societies have historically been based. In all these respects, the constitutive economic processes – production and commodification, accumulation and crisis, distribution and conflict – are embedded in a range of institutional forms. These serve to integrate the 'anarchy' of private commodity production with the process of social provisioning.

In the second part of the book, we examined how these core institutions regulate market society giving 'unity and stability, structure and function' to actual existing economies (Polanyi 1957, p. 249). We examined how the state and market developed alongside each other with the state creating and regulating markets and the private corporation. We argued that the market itself is an important regulatory institution. Its competitive forces provide strong incentives for people to act in certain ways, which is reinforced by the dependence of most people on market income to survive. However, these competitive forces have themselves been shaped by the rise of large corporations which have also become powerful political actors. These three regulatory institutions also profoundly shape our experience of the economy and everyday life.

In the final section of the book, we examined this experience by broadening the analysis to include consideration of people's reality as workers and consumers, as well as within the family, the community and the environment. This focus goes beyond concerns with producing and consuming to include reproduction of the social and ecological relations that underpin the economy and our quality of life. We looked not only at how economic forces shape these experiences, but also at how the discursive and contentious practices of civil society set limits on the 'social license' of corporations and on the legitimacy of the state. Civil society is where communities are built, where social connections are formed and where norms and politics are debated. Ultimately, it is where market society itself is remade. Through understanding the economic and social processes discussed in the book, we can critically reflect on the nature of market society and our potential to transform its institutions in order to realise a more just way of life.

# References

Ackerman, F 2002, 'Still dead after all these years: interpreting the failure of general equilibrium theory', *Journal of Economic Methodology*, vol. 9, no. 2, pp. 119–39.

Ackermann, P, DuVall, J 2000, *A force more powerful: a century of nonviolent conflict*, Palgrave, New York.

Adorno, T 1991, *The culture industry: selected essays on mass culture*, Routledge, London.

Akerlof, G, Shiller, R 2009, *Animal spirits: how human psychology drives the economy, and why it matters for global capitalism*, Princeton University Press, Princeton.

Alcott, B 2005, 'Jevons' paradox', *Ecological Economics*, vol. 54, pp. 9–21.

Altvater, E 1994, 'Ecological and economic modalities of time and space', in M O'Connor (ed), *Is capitalism sustainable? Political economy and the politics of ecology*, The Guilford Press, New York.

Amin, A 1994, 'Post-Fordism: models, fantasies and phantoms of transition', in A Amin (ed), *Post-Fordism: a reader*, Blackwell, Oxford.

Andrews, D, Leigh, A 2009, 'More inequality, less social mobility', *Applied Economic Letters*, vol. 16, pp. 1489–92.

Angus, I 2008, 'The myth of the tragedy of the commons', *MR Zine*, 25 August 2008, <http://mrzine.monthlyreview.org/2008/angus250808.html>. Accessed August 2011.

Arthur, B 1994, *Increasing returns and path dependence in the economy*, University of Michigan Press, Ann Arbor.

Atkinson, AB 2003, 'Income inequality in OECD countries: data and explanations', *CESifo Economic Studies*, vol. 49, 4/2003, pp. 479–513.

Australian Broadcasting Corporation 2006, 'Robert McCullough and John Falzon', *The Religion Report*, ABC Radio, 23 August.

Australian Bureau of Statistics 1997, 'Basic timeuse survey', Cat. No. 4151.0, ABS, Canberra.

Australian Bureau of Statistics 2006, 'How Australians use their time', 4153.0, ABS, Canberra.

Australian Bureau of Statistics 2011, 'Balance of payments – exports and imports', Cat. No. 5302.0, Table H3, ABS, Canberra.

Australian Fair Trade and Investment Network (AFTINET) n.d., 'World Trade Organisation', available at <http://aftinet.org.au/cms/world-trade-organisation>. Accessed August 2011.

Australian Government 1975, 'Commonwealth Commission of Inquiry into Poverty', available at <http://nla.gov.au/nla.party-554637>. Accessed August 2011.

Australian Treasury 2010, *Intergenerational report 2010*, AGPS, Canberra.

Baek, SW 2005, 'Does China follow the "East Asian development model"?', *Journal of Contemporary Asia*, vol. 35, no. 4, pp. 485–98.

Baldwin, P 1990, *The politics of social solidarity: class bases of the European welfare state 1875–1975*, Cambridge University Press, Cambridge.

Banerjee, SB 2007, *Corporate social responsibility: the good, the bad and the ugly*, Edward Elgar, Cheltenham.

Bank of International Settlements 2010, 'Triennial Central Bank survey: foreign exchange and derivatives market activity in April 2010', preliminary results, Monetary and Economic Department, Basel, Switzerland, <http://www.bis.org/publ/rpfxf10t.htm>. Accessed January 2010.

Baran, P, Sweezy, P 1966, *Monopoly capital: an essay on the American economic and social order*, Monthly Review Press, New York.

Barber, WJ 1967, *A history of economic thought*, Penguin Books, London.

Barbier, E 2010, *A global green new deal: rethinking the economic recovery*, Cambridge University Press, Cambridge.

Barker, DK 1999, 'Gender', in J Peterson and M Lewis (eds), *The Elgar companion to feminist economics*, Edward Elgar, Cheltenham, pp. 390–6.

Baudrillard, J 1998, *The consumer society: myths and structures*, Sage Publications, Thousand Oaks, CA.

Bauman, Z 2000, *Liquid modernity*, Polity, Cambridge.

Beck, U 1992 [1986], *Risk society: towards a new modernity*, Sage, New Delhi (trans. from *Risikogesellschaft*).

Beck, U 2000, *The brave new world of work*, Polity Press, Malden.

Beck, U, Giddens, A, Lash, S 1994, *Reflexive modernization: politics, tradition and aesthetics in the modern social order*, Polity, Cambridge.

Becker, G 1993 [1964], *Human capital: a theoretical and empirical analysis, with special reference to education*, 3rd edn, University of Chicago Press, Chicago.

Becker, GS 1981, *A treatise on the family*, Harvard University Press, Cambridge, MA.

Beder, S 2000, *Selling the work ethic: from puritan pulpit to corporate PR*, Zed Books, London.

Beder, S 2002, 'bp: beyond petroleum?', in E Lubbers (ed), *Battling big business: countering greenwash, infiltration and other forms of corporate bullying*, Green Books, Devon, pp. 26–32. Available at <http://www.uow.edu.au/~sharonb/bp.html>.

Bell, D 1999, *The coming of post-industrial society: a venture in social forecasting*, Basic Books, New York.

Bellamy Foster, J 1999, 'Marx's theory of Metabolic Rift: classical foundations for environmental sociology', *The American Journal of Sociology*, vol. 105, no. 2, pp. 366–405.

Bellamy Foster, J 2007, 'The financialization of capitalism', *Monthly Review*, vol. 58, no. 11.

Bellamy Foster, J 2010, 'The financialization of accumulation', *Monthly Review*, vol. 62, no. 5.
Bello, W 2009, *Food wars*, Verso, New York.
Bergmann, B 1995, 'Becker's theory of the family: preposterous conclusions', *Feminist Economics*, vol. 1, no. 1, pp. 141–50.
Berle, A, Means, G 1932, *The modern corporation and private property*, Transaction Publishers, New Brunswick.
Berlin, I 1969, *Four essays on liberty*, Oxford University Press, London.
Boggs, J 1970, *Racism and the class struggle: further pages from a black worker's notebook*, Monthly Review Press, New York.
Böhm-Bawerk, E, von 1949 [1896], *Karl Marx and the close of his system by Eugen Böhm-Bawerk and Böhm-Bawerk's criticism of Marx by Rudolf Hilferding with an appendix by L von Bortkiewicz*, Sweezy, P (trans) from 'Zum Abschluss des Marxschen Systems', *Festgabe für Karl Knies*, Berlin.
Bookchin, M 1971, *Post-scarcity anarchism*, Berkeley Ramparts Press, Berkeley.
Bourdieu, P 1984, *Distinction: a social critique of the judgement of taste*, Harvard University Press, Cambridge.
Bourdieu, P 1986, 'The forms of capital', in JE Richardson (ed), Nice, R (trans), *Handbook of theory of research for the sociology of education*, Greenwood Press, New York, pp. 241–58.
Bourdieu, P 1990, *The logic of practice*, Polity Press, Cambridge.
Boyer, R, Saillard, Y 1995, 'A summary of regulation theory', in R Boyer and Y Saillard (eds), Shread, C (trans), *Regulation theory: the state of the art*, Routledge, London, pp. 36–44.
Braverman, H 1975, *Labour and monopoly capital: the degradation of work in the twentieth century*, Monthly Review Press, New York.
Brecher, J, Costello, T 2000, *Globalization from below: the power of solidarity*, South End Press, Cambridge.
Brennan, S, Behrendt, LY, Strelein, L, Williams, GJ 2005, *Treaty*, Federation Press, Sydney.
Brenner, R 1989, 'Bourgeois revolution and transition to capitalism', in AL Beier et al (eds), *The first modern society: essays in English history in honour of Lawrence Stone*, The Press Syndicate of the University of Cambridge, Cambridge.
Brenner, R 2002, *The boom and the bubble: the US in the world economy*, Verso, London.
Brenton, T 1994, *The greening of Machiavelli: the evolution of international politics*, Earthscan Publications, London.
Brown, VA 1998, 'The Titanic or the Ark?: indicators of national progress towards environmental sustainability', in R Eckersley (ed) *Measuring progress: is life getting better?*, CSIRO Publishing, Collingwood, Victoria.
Bryan, D, Rafferty, M 2006, *Capitalism with derivatives*, Palgrave Macmillan, London.
Buchanan, JM, Tullock, G 1962, *The calculus of consent*, University of Michigan Press, Ann Arbor.
Burawoy, M 1985, *The Politics of production: factory regimes under capitalism and socialism*, Verso, London.
Burke, E 1790, *Reflections on the Revolution in France*, available at <http://www.constitution.org/eb/rev_fran.htm>. Accessed June 2011.
Bushell-Embling, D 2010, 'Indian minister quits over 2G scandal', *Telecomasia.net*, 15 November.

Cadbury n.d., available at <http://www.cadbury.com.au/About-Cadbury.aspx>. Accessed August 2011.
Calhoun, C 1993 'Nationalism and civil society: democracy, diversity and self-determination', *International Sociology*, vol. 8, no. 4, pp. 387–411.
Callon, M (ed) 1998, *The laws of markets*, Blackwell, Oxford.
Carmton, P, Kurr S 2002, 'Tradeable carbon permit auctions: how and why to auction not grandfather', *Energy Policy*, vol. 30, no. 4, pp. 333–45.
Carrier, J, Heyman, J 1997, 'Consumption and political economy', *Journal of the Royal Anthropological Institute*, vol. 3, no. 2, pp. 355–73.
Castles, FG 1985, *The working class and welfare*, Allen & Unwin, Sydney.
Castles, FG 1994, '"The wage earners" welfare state revisited: refurbishing the established model of Australian social protection, 1983–1993', *Australian Journal of Social Issues*, vol. 29, no. 2, pp. 120–45.
Castles, FG 2001, 'A farewell to Australia's welfare state', *International Journal of Health Services*, vol. 31, no. 3, pp. 537–44.
Castles, S 2000, 'International migration at the beginning of the twenty-first century: global trends and issues', *International Social Science Journal*, vol. 165, pp. 269–81.
Castles, S 2001, 'Globalisation from below: migrants of the twenty-first century', *Arena Magazine*, vol. 49, pp. 45–7.
Chancellor, T 1988, 'Imputed income and the ideal income tax', *Orlando Law Review*, 561.
Chandhoke, N 2005, 'What the hell is civil society', available at *Open Democracy*, <http://www.opendemocracy.net/democracy-open_politics/article_2375.jsp>. Accessed August 2011.
Chandler, A 1977, *The visible hand: the managerial revolution in American business*, Harvard University Press, Harvard.
Chandler, A, Amatori, F, Hikino T 1997, 'Historical and comparative contours of big business', in A Chandler, F Amatori and T Hikino (eds), *Big business and the wealth of nations*, Cambridge University Press, Cambridge.
Chang, L 2008, *Factory girls: from village to city in a changing China*, Spiegel & Garu, New York.
Chant, S 2008, 'The "feminisation of poverty" and the "feminisation of anti-poverty programmes": room for revision?', *Journal of Development Studies*, vol. 44, no. 2, pp. 165–97.
Chessell, J 2011, 'Big four tighten grip on deposits and home loans', *The Australian*, 1 January 2011.
Clark, B, York, R 2005, 'Carbon metabolism: global capitalism, climate change and the biospheric rift', *Theory and Society*, vol. 34, no. 4, pp. 391–428.
Coase, R 1937, 'The nature of the firm', *Economica*, vol. 4, no. 16, pp. 386–405.
Coase, R 1972, 'The problem of social cost', in R Dorfman and NS Dorfman (eds), *Economics of the environment: selected readings*, Norton, New York.
Cockett, R 1995, *Thinking the unthinkable: think-tanks and the economic counter-revolution 1931–1983*, HarperCollins, London.
Coleman, J 1990, *Foundations of social theory*, The Belknap Press, Cambridge, MA.

Communitarian Network n.d., 'The responsive communitarian platform', The Communitarian Network, available at <http://communitariannetwork.org/about-communitarianism/responsive-communitarian-platform/>. Accessed August 2011.

Connell, RW 2002, *Gender*, Polity Press, Cambridge.

Cornell, S, Jorgensen, M, Kalt, JP, Spilde, KA 2005, 'Seizing the future: why some native nations do and others don't', Joint Occasional Papers on Native Affairs, 2005–2001, Native Nations Institute/Harvard Project on American Indian Economic Development, Tucson & Cambridge.

Cox, E 1995, *A truly civil society*, ABC Books, Sydney.

Cross, G 1993, *Time and money: the making of consumer culture*, Routledge, London.

Crough, G, Wheelwright, T 1982, *Australia: a client state*, Penguin, Ringwood.

Daly, H 1996, *Beyond growth: the economics of sustainable development*, Beacon Press, Boston.

Daly, HE, Townsend, KN 1993, *Valuing the Earth: economics, ecology, ethics*, MIT Press, Cambridge, MA.

Dasgupta, P, Serageldin, I (eds) 2000, *Social capital: a multifaceted perspective*, World Bank, Washington.

Davis, M 2006, *Planet of slums*, Verso, London.

de Graff, J, Wann, D, Naylor, TH 2001, *Affluenza: the all-consuming epidemic*, Berrett-Koehler, San Francisco.

DeBord, G 1956, 'Methods of detournement', *Le Levres Nues*, 8, available at <http://library.nothingness.org/articles/all/en/display/3>.

Domar, E 1946, 'Capital expansion, rate of growth, and employment', *Econometrica*, vol. 14, pp. 137–47.

Drago, R, Wooden, M, Black, D 2009, 'Long work hours: volunteers and conscripts', *British Journal of Industrial Relations*, vol. 47, pp. 571–600.

Driesen, DM 1998, 'Is emissions trading an economic incentive program? Replacing the command and control/economic incentive dichotomy', *Washington and Lee Law Review*, vol. 55, pp. 289–350.

Drucker, PF 1999, *Management challenges of the 21st century*, Harper Business, New York.

Dugger, WM 1996, *Inequality: radical institutionalist views on race, gender, class and nation*, Greenwood Press, Westport.

Durkheim, E 1984 [1893], *The division of labour in society*, Macmillan, Basingstoke.

Edgell, S 2006, *The sociology of work: continuity and change in paid and unpaid work*, Sage, London.

Edwards, S 1987, 'In defense of environmental economics', *Environmental Ethics*, vol. 9, no. 1, pp. 73–85.

Ehrenreich, B 2001, *Nickel and dimed: on (not) getting by in America*, Metropolitan Books, New York.

Ehrlich, P 1969, *The population bomb*, Sierra Club, San Francisco.

Engels, E 1942 [1884], *The origin of the family, private property and the state*, Lawrence & Wishart, London.

Esping-Anderson, G 1990, *The three worlds of welfare capitalism*, Polity Press, Cambridge.

Etzioni, A 1993, 'The spirit of community: rights, responsibilities, and the communitarian agenda', Crown Publishers, New York.

Fine, B 2010, *Theories of social capital: researchers behaving badly*, Pluto Press, London.

Fine, B, Saad-Filho, A 2004, *Marx's Capital*, Pluto Press, London.

Florida, R 2002, *The rise of the creative class: and how it's transforming work, leisure, community and everyday life*, Basic Books, New York.
Folbre, N 1994, *Who pays for the kids? Gender and the structures of constraint*, Routledge, New York.
Foucault, M 1982, 'The subject and power', in HL Dreyfus and P Rabinow (eds), *Michel Foucault: beyond structuralism and hermeneutics*, University of Chicago Press, Chicago.
Foucault, M 1991, 'Governmentality, in G Burchell, C Gordon and P Miller (eds), *The Foucault effect: studies in governmentality*, University of Chicago Press, Chicago.
Foucault, M 1997, *Ethics: subjectivity and truth*, The New Press, New York.
Fox-Piven, F, Cloward, R 1971, *Regulating the poor: the functions of public welfare*, Tavistock, London.
Frank, R 2000, *Luxury fever: money and happiness in an era of excess*, Princeton University Press, Princeton.
Frankel, B 1997, 'Beyond labourism and socialsim: how the Australian Labor Party developed the model of "New Labour"', *New Left Review*, vol. 221, pp. 3–33.
Fraser, N 1997, 'From redistribution to recognition? Dilemmas of justice in a "postsocialist" age', *Justice Interruptus*, Routlegde, London.
Fraser, N, Gordon, L 1994, 'A genealogy of "dependency": tracing a keyword of the U.S. welfare state', *Signs*, vol. 19, no. 2, pp. 309–36.
Fraser, N, Honneth, A 2003, *Redistribution of recognition? A political-philosophical exchange*, Verso, New York.
Friedman, M 1970, 'The social responsibility of business is to increase its profits', *The New York Times Magazine*, 13 September.
Friedman, M, Friedman, R 1980, *Free to choose*, Secker and Warburg, London.
Friedman, T 1999, *The Lexus and the olive tree*, Harper Collins, London.
Fukuyama, F 1992, *The end of history and the last man*, Free Press, New York.
Fukuyama, F 1995, *Trust: the social virtues and the creation of prosperity*, Free Press, New York.
Galbraith, JK 1967, *The new industrial state*, Houghton Mifflin Company, Boston.
Galbraith, JK 1976 [1958], *The affluent society*, 3rd edn, Houghton Mifflin, Boston.
Game, A, Pringle, R 1983, *Gender at work*, Allen & Unwin, Sydney.
Garnaut, R 2008, *The Garnaut climate change review*, Cambridge University Press, Melbourne.
Gaud, WS 1968, 'The Green Revolution: accomplishments and apprehensions', speech to Society for International Development, Washington, available at <http://www.agbioworld.org/biotech-info/topics/borlaug/borlaug-green.html>. Accessed August 2011.
George, S 1998, *A fate worse than debt*, Penguin Books, London.
George, S 1999, 'Neoliberalism: nothing owed to the losers', conference on *Economic sovereignty in a globalising world*, Bangkok, 24–26 March, available at <http://www.aislingmagazine.com/aislingmagazine/articles/TAM26/Neoliberalism.html>.
Georgescu-Roegen, N 1971, *The entropy law and the economic process*, Harvard University Press, Cambridge, MA.
Giddens, A 1998, *The third way: the renewal of social democracy*, Polity Press, Cambridge.
Gintis, H 1972, 'Consumer behavior and the concept of sovereignty: explanations of social decay', *American Economic Review*, vol. 62, no. 1/2, pp. 267–78.

Goodman, E, Bamford, J (eds) 1989, *Small firms and industrial districts in Italy*, Routledge, London.

Gordon, D, Edwards, R, Reich, M 1982, *Segmented work, divided workers: the historical transformation of labor in the United States*, Cambridge University Press, New York.

Gordon, D, Edwards, R, Reich, M 1994, 'Long swings and stages of accumulation', in K David, T McDonough and M Reich (eds), *Social structures of accumulation: the political economy of growth and crisis*, Cambridge University Press, New York.

Grampp, WD 1965, *Economic liberalism: the classical view*, vol. 11, Random House, New York.

Gramsci, A 1971, *Selections from the Prison Notebooks*, Lawrence & Wishart, London.

Granovetter, M 1973, 'The strength of weak ties', *American Journal of Sociology*, vol. 78, no. 6, pp. 1360–80.

Granovetter, M 1985, 'Economic action and social structure: the problem of embeddedness', *American Journal of Sociology*, vol. 91, no. 3, pp. 481–510.

Green, D 1993, *Reinventing civil society*, Institute of Economic Affairs, London.

Green, R, Wilson, A 1999, 'Labor's Trojan Horse: the "Third Way" on employment policy', in D Glover and G Patmore (eds), *New voices for social democracy. Labor essays 1999–2000*, Pluto Press, Annandale, pp. 63–85.

Greens NSW n.d., 'Democracy for Sale Project', available at <http://www.democracy4sale.org/>. Accessed August 2011.

Habermas, J 1987, *The theory of communicative action*, McCarthy, T (trans), Polity, Cambridge.

Habermas, J 1989 [1964], *The structural transformation of the public sphere: an inquiry into a category of bourgeois society*, Polity Press, Oxford.

Habib, B, Narayan, A, Olivieri, S, Sanchez-Paramo, C 2010, 'Assessing ex ante the poverty and distributional impact of the global crisis in the Philippines: a micro-simulation approach with application to Bangladesh', Policy Research Working Paper, World Bank, Dhaka.

Hacker, J, Pierson, P 2010, 'Winner-take-all politics: public policy, political organization, and the preciptitous rise of top incomes in the United States', *Politics and Society*, vol. 38, no. 2, pp. 152–204.

Haggard, S 2004, 'Institutions and growth in East Asia', *Studies in Comparative International Development*, vol. 38, no. 4, pp. 53–81.

Hall, P, Soskice, D 2001, *Varieties of capitalism: the institutional foundations of comparative advantage*, Cambridge University Press, Cambridge.

Hamilton, C 1997, 'The genuine progress indicator: a new index of changes in well-being in Australia', Australia Institute Paper no. 14, Australia Institute, Canberra.

Hamilton, C, Denniss, R 2005, *Affluenza: when too much is never enough*, Allen & Unwin, Sydney.

Harcourt, G 1972, *Some Cambridge controversies in the theory of capital*, Cambridge University Press, New York.

Hardin, G 1968, 'The tragedy of the commons', *Science*, 13 December.

Hardt, M, Negri, A 2004, *Multitude: war and democracy in the Age of Empire*, The Penguin Press, New York.

Hargreaves Heap, S, Hollis, M, Lyons, R, Sugden, R, Weale, A (eds) 1994, *The theory of choice: a critical guide*, Blackwell, Oxford.

Harrod, R 1939, 'An essay in dynamic theory', *Economic Journal*, vol. 49, pp. 14–33.
Harvey, D 1990, *The condition of postmodernity: an inquiry into the origins of cultural change*, Blackwell, Oxford.
Hayek, FA 1967, 'The results of human action but not of human design' in *Studies in philosophy, politics and economics*, Routledge, London, pp. 96–105.
Hayek, FA 1991, *The fatal conceit: the errors of socialism*, University of Chicago Press, Chicago.
Hayek, FA 1994 [1944], *The road to serfdom*, University of Chicago Press, Chicago.
Heilbroner, R 1978, *Beyond boom and crash*, Norton, New York.
Heilbroner, R 1980, *The worldly philosophers: the lives, times and ideas of the great economic thinkers*, 5th edn, Touchstone, New York.
Herman, E, Chomsky, N 1988, *Manufacturing consent: the political economy of the mass media*, Pantheon Books, New York.
Hesmondhalgh, D, Baker, S 2009, '"A very complicated version of freedom": conditions and experiences of creative labour in three cultural industries', *Poetics*, vol. 38, no. 1, pp. 4–20.
Hilton, R 1985, *Class conflict and the crisis of feudalism: essays in medieval social history*, The Hambledon Press, London.
Hindess, B 1996, *Discourses of power: from Hobbes to Foucault*, Blackwell Publishers, Oxford.
Hingst, R 2006, 'Perceptions of working life in call centres, *Journal of Management Practice*, vol. 7, no. 1, pp. 1–9.
Hirst, P, Thompson, G 1996, *Globalization in question*, Polity Press, Oxford.
Hobsbawm, E 1987, *Age of Empire 1875–1914*, Pantheon Books, New York.
Hochschild, A 1983, *The managed heart: the commercialization of human feeling*, University of California Press, Berkeley.
Hochschild, A, Ehrenreich, B (eds) 2002, *Global woman: nannies, maids and sex workers in the new economy*, Owl Books, Henry Holt and Company, New York.
Holden C 2003, 'Decommodification and the workfare state', *Policy Studies Review*, vol. 1, pp. 303–16.
Holt, R, Pressman, S, Spash, C (eds), 2009, *Post-Keynesian economics: confronting environmental issues*, Edward Elgar, Cheltenham.
Honey, M 1995, 'Remembering Rosie: advertising imagines of women in World War II', in K O'Brien and L Parsons (eds), *The home-front war: World War II and American society*, Greenword, Westport.
Honneth, A 1996, *The struggle for recognition: the moral grammar of social conflicts*, Polity, Cambridge.
Hopkins, T, Wallerstein, I 1986, 'Commodity chains in the world-economy prior to 1800', *Review Journal of the Fernand Brandel Center*, vol. 10, no. 1, pp. 157–70.
Huber, J 2000, 'Towards industrial ecology: sustainable development as a concept of ecological modernization', *Journal of Environmental Policy and Planning*, vol. 2, no. 4, pp. 269–85.
Hughes, V 2011, 'Non-profits lose sight of volunteer heritage', *Sydney Morning Herald*, 4 February.
Hutt, W 1940, 'The concept of consumer sovereignty', *Economic Journal*, pp. 66–77.
Inglehart, R 1972, *The silent revolution*, Princeton University Press, Princeton.
Inglehart, R 1990, *Culture shift in advanced industrial society*, Princeton University Press, Princeton.

International Labor Organisation (ILO) 2004, 'Economic security for a better world', International Labour Office, Socio-Economic Security Programme, Geneva.

International Monetary Fund (IMF) 2011, World Economic Outlook Database, April, available at <http://www.imf.org/external/pubs/ft/weo/2011/01/weodata/index.aspx>. Accessed August 2011.

Iversen, T, Wren, A 1998, 'Equality, employment, and budgetary restraint: the trilemma of the service economy', *World Politics*, vol. 50, no. 4, pp. 507–46.

Jackson, T. 2009, *Prosperity without growth: economics for a finite plant*, Earthscan, London.

Jacobs, M 1991, *The green economy*, Pluto Press, London.

Jefferson, T 2009, 'Women and retirement pensions: a research review', *Feminist Economics*, vol. 15, no. 4, pp. 115–45.

Jenkins, JC 1983, 'Resource mobilization theory and the study of social movements', *Annual Review of Sociology*, vol. 9, pp. 527–53.

Jessop, B 1997, 'Survey article: the regulation approach', *Journal of Political Philosophy*, vol. 5, no. 3, pp. 287–326.

Jessop, B 2007, 'Knowledge as a fictitious commodity: insights and limits of a Polanyian perspective', in A Buğra and K Ağartan (eds), *Reading Karl Polanyi for the twenty-first century: market economy as a political project*, Palgrave Macmillan, New York.

Jevons, WS 1865, *The coal question: an enquiry concerning the progress of the nation, and the probable exhaustion of our coal-mines*, Macmillan, London.

Jevons, WS 1871, *The principles of political economy*, Macmillan, London.

Kates, S 2003, 'Producing and consuming gendered representations: an interpretation of the Sydney Gay and Lesbian Mardi Gras', *Consumption Markets and Culture*, vol. 6, no. 1, pp. 5–22.

Keating, M 2004, *Who Rules? How government retains control of a privatised economy*, Federation Press, Sydney.

Kelly, J, Graziani, R 2004, 'International trends in company tax rates – implications for Australia', *Economic Roundup*, Spring, Australian Treasury, Canberra.

Kesselman, M, Krieger, J, Joseph, WA 2004, *Introduction to comparative politics: political challenges and changing agendas*, Houghton Mifflin, Boston.

Keynes, J 1919, *The economic consequences of the peace*, Macmillan, London.

Keynes, JM 1937, 'The general theory of employment', *Quarterly Journal of Economics*, vol. 51, pp. 209–23.

Keynes, JM 1965 [1936], *The general theory of employment, interest and money*, Harcourt, Brace & World, New York.

Kindleberger, C 1996, *Manias, panics and crashes: a history of financial crisis*, 3rd edn, John Wiley & Sons, Chichester.

Klein, N 2007, *The shock doctrine: the rise of disaster capitalism*, Allen Lane, Camberwell.

Knudtson, P, Suzuki, D 1992, *Wisdom of the elders: honoring sacred native visions of nature*, Bantam Books, New York.

Korpi, W 2000, 'Faces of inequality: gender, class, and the patterns of inequality in different types of welfare state', *Social Politics*, vol. 7, no. 2, pp. 127–91.

Kossoudji, S, Dresser, L 1992, 'Working class Rosies: women industrial workers during World War II', *Journal of Economic History*, vol. 52, no. 2, pp. 431–46.

Kotz, D, McDonough, T, Reich, M (eds) 1994, *Social structures of accumulation: the political economy of growth and crisis*, Cambridge University Press, New York.

Krippner, GR 2005, 'The financialization of the American economy', *Socio-Economic Review*, vol. 3, no. 2, pp. 173–208.
Krugman, P 1999, *The return of depression economics*, W. W. Norton, New York.
Krugman, P 2007, *The conscience of a liberal: reclaiming America from the Right*, Penguin Books, London.
Matthews E et al 2000, *Weight of nations*, World Resources Institute, Washington DC.
Kuznets, S 1934, 'National income, 1929–1932', 73rd US Congress, 2nd session, Senate document no. 124.
Kuznets, S 1955, 'Economic growth and income inequality', *The American Economic Review*, vol. 45, no. 1, pp. 1–28.
Lakoff, G 2004, *Don't think of an elephant: know your values and frame the debate*, Chelsea Green Publishing, San Fransisco.
Laslett, B, Brenner, J 1989, 'Gender and social reproduction: historical perspectives', *Annual Review of Sociology*, vol. 15, pp. 381–404.
Le Grand, J 2003, *Motivation, agency, and public policy: of knights and knaves, pawns and queens*, Oxford University Press, Oxford.
Lebowitz, M 1992, *Beyond capital: Marx's political economy of the working class*, Macmillan, Basingstoke.
Leontief, W 1954, 'Domestic production and foreign trade; the American capital position re-examined', *Proceedings of the American Philosophical Society*, vol. 97, no. 4, pp. 332–49.
Levi-Faur, D 2005, 'The global diffusion of regulatory capitalism' *The ANNALS of the American Academy of Political and Social Science*, vol. 598, no. 21, pp. 12–32.
Lipset, SM, Rokkan S 1967, *Party systems and voter alignments: cross-national perspectives*, Toronto, The Free Press.
Locke, J 1967 [1689], *Two treatises of government*, Cambridge University Press, Cambridge.
Machiavelli, N 1969 [1640], *The Prince*, Scolar Press, Menston, UK.
MacKenzie, D 2006, *An engine, not a camera: how financial models shape markets*, The MIT Press, Cambridge.
Malthus, T 1992 [1798], *An essay on the principle of population*, Cambridge University Press, Cambridge.
Marcuse, H 1991 [1964], *One-dimensional man: studies in the ideology of advanced industrial society*, 2nd edn, Routledge, London.
Marshall, TH 2009 [1950], 'Citizenship and social class', in J Manza and M Sauder (eds), *Inequality and society*, W.W. Norton, New York.
Martin, B 2005, 'How nonviolence works', *Borderlands*, vol. 4, no. 3.
Marx, K 1871a, *Political action and the working class*, The International Workingmen's Association, London.
Marx, K 1871b, *Marx and Engels correspondence*, International Publishers, New York.
Marx, K 1894, *Capital*, vol. 3, F Engels (ed), International Publishers, New York.
Marx, K 1959 [1844], *Economic and philosophic manuscripts*, Progress Publishers, Moscow.
Marx, K 1963 [1847], *Poverty of philosophy*, International Publishers, New York.
Marx, K 1971 [1875], *Critique of the Gotha Program*, Progress Publishers, Moscow.
Marx, K 1976 [1867], *Capital: a critique of political economy*, vol. 1, Penguin Books, Harmondsworth.

Marx, K 1992 [1884], *Capital: a critique of political economy*, vol. 2, Penguin Books, Harmondsworth.
Marx, K, Engels, F 1977 [1848], *The Communist Manifesto*, Penguin, Middlesex.
Matthaei, J 1999, 'Patriarchy', in J Peterson and M Lewis (eds) *The Elgar companion to feminist economics*, Edward Elgar, Cheltenham, pp. 592–600.
Maurer-Fazio, M, Connelly, R, Lin, C, Tang, L 2009, 'Childcare, eldercare, and labor force participation of married women in urban China 1982–2000', Discussion paper no. 4204, IZA, Bonn, Germany.
McAdam, D, McCarthy, J, Zald, M (eds) 1996, 'Introduction: opportunities, mobilizing structures and framing processes', *Comparative perspectives on social movements*, Cambridge University Press, Cambridge and New York.
McDermott, K 2007, 'Whatever happened to frank and fearless? The systems of New Public Management and the ethos and beahviour of the Australian Public Service', Discussion paper 20/07, *Democratic audit of Australia*, Australian National University, Canberra.
McDonald, RL 2006, *Derivatives markets*, Addison-Wesley, Boston.
Mead, L 1997, 'The rise of paternalism', in L Mead (ed) *The new paternalism: supervisory approaches to poverty*, Brookings Institute Press, Washington, pp. 1–27.
Meadows, DH, Meadows, DL, Randers J, Behrens, W 1972, *The limits to growth: a report for the Club of Rome's Project on the Predicament of Mankind*, Earth Island Limited, London.
Mehigan, J, Rowe, A 2007, 'Problematizing prison privatization: an overview of the debate', in Y Jewkes (ed), *Handbook on prisons*, Willan, Portland.
Mendes, P 2009, 'Retrenching or renovating the Australian welfare state: the paradox of the Howard government's neo-liberalism', *International Journal of Social Welfare*, vol. 18, no. 1, pp. 102–10.
Menger, C 1951 [1871], *Principles of economics*, The Free Press, New York.
Merchant, C 1992, *Radical ecology: the search for a livable world*, Routledge, New York.
Mertes T 2004, *A movement of movements: is another world really possible?*, Verso, London.
Michalos, A, Sharpe, A, Arsenault, J, Muhajarine, A et al 2010, *An approach to the Canadian Index of Wellbeing: a report of the Canadian Index of Wellbeing*, Canadian Index of Wellbeing, Toronto.
Mill, JS 1909 [1848], *Principles of political economy*, in WJ Ashley (ed), Longmans Green and Co, London.
Mill, JS 1970 [1869], *The subjection of women*, MIT Press, Cambridge, MA.
Mill, JS 1975 [1859], *On liberty*, Norton, New York.
Minsky, HP 1986, *Stabilizing an unstable economy*, Yale University Press, New Haven.
Monbiot, G 2008, 'Population growth is a threat. But it pales against the greed of the rich', *Guardian*, 29 January.
Myrdal, G 1944, *An American dilemma*, New York, Harper & Bros.
Nader, R 1965, *Unsafe at any speed: the designed-in dangers of the American automobile*, Grossman, New York.
Nettlau, M 2000, *A short history of anarchism*, Freedom Press, London.
Nevins, A 1940, *John D. Rockefeller: the heroic age of American enterprise*, Charles Scribner's Sons, New York.

Nike n.d., available at <http://media.corporateir.net/media_files/IROL/10/100529/nike-gs09/connection.html>. Accessed August 2011.

Nordhaus, WD 1994, *Managing the global commons: the economics of climate*, MIT Press, Cambridge, MA.

Norris, P 2002, 'New social movements, protest politics and the internet', *Democratic phoenix: reinventing political activism*, Cambridge University Press, New York.

North, D 1990, *Institutions, institutional change, and economic performance*, Cambridge University Press, New York.

Northrop, EM 1990, 'The feminization of poverty: The demographic factor and the composition of economic growth', *Journal of Economic Issues*, vol. 24, no. 1 pp. 145–60.

Nozick, R 1974, *Anarchy, state and utopia*, Basil Blackwell, Oxford.

Nyland, C 1996, 'Taylorism, John R. Commons, and the Hoxie Report', *Journal of Economic Issues*, vol. 30, no. 4, pp. 985–1016.

O'Connor, J 1973, *The fiscal crisis of the state*, St Martin's Press, New York.

O'Connor, J 1998, *Natural causes: essays in ecological Marxism*, Guilford Press, New York.

Offe, C 1984, *Contradictions of the welfare state*, Hutchinson, London.

Olson, M 1965, *The logic of collective action; public goods and the theory of groups*, Harvard University Press, Cambridge, MA.

Organisation for Economic Co-operation and Development (OECD) 2005, *OECD Employment Outlook*, OECD, Paris.

Organisation for Economic Co-operation and Development 2008, 'Counting the Hours', *OECD Observer*, 266, March.

Organisation for Economic Co-operation and Development 2010, *Growing unequal? income distribution and poverty in OECD countries*, OECD, Paris.

Organisation for Economic Co-operation and Development 2011, 'Ranking nations by the good life: how the U.S. stacks up depends on your priorities', *National Journal*, 2 June.

Ostrom, E 1990, *Governing the commons: the evolution of institutions for collective action*, Cambridge University Press, New York.

Otter, S den 1997, 'Thinking in communities: late nineteenth-century liberals, idealists and the retrieval of community', *Parliamentary History*, vol. 16, no. 1, pp. 67–84.

Oxfam 2008, 'Square pegs in round holes: how the Farm Bill squanders chances for a pro-development trade deal', Oxfam Briefing Note, 21 July, available at <http://www.oxfam.org/sites/www.oxfam.org/files/us-farm-bill-square-pegs-in-round-holes-0807.pdf>. Accessed August 2011.

Oxfam 2009, 'Empty promises: what happened to "development" in the WTO's Doha Round?', Briefing Paper, 16 July, available at <http://www.oxfam.org/sites/www.oxfam.org/files/bp131-empty-promises.pdf". Accessed August 2011.

Oxfam n.d., 'Burkina Faso: cotton story', Oxfam Website, available at <http://www.oxfam.org/en/campaigns/trade/real_lives/burkina_faso>. Accessed August 2011.

Packard, V 1978, *The waste makers*, David McKay Co., New York.

Page, D, Bonikowski, B, Western, B 2009, 'Discrimination in a low wage labour market', *American Sociological Review*, vol. 74, pp. 777–99.

Painter, J, Jeffrey, A 2009. *Political geography*, 2nd edn, Sage, London.

Pakulski, J, Waters, M 1996, *The death of class*, Sage, London.

Pareto, V 1972 [1906], *Manual of political economy*, Schwier, AS, Page, AN (trans), Macmillan, London.
Park, JH 2002, 'The east Asian model of economic development and developing countries', *Journal of Developing Societies*, vol. 18, pp. 330–53.
Parker, D 2009, *The official history of privatisation*, Routledge, New York.
Pateman, C 1988, *The sexual contract*, Polity Press, Cambridge.
Pearce, DW 1976, *Environmental economics*, Longman, London.
Peck, J 2001, *Workfare states*, Guilford Press, New York.
Phillips, A 1987, *Divided loyalties: dilemmas of sex and class*, Virago Press, London.
Pierson, P 1994, *Dismantling the welfare state? Reagan, Thatcher, and the politics of retrenchment*, Cambridge University Press, Cambridge.
Pigou, AC 1938 [1920], *The economics of welfare*, 4th edn, Macmillan, London.
Piore, MJ, Sabel, CF 1984, *The second industrial divide: possibilities for prosperity*, Basic Books, New York.
Pixley, J 2004, *Emotions in finance: distrust and uncertainty in global markets*, Cambridge University Press, Cambridge.
Pocock, B 2003, *The work/life collision: what work is doing to Australians and what to do about it*, Federation Press, Annandale.
Polanyi, K 1944, *The great transformation*, Farrar & Rinehart, New York.
Polanyi, K 1957, 'The economy as instituted process', in K Polanyi, C Arensberg and H Pearson (eds), *Trade and market in early empires: economics in history and theory*, Free Press, Glencoe.
Polanyi, K 2001 [1944], *The great transformation: the political and economic origins of our time*, 2nd edn, F Block (ed), Beacon Press, Boston.
Ponting, C 1991, *A green history of the world*, Penguin Books, London.
Porter, M 1990, *The competitive advantage of nations*, Macmillan, London.
Porter, R 2000, *Enlightenment: Britain and the creation of the modern world*, Penguin Books, London.
Powell, M 2000, 'New Labour and the third way in the British welfare state: a new and distinctive approach?', *Critical Social Policy*, vol. 20, no. 1, pp. 39–60.
Pusey, M 2003, *The experience of middle Australia: the dark side of economic reform*, Cambridge, Melbourne.
Putnam, R (with R Leonardi and RY Nanetti) 1993, *Making democracy work: civic traditions in modern Italy*, Princeton University Press, Princeton.
Putnam, R 2000, *Bowling alone: the collapse and revival of American community*, Simon & Schuster, New York.
Rawls, J 1971, *A theory of justice*, Oxford University Press, London.
Ricardo, D 1949 [1817], *The principles of political economy and taxation*, Dent, London.
Ritzer, G 1983, 'The McDonalization of society', *Journal of American Culture*, vol. 6, no. 1, pp. 100–7.
Ritzer, G 1998, 'McJobs: McDonaldization and the workplace', in G Ritzer (ed) *The McDonaldization thesis: explorations and extensions*, Sage, London.
Robbins, L 1945, *An essay on the nature and significance of economic science*, Macmillan, London.
Romer, P 1986, 'Increasing returns and long-run growth', *Journal of Political Economy*, vol. 94, no. 5, pp. 1002–37.

Romer, P 1990, 'Endogenous technological change', *Journal of Political Economy*, vol. 98, no. 5, pp. S71–S102.
Rose, N, Miller P 1992, 'Political power beyond the state: problematics of government', *The British Journal of Sociology*, vol. 43, no. 2, pp. 173–205.
Rossi, U 2006, 'The struggles of precarious researchers and the demands for social change in (post-) Berlusconian Italy', *ACME: An International E-journal for Critical Geographies*, vol. 4, no. 2, pp. 277–86.
Roth, AE 1993, 'The early history of experimental economics', *Journal of the History of Economic Thought*, vol. 15, pp. 184–209.
Roy, WG 1997, *Socializing capital: the rise of the large industrial corporation in America*, Princeton University Press, Princeton.
Rudy, K 2001, 'Radical feminism, lesbian separatism and queer theory', *Feminist Theory*, vol. 27, no. 1, pp. 190–222.
Sachs, J 1998, 'International economics: unlocking the mysteries of globalization', in P O'Meara, HD Mehlinger and M Krain (eds) 2000, *Globalization and the challenges of a new century*, Indiana University Press, Bloomington.
Sagoff, M 1994, 'Four dogmas of environmental economics', *Environmental Values*, vol. 3, pp. 285–310.
Salleh, A 2009, 'From eco-sufficiency to global justice', in A Salleh (ed) *Eco-sufficiency & global justice: women write political ecology*, Pluto Press and Spinifex Press, New York.
Sandel, M 1982, *Liberalism and the limits of justice*, Cambridge University Press, Cambridge.
Sassatelli, R 2007, *Consumer culture: history, theory and politics*, Sage, London.
Sassen, S 1988, *The mobility of labor and capital. A study in international investment and labor flow*, Cambridge University Press, Cambridge.
Sassen, S 2006, *Cities in a world economy*, 3rd edn, Pine Forge Press, California.
Sawer, M 2003, *The ethical state: social liberalism in Australia*, Melbourne University Publishing, Carlton, VIC.
Scalmer, S, Irving, T 2005, 'Labour intellectuals in Australia: modes, traditions, generations, transformations', *International Review of Social History*, vol. 50, no. 1, pp. 1–26.
Schor, J 1992, *The overworked American: the unexpected decline of leisure*, Basic Books, New York.
Schor, J 1998, *The overspent American: upscaling, downshifting, and the new consumer*, Basic Books, New York.
Schor, J 2004, *Born to buy*, Scribner, New York.
Schumpeter, J 1943, *Capitalism, socialism and democracy*, Allen & Unwin, London.
Scott, AJ 1988, *New industrial spaces: flexible production organization and regional development in North America and Western Europe*, Pion, London.
Screpanti, E, Zamagni, S 1993, *An outline of the history of economic thought*, Oxford University Press, Oxford.
Shapiro, C, Stiglitz, J 1984, 'Equilibrium unemployment as a worker discipline device', *The American Economic Review*, vol. 74, no. 3, pp. 433–44.
Shiva, V 1988, *Staying alive: women, ecology and survival in India*, Zed Books, New Delhi.
Shiva, V 1991, *The violence of the green revolution: third world agriculture, ecology and politics*, Zed Books, London.
Simon, H 1957, *Models of man*, John Wiley & Sons, New York.

Skocpol, T 1992, *Protecting soldiers and mothers: the political origins of social policy in the United States*, Belknap Press, Cambridge.
Slater, D 1997, *Consumer culture and modernity*, Polity Press, Oxford.
Smart, B 2010, *Consumer society: critical issues and environmental consequences*, Sage, Los Angeles.
Smith, A 1904 [1776], *An inquiry into the nature and causes of the wealth of nations*, Edwin Cannan (ed), Library of Economics and Liberty, available at <http://www.econlib.org/library/smith/smWN.html>. Accessed May 2011.
Smith, K, Marsh, I 2007, 'Wine and economic development: technology and corporate change in the Australian wine industry', *International Journal of Technology and Globalisation*, vol. 3, no. 2–3, pp. 224–46.
Soja, EW 2000, *Postmetropolis: critical studies of cities and regions*, Basil Blackwell, Oxford.
Solow, R 1956, 'A contribution to the theory of economic growth', *Quarterly Journal of Economics*, vol. 70, no. 1, pp. 65–94.
Standing, G 2009, *Work after globalization: building occupational citizenship*, Edward Elgar, Cheltenham.
Stearns, P 2001, *Consumerism in world history: the global transformation of desire*, Routledge, London.
Stern, N 2006, *The Stern Review on the economics of climate change*, HM Treasury, UK Government, available at <http://www.hmtreasury.gov.uk/independent_reviews/>. Accessed August 2011.
Stiglitz, J 1996, 'Some lessons from the East Asian Miracle', *World Bank Research Observer*, vol. 11, no. 2, pp. 151–77.
Stilwell, F 2006, *Political economy: the contest of Economic Ideas*, 2nd edn, Oxford University Press, Melbourne.
Strange, S 1996, *The retreat of the state: the diffusion of power in the world economy*, Cambridge University Press, Cambridge.
Tann, J 1979, 'Arkwright's employment of steam power', *Business History*, vol. 21, no. 2, pp. 247–50.
Tari, M, Vanni, I 2005, 'On the life and deeds of San Precario, patron saint of Precarious workers and lives', *Fibreculture Journal*, 5.
Tarrow, S 1998, *Power in movement: social movements and contentious politics*, Cambridge University Press, Cambridge and New York.
Taylor, FW 1911, *The principles of scientific management*, Harper, New York.
Thompson, EP 1971, 'The moral economy of the English crowd in the eighteenth century', *Past and Present*, vol. 50, no. 1, pp. 76–136.
Thompson, EP 1980, *The making of the English working class*, Penguin, Harmondsworth.
Thrift, NJ 2005, *Knowing capitalism*, Sage, London.
Tilly, C 2004, 'Social movements as politics', *Social Movements, 1768–2004*, Paradigm, London.
Titmuss, R 1958, *Essays on the welfare state*, Unwin University Books, London.
Trainer, T 2002, 'Recognising the limits to growth: a challenge to political economy', *Journal of Australian Political Economy*, vol. 50, pp. 163–78.
Trigilia, C 2002, *Economic sociology: state, market, and society in modem capitalism*, Blackwell, Oxford.
Trinca, H, Davies, A 2000, *Waterfront: the battle that changed Australia*, Doubleday, Millers Point.

Tullock, G, Seldon, A, Brady, GL 2002, *Government failure: a primer in public choice*, Cato Institute, Washington.
United Nations Development Programme (UNDP) 1990–2011, *Human development reports*, UN, New York, available at <http://hdr.undp.org/en/reports/>. Accessed August 2011.
United Nations HABITAT 2008, *State of the world's cities 2008/2009: harmonious cities*, UN, Geneva.
US Government Printing Office (GPO) 1996, *Public Law 104–193 Personal Responsibility and Work Opportunity Reconciliation Act of 1996*, available at <http://www.gpo.gov/fdsys/pkg/PLAW-104publ193/content-detail.html>. Accessed April 2011.
Vanberg, V 2007, 'Corporate social responsibility and the "Game of Catallaxy": the perspective of constitutional economics', *Constitutional Political Economy*, vol. 18, no. 2, pp. 199–222.
Varoufakis, Y 2001, *Game theory: critical concepts in the social sciences*, Routledge, New York.
Veblen, T 1899, *Theory of the leisure class: an economic study in the evolution of institutions*, Macmillan, New York.
Veblen, T 1904, *The theory of the business enterprise*, Transaction Books, New Brunswick.
Viner, J 1958, *The long view and the short: studies in economic theory and policy*, The Free Press, Glencoe.
Vogel, S 1996, *Freer markets, more rules: regulatory reform in advanced industrial countries*, Cornell University Press, Ithaca.
Wachtel, H 1986, *The money mandarins: the making of a new supranational order*, Pantheon Books, New York.
Wade, R 1990, *Governing the market: economic theory and the role of government in East Asian industrialization*, Princeton University Press, Princeton.
Waldrop, MM 1992, *Complexity: the emerging science at the edge of order and chaos*, Viking, London.
Wall, JF 1981, 'Image and reality: the railway corporate-state metaphor', *Business History Review*, vol. 55, no. 4, pp. 491–516.
Wall, JF 1989, *Andrew Carnegie*, University of Pittsburgh Press, Pittsburgh.
Wallerstein, I 1974, *The modern world-system*, Academic Press, New York.
Wallerstein, I 2004, *World-systems analysis: an introduction*, Duke University Press, Durham, North Carolina.
Wallison, PJ 2009, 'The true origins of this financial crisis', *The American Spectator*, February, available at <http://spectator.org/archives/2009/02/06/the-true-origins-of-this-finan>. Accessed December 2011.
Walras, L 1954 [1874], *Elements of pure economics, or the theory of social wealth*, Jaffe, W (trans), Allen & Unwin, London.
Waring, M 1988, *Counting for nothing*, George Allen & Unwin, Wellington.
Warren, E 2007, 'The new economics of the middle class: why making ends meet has gotten harder', Testimony before Senate Finance Committee, 10 May, Washington.
Weber, M 1918, *Politics as a vocation*, available at <http://www.ne.jp/asahi/moriyuki/abukuma/weber/lecture/politics_vocation.html>. Accessed February 2011.
Weber, M 1978 [1922], *Economy and society: an outline of interpretive sociology*, G Roth and C Wittich (eds), University of California Press, Berkley.
Weber, M 2002 [1905], *The protestant ethic and the spirit of capitalism*, Baehr, P, Wells, G (trans), Penguin Books, London.

Wheelwright, EL 1999, 'Economic rationalism or liberalism', in P O'Hara (ed), *Encyclopedia of Political Economy*, Routledge, London.
Wheelwright, EL, Crough, GJ, 1982, *Australia: a client state*, Penguin Books, Ringwood, Victoria.
Wiarda, HJ 1997, *Corporatism and comparative politics: the other great 'ism'*, ME Sharpe, New York.
WikiLeaks 2010, 'Collateral Murder', available at <http://www.collateralmurder.com/>. Accessed August 2011.
Wilkinson, R, Pickett, K 2009, *The spirit level: why more equal societies almost always do better*, Allen Lane, London.
Williams, R 1988, *Keywords: a vocabulary of culture and society*, Croom Helm, London.
Williamson, OE 1975, *Markets and hierarchies*, Free Press, New York.
Williamson, OE 1987, 'Transaction cost economics', *Journal of Economic Behaviour and Organization*, vol. 8, pp. 617–25.
Wiwa v Shell n.d., 'The case Against Shell', Wiwa v Shell website, available at <http://wiwavshell.org/about/about-wiwa-v-shell/>. Accessed August 2011.
Wolf, N 1992, *The beauty myth: how images of beauty are used against women*, Anchor, New York.
Wollstonecraft, M 1978 [1792], *A vindication of the rights of woman*, Penguin Books, Harmondsworth.
Wood, EM, Wood, N 1997, *A trumpet of sedition: political theory and the rise of capitalism, 1509–1688*, New York University Press, New York.
Wood, EM 1999, *The origin of capitalism*, Monthly Review Press, New York.
World Bank 1987, *World development report 1987*, Oxford University Press, New York.
World Bank 1994, *Averting the old age crisis: policies to protect the old and promote growth*, World Bank, New York.
World Bank 2008, *Global economic prospects 2009*, World Bank, New York.
World Commission on Environment and Development 1987, *Our common future: World Commission on Environment and Development (The Brundtland Report)*, Oxford University Press, Oxford.
World Economic Forum 2010, *The global competitiveness report 2010–2011*, World Economic Forum, Geneva.
Wright, EO 1997, *Class counts: comparative studies in class analysis*, Cambridge University Press, Cambridge.
Wright, EO 2009, 'Understanding class: towards an integrated analytical approach', *New Left Review*, vol. 60, pp. 101–16.
Yates, C 2009, 'Four pillars policy saved us: Macfarlane', *Sydney Morning Herald*, 3 March.
Zeldich, M 2001, 'Theories of legitimacy', in J Jost and B Major (eds), *The psychology of legitimacy: emerging perspective on ideology, justice and intergroup relations*, Cambridge University Press, Cambridge, pp. 33–55.

# Index

activism, 225–30
*Ad Busters* magazine, 224
Adorno, Theodore, 224
advertising, 29, 33, 180
affluenza, 184, 185
Africa, 86
agricultural sector
   application of scientific principles in, 199
   declining employment in, 156
   Green Revolution, 198
anarchism, 98
Arkwright, Richard, 140
Asian 'tiger economies', 56–7, 109–10
Atkinson, 174
austerity measures, 128–9
Australia, 235
   banking sector, 150
   compulsory conciliation and arbitration system, 107
   deregulation, 146
   economic stability, 147
   'Four Pillars' policy, 146
   Harvester case, 107
   poverty line, 71
   privatisation, 146
   Reserve Bank, 147
   wage-earner model of the welfare state, 106–7
Australian Institute, 47
Australian settlement, 107
authority, 94, 124

Baran, Paul, 149–50, 182
Baudrillard, J, 183
Bauman, Zygmunt, 175, 183
Beck, Ulrich, 63
Becker, Gary, 54, 191, 231
Beder, Sharon, 159, 170
Bell, Daniel, 177

Bellamy Foster, John, 129, 206
Berle, Adolf, 155
Berlin, Isaiah, 73, 217
Bohm-Bawerk, Eugen von, 74
Bolsheviks, 99, 100
   collectivisation of land and factories
Bookchin, Murray, 212
Bourdieu, Pierre, 184
   field theory, 12, 222
   social capital, 81, 232
bourgeoisie, 77, 223
BP, 159
Braverman, Harry, 168
Bretton Woods negotiations, 102, 130
British East India Company, 142
Bruntland report, 63, 205
Buchanan, James, 112
BUGA UP, 224
Burawoy, Michael, 153
bureaucracy, 112, 166
business cycle, 57

Cadbury, George, 215
Callon, Michel, 120
Canadian Index of Wellbeing, 47
capital accumulation, 43–52, 54, 66, 87
   flexible, 174
   social structures of, 56
capital flight, 120
capital gains, 70
capital–labour relationship, 153, 154
capitalism, 12
   early development of, 4, 34
   expansion and contraction, 57
   exploitative character of, 99
   and inequality, 71–5
   knowing capitalism, 180
   Marxian critique of, 31–3, 34

257

capitalism (cont.)
  social relations underpinning, 32
  varieties of, 109–10
care work, unpaid, 84, 186, 191, 195–7
  gendered nature of
Carnegie Steel Company, 142
Castles, Francis, 106
casual and contract employment, 134, 151, 175, 187
central banks, 135
Chang, Leslie, 167
change, 108–9, 225–30
  and 'the multitude', 81
child labour, 193
childcare, paid, 37
Chomsky, Noam, 225
circuit of capital, 51, 52, 58
citizenship, 219
civil disobedience, 227–8
civil society, 15, 159, 214–37
  classical liberalism and, 216–18
  communitarian approaches to, 219–21
  and critical theory, 221–4
  economic role of, 215
  in practice, 225
  theories of, 214–16
  and the welfare state, 234–6
class
  class-based organisation of production, 99
  cross-class solidarity, 105
  definitions of, 78
  diminishing importance of, 80–1
  and inequality, 75–9
  Marxian account of, 77–8
  and politics, 79–81
  theories of, 76
  Weberian account of, 78–9
classical political economy, 8–9
  class, 76
  financial markets, 127
  firms, 145
climate change, 63, 197, 201, 211
  and the 'steady state' economic model
Coase, Ronald, 151–2, 209
coffee, 88
Coleman, James, 231
collective action, 226, 231
collectivism, 111, 112
colonialism, 7, 82, 84–5, 88
commodification, 19–34, 42, 73, 190
  and decommodification, 39–41
  of experience, 183
  and recommodification, 39–40
  and regulation, 40
  and social institutions, 37
commodities, 19
commodity chains, 157–8

commodity fetishism, 32–4
common good, 220
communitarian approaches to civil society, 235
The Communitarian Network, 220
community, 214–33, 237
comparative advantage, 49
comparative statistics, 53, 58
competition, 8, 26, 139–61
  for access to land, 5
  competitive selling, 149
  corporations and, 11
  global, 122
  imperfect, 95
  implicit, 150
  in manufacturing, 131
  monopolistic, 146
  and New Public Management theory, 136
  non-price competition, 149
  oligopolistic, 146–7
  perfect, 11, 26, 27, 30, 95, 147, 201
  in technical and organisational innovation, 55
competitive advantage, 49, 57
confidence, 61, 103, 125
conflict, 61–2, 67–90, 181
  class, 77, 79
  and crisis, 61–2
  and inequality, 81–6
  sources of, 61
  in the workplace, 152–3
Connell, RW, 194
consumer sovereignty, 22–3, 26, 28, 180
consumerism, 170, 179
  and debt, 185
  and happiness, 184–5
  and identity, 183
  and planned obsolescence, 182
  and 'positional goods', 184
  rise of, 182–4
  and sales effort, 182
  social movements contesting, 183
consumption, 165–79, 188
  aesthetic of, 183
  approaches to, 179–84
  under consumption, 61
  and leisure, 180–1
  luxury consumption, 180
  mass consumption, 181, 191
  and production, 20
  social meaning of, 184
cooperation, 55, 63
corporate social responsibility, 158–9
corporations, 14, 139–61
  advertising and marketing, 29, 149
  competition and, 11
  complexity of, 140, 154
  cultural and political factors in, 143

and democracy, 159–60
development of, 140, 141–3
and economic stability, 150
externalising of costs, 145
and the global economy, 155–6
limited liability, 142
multi-divisional structure, 143, 144
organisation of, 143–5
political donations, 160
power of, 118, 129, 145, 156, 157
public, 142
race to the bottom, 156–9
role in economic growth, 139
separation of ownership and control, 155
transnational, 81, 144, 145, 150
and the workplace, 152–5
*see also* firms
cost-benefit analysis, 203
creative destruction, 56, 150
credit, 125, 129, 170
credit default swaps, 128
crisis, 43–66, 96
and austerity measures, 128–9
and change, 80
and conflict, 61–2
of disproportionality, 62
and economic growth, 57–8
endogenous theories of, 59
environmental, 201
exogenous theories of, 58
financial, 127
macroeconomic, 128
political, 64
and political reform, 101
politics of, 64–5
theories of, 58–64
and uncertainty, 59–61
critical theory and civil society, 221–4, 236
cultural capital, 81, 89
cultural norms, 221–2
culture, influence of, 11
culture jammers, 224
culture of dependency, 75
currencies, 103, 121

Daly, Herman, 211
debt, 128, 185
Declaration of the Rights of Man and of the Citizen, 218
decommodification, 39–40, 105
deep ecology, 208
defensive expenditure, 47
deindustrialisation, 130, 178
demand, 182
 elasticity of, 25
 marginal theory of, 24
democracy, and corporations, 159–60

dependency theory, 87
deregulation, 112, 120, 157
 financial, 122
derivatives, 126, 128
developing countries, 85, 156, 157, 178
 environment movement in, 212
 and the Green Revolution, 198
 manufacturing in, 156
 market access, 132
 population growth, 198
development, free market model of, 131
development state, 109
diminishing marginal utility, 23, 24
distribution of resources, 67–8, 90
 regulation of, 73
 role of the state in, 75
 through markets, 73–5
division of labour, 165–6, 192
 social, 215, 217
Domar, Evsey, 54
double movement, 38
Durkheim, Emile, 86, 215
 specialisation, 165–6
 structural functionalism, 166

East Asian development model, 109–10
ecology
 feminist, 207, 208, 212
 social, 212
economic growth, 13, 43–66, 211
 alternative measures of, 47
 and competition, 8
 and consumption, 181
 and crises, 57–8
 decreasing marginal returns, 54
 definition of, 44–6
 division of labour, 48
 endogenous models of, 54–5
 exogenous models of, 54
 and human welfare, 45
 impact on social relationships, 63
 institutional perspectives on, 55–6
 and legitimacy, 64–5
 limits to, 62–4
 in market societies, 43–4
 mechanisms of, 47–9
 politics of modelling, 49–50
 problems of, 45–6
 qualitative dimension of, 44, 63
 quantitative dimension of, 44
 role of corporations, 139
 and social and cultural traditions, 55
 social and environmental costs of, 46
 theories of trade, 48–9
 and trade, 8
 and unemployment, 45
economic instability, and the finance sector, 127

economic participation, 69
economic sociology, 12, 28–31, 171, 231
economic welfare, and markets, 26–8
economics
  behavioural and experimental, 3
  of care, 195
  environmental, 201, 202
  and environmental exploitation, 206–7
  experimental, 31
  of the family, 191–2
  institutional, 28–31
  neoclassical, 3, 9
  regulation school, 2, 11, 56
  sociological, 28–31
  welfare economics, 27
economy
  coordinated market, 109
  liberal market, 109
  markets and, 1
  post-war economic order, 121–3
  and the market society, 2
education, 81, 168, 194
efficiency, 50–4, 57, 59, 74, 128, 141, 172, 201
Ehrlich, Paul, 198
emissions trading schemes, 210
employment, part-time, 175
employment, stability of, 170, 187
  and identity, 170
  industrial legislation supporting, 170
energy efficiency, 200
Engels, Friedrich, 193
England
  agricultural sector, 5
  democracy, 97
  Factory Acts, 35–6, 193
  feudal system, 4
  imperialism, 85
  industrial revolution, 140
  political rights in, 94
  poor laws, 176
  regulation of the industrial workforce, 98
  revolution in, 94, 218–19
Enlightenment ideas, 71
environment, 14, 189–213
  alternative approaches to, 205
  commodification of, 199
  decommodification of, 210–11
  and the economy, 62–4
  and the limits to growth, 200–1
  and the market society, 197
  regulation and, 210–11
  valuation of environmental assets, 204, 206–7
environmental challenges, economic responses to, 201–5
environmental degradation, 197–201, 209
  alternative approaches to, 211–12
  use of taxes to deal with, 209

equality
  before the law, 72
  formal, 72
equity, intergenerational, 206
Esping-Andersen, Gosta, 39, 105, 106, 108
Etzioni, Amitai, 220
European Union, 131, 135
exchange rates, 103
  fixed, 121
  floating, 122
expectations, 61
experimental economics, 31
exploitation, 153
externalities, 46, 95, 201

Fabian Society, 101
factory system, 6
  regulation of the conditions of work, 6, 193
Falzon, John, 236
families, 189–213
  affective relationships in, 191
  development of, 193–5
  economising of, 190–2
  in the market society, 193–5
  non-market support systems, 14
  nuclear family, 193
  and social reproduction, 192–3
fascism, 114
feminism, 82–4, 194
  ecological, 207, 208, 212
  first wave, 82–3
  second wave, 83–4
  third wave, 84
feudal system, 4, 5, 165
fictitious commodities, 34–6, 67, 124, 192, 199
finance, 126–30, 142
  corporations' access to, 141
  liberalisation of, 120
financial markets
  and economic instability, 127
  economic and social significance of, 126
  growth of, 126–30
  and inequality, 127, 130
  speculation in, 126, 127, 129
financial repression, 121, 126
financialisation, 126, 127
Fine, Ben, 232
FIRE industries (Finance, Insurance and Real Estate), 126, 131
firms, 139–61
  and competition, 145–50
  economic importance of, 148
  hierarchical nature of, 151
  history of, 140–5
  rise of smaller, 172
  theories of, 145–7
  *see also* corporations
fiscal policy, 104

# INDEX

flexible employment practices, 134, 171, 174, 187
  negative aspects of, 173
  and productivity, 173
Folbre, Nancy, 194
Ford, Henry, 181
Ford Motor Company, 144, 168–71
Fordism, 168–71
Foucault, Michel, 117
framing, 227
Frank, Robert, 184
Frankfurt School, 224
Fraser, N, 193, 229
free trade agreements, 131
freedom: *see* liberty
French Revolution, 218–19
Friedman, Milton, 58, 73, 74, 96, 110, 111, 159
Friedman, Rose, 58
Friedman, Thomas, 120

Galbraith, John Kenneth, 102, 182
  competitive sector of the economy, 149
  corporations, 149
  dependence effect, 30
  planned sector of the economy, 149
  producer sovereignty, 29–30
game theory, 12, 30–1, 119, 155, 232–3
  advantages of, 30
Gandhi, Mohandas, 227
Garnaut Review, 201
gender, and inequality, 82–6
gender norms, 194
General Agreement on Tariffs and Trade, 130
general equilbrium theory, 53
General Motors, 154
Genuine Progress Index, 47
Genuine Progress Indicator, 47, 186
Georgescu-Roegen, Nicholas, 208
Germany, corporations in, 143
Giddens, Anthony, 63, 206, 234–5
Gini, Corrado, 69
Gini coefficient, 69
Gintis, Herbert, 30
global care chains, 197
global economy, corporations and, 155–6
Global Financial Crisis, 58, 112, 121, 128–9, 130
global justice movement, 230
globalisation, 81, 86, 108, 116–38, 144, 178, 234
  and markets, 120–4
Gorbachev, Mikhail, 123
Gordon, L, 193
governance
  international, 156
  and markets, 117–18
government, 'big', 112

Gramsci, Antonio, 221–2
Granovetter, Mark, 231
  embeddedness, 12, 38
  network theory, 125, 231
Great Depression, 58, 61
Green New Deal, 211
Green Revolution, 198
  negative consequences of, 198
greenhouse gas emissions, 200
Gross Domestic Product, 44
  exclusions from, 44, 45
  and Human Development Index, 46
  'real', 44
  and social and environmental costs of growth, 47

Habermas, Juergen, 222–3, 228
  bourgeoisie, 223
  public sphere, 222, 223, 226
Hacker, J, 160
Hall, Peter, 109
happiness, and consumerism, 184–5
Hardin, Garrett, 202
Hardt, Michael, 81, 230
Harrod, Roy, 54
Harvey, David, 174
Hayek, Friedrich von, 26, 110, 111, 112, 127
hegemony, 221
Henderson Poverty Line, 71
Herman, Edward, 225
Hirst, P, 157
historical materialism, 10
Hochschild, Arlie, 195
*homo economicus*, 28, 31
Honneth, Axel, 229
household income, 69, 190
households
  the family and, 190
  functions of, 4
  roles of, 190
  sexual contract, 193
Hughes, Vern, 235
human capital, 54
Human Development Index, 47, 186
  and Gross Domestic Product, 46
Hutt, William, 22

identity, consumption and, 183
imperialism, 85–6, 200
income, 68, 69
income policy, 60, 104
India, 85, 160
indigenous people, 81, 88, 207
industrial revolution, 6, 140
industrialisation, 199
industrialists, 148
industry, regulation of, 130–3

inequality, 13, 67–71, 90, 118, 134, 232
   and capitalism, 71–5
   changing patterns of, 81
   and class, 75–9
   and conflict, 81–6
   contemporary challenges of, 86–9
   cumulative causation theory of, 89
   economic, 72
   and the finance sector, 127, 130
   and gender, 82–6
   in households, 196
   measurement of, 68, 69
   political, 71
   race, colonialism and empire, 84–5
   racial, 88
   and social dysfunction, 71
   and value, 74–5
information technology, 173, 215
Inglehart, Ronald, 80, 177
innovation, 150, 177
institutional economics, 28–31, 102
   competition, 148
   consumption, 180, 182
   corporations, 148
institutional theory, 11–12
institutions, 2, 13, 93–4, 118
   and changes in work, 187
   and commodification, 37
   political, 65
   structure of, 135–6
intellectual property, 37
interest rates, 104, 125, 135
International Labour Organization, 187
International Monetary Fund, 86, 103
   Structural Adjustment Programs, 122–3
international trade, 87
interpretive sociology, 166
intervention in markets, 28, 53, 64, 96
investment, 54, 178
   and the environment, 202
   regulation of, 126
'invisible hand', 96, 114, 148
Italy, 172

Jackson, Tim, 211
Japan, industrial development, 143
Jevons, William Stanley, 24, 58, 200
Jevons paradox, 200
just price, 4, 41

Keating, Michael, 235
Keynes, John Maynard, 121
   capital accumulation, 54
   consumption, 181
   crisis, 59
   economic management, 110
   environmental degradation, 209
   Great Depression, 59
   macroeconomics, 11, 103–5
   socialising investment, 211
   uncertainty, 60
   unemployment, 102
Klein, Naomi, 114
knowledge creation, 55
knowledge workers, 178, 187
Krippner, GR, 126
Krugman, Paul, 81, 130
Kuznets, Simon, 72

labour
   and the ageing population, 196
   bargaining position of, 122
   casual and contract, 134
   division of, 48, 83, 84, 165–6, 192, 215, 217
   emotional labour, 195
   as a fictitious commodity, 35, 60
   market for, 38
   regulation of conditions of, 35–6, 38
   reproductive, 82
   segmented system, 171
   and value, 8
   wage labour relationship, 36
labour market, 6, 59–60
   and civil society, 235
   deregulation, 173
   primary and secondary, 171
   regulation of, 134
labour theory of value, 21, 52, 62, 74, 127
*laissez-faire*, 95–7, 101, 220
Lakoff, George, 227
land
   as a fictitious commodity, 35, 199
   integration into self-regulating markets, 199
   regulation of access to, 5, 38, 199
   tragedy of the commons, 202–3
Le Grand, Julian, 136
legitimacy, 64–5
   conflict models of, 65
   political, 64
   sources of, 65
leisure, and consumption, 180–1
Lenin, Vladimir, 86
Leontief, Wassily, 49
liberalism, 95–7, 219
   and civil society, 216–18
   classical, 95
liberty, 71, 94, 217
   positive and negative, 73, 217
*The Limits to Growth*, 63, 201
living standards, 43, 181, 184–8
lobby groups, 112
Locke, John, 71, 216

# INDEX 263

Maastricht Treaty, 135
MacFarlane, Ian, 147
MacKenzie, Donald, 120
macroeconomics, 12, 104
Major, John, 39
Malthus, Thomas, 8, 197–8
management, 141, 154–5, 235
  bonuses, 155
  declining employment in, 156
managerial revolution, 155
  scientific, 169
manufacturing
  corporations in, 142
  declining employment in, 173
  protection of, 144
  see also production
Marcuse, Herbert, 183, 224
marginal utility curve, 24–5
marginalism, 23–5
market failure, 95–6, 201, 209
market society, 1–15
  economic growth in, 43–4
  and the environment, 197
  experience of living in, 14
  and the family, 193–5
  historical perspective on, 4–8
  legitimacy of, 205
  and political and cultural change, 71
  and social movements, 229
  theories of, 8–12
marketisation, 34, 37, 112, 120
markets
  coordinated, 109
  creation of, 37–41
  distribution of resources through, 73–5
  and economic welfare, 26–8
  and the economy, 1, 53
  equilibrium, 53
  free, 27, 28, 114, 131
  global, 124
  and globalisation, 120–4
  and governance, 117–18
  importance of, 1, 2, 13
  incentives in, 74, 118
  as institutions of allocation, 22, 28, 53, 59, 73, 116–17
  intervention in, 28, 53, 64, 96
  for land, labour and money, 35
  liberal, 109
  management of, 235
  regulation of, 13, 103, 114, 116–17
  and risk, 116–38
  self-regulating nature of, 26
  stability of, 58
Marshall Plan, 144
Marx, Karl, 19
Marxian political economy, 9–10, 31–3, 34
  alienation, 167, 180
  analysis of capitalism, 3
  challenge to capitalism, 98–101
  circuit of capital, 50, 51
  class, 77–8
  commodity fetishism, 32–4, 180
  competition, 147
  consumption, 180, 182
  crisis, 59, 61
  influence in sociology, 10
  investment-production cycle, 50
  labour theory of value, 21
  power, 118
  power and conflict in the workplace, 152
  private ownership of productive resources, 77
  social metabolism, 206
  social movements, 226
  and the state, 98–101
  strategic action, 62
  wage labour, 167
mass culture, 224
Mead, Laurence, 75
Means, Gardiner, 155
Menger, Carl, 24
mercantilism, 85
methodological individualism, 9, 28, 152, 192
microeconomics, 53
middle class, 228
migration, 178, 198
Mill, John Stuart, 8, 71
  class, 76
  consumption, 181
  liberalism, 97
  liberty, 217
  rights of women, 82
minimum wage legislation, 60
Minsky, Hyman, 127–8
Mitchell, Wesley, 102
modernisation, 86
modernity, 7
  liquid, 175
  and rationalisation, 64
monetary policy, 104, 134
money
  as a fictitious commodity, 35
  and trust, 124–9
monopoly, 146
Mont Pelerin Society, 111
the 'multitude', 81

Nader, Ralph, 183
nation state, 7, 13
nationalisation of industries, 39
nature, value of, 208, 209–10
  see also environment

Negri, Antonio, 81, 230
neoclassical economics, 3, 9
  assumptions of, 9, 28
  competition, 149
  consumer choice, 184
  consumption, 179
  corporations, 149
  critiques of, 28–31
  efficiency, 52–4
  and environmental degradation, 209–10
  equilibrium, 58
  expansionary policies, 121
  financial markets, 127
  and inequality, 74
  labour market, 173
  methodological individualism, 9, 28
  preference theory of value, 21
  price theory, 26
  role of the state, 102
  theory of supply and demand, 22
  value, 204
neoliberalism, 9, 105, 111, 114, 120, 157
  and civil society, 217, 220
  economic reforms, 220
  role of the state, 133, 234
  theories, 111
network theory, 31, 87, 125
networks, 229–30
New Institutional Economics, 2, 11, 31, 55–6, 108, 151, 152
New Public Management theory, 135, 136
newly industrialised country, 178
Nike shoes
non-violent direct action, 227–8
Nordhaus, William, 204
Norris, Pippa, 233
North, Douglass, 55, 88
North American Free Trade Agreement, 131
Nozick, Robert, 75, 97

O'Connor, James, 207, 212
Offe, Claus, 40
Olin, Erik, 81
Olson, Mancur, 226
OPEC, 122
Organisation for Economic Co-operation and Development, 69
  Better Life Initiative, 47
Ostrom, Elinor, 55, 203
outsourcing, 144, 151
Owen, Robert, 36
Oxfam, 132

Pareto, Vilfredo, 27
participation, political, 214–33, 237
Pateman, Carole, 193
patents, 6

peak oil, 63, 200
perfect competition, 26, 30
performativity, 120
Pierson, Paul, 113, 160
Pigou, AJ, 27, 209
Piore, Michael, 172, 174
Pocock, Barbara, 186
Polanyi, Karl, 2
  affluence, 29
  commodification, 38, 199
  double movement, 38
  embeddedness, 38
  fictitious commodities, 34, 60, 124, 192, 199
  welfare state, 105
policy-making, politics of, 113
political economy, 2
  classical, 8–9, 76
  consumption, 180
  Marxian, 9–10
  of the welfare state, 101
political opportunity structure, 227
political parties, and trade and labour unions, 79
politicians, 112
politics, 93–115
  and class, 79–81
  and policy-making, 113
  post-materialist, 80
pollution, 202
poor relief, 6
  see also welfare state
Popper, Karl, 111
population levels, 197–8
Porter, Michael, 49, 57
post-Fordism, 171–6
  impact on skills of workers, 174
  and social welfare, 176–7
post-industrial society, 177–9
poverty, 70–1, 215
  absolute, 70
  and free trade, 132
  perceptions of the poor, 107
  relative, 70
  working poor, 176
power, 65, 221, 232, 235–6
  of corporations, 156
  and credit, 125
  economic, 80, 117
  labour power, 77
  patriarchal, 83
  political, 7, 215
  of states, 156
'precariat', 187–8
precautionary principle, 205–6
price
  regulating force of, 26–8
  and supply and demand, 25

price theory, neoclassical, 26
Prisoner's Dilemma, 226, 231, 232–3
private property, 72, 98
  see also property rights
privatisation, 34, 37, 39, 41, 112, 120, 157
probability and uncertainty, 119
producer sovereignty, 29
production, 1, 19–42
  the commodity production system, 19–20
  and consumption, 20
  control of, 99
  factors of, 25, 67, 73, 190
  globalised, 156
  and the household, 191
  mass production, 181
  overproduction, 61
  post-Fordist, 145, 167
  regulation of, 130
  separation from the household, 140
  social relations underpinning, 33
  team-based models, 172
productivity, 5, 44, 141, 173
  and care services, 196
proletariat, 77
property rights, 37, 71, 117, 203, 217
  over the environment, 209
Proudhon, Pierre-Joseph, 98
public choice theory, 96, 112
public–private partnerships, 136
public service, 135
  outsourcing of, 136
Putnam, Robert, 230, 231, 233

quality of life, 165–88
  consumerism and happiness, 184–5
  measurement of, 185–6
  subjective measures of, 186
quasi-markets, 136–7, 235

race and inequality, 84–5
race to the bottom, 156–9
racial superiority, theories of, 86
rational choice theory, 9, 12, 30, 232
rationalisation, 64, 166, 190
rationality, 27, 31, 192, 203, 223
Reagan, Ronald, 111
recession, 43, 58, 104
recognition, 229
regulation, and the environment, 210–11
regulation school of economics, 2, 11, 56
religion, 7, 107
resources
  distribution of, 27
  non-renewable, 200
  optimal use of, 203–5

revolutionary movements, 79, 100
Ricardo, David, 8, 49
  class, 76
  colonialism, 85
  comparative advantage, 49
  international trade, 48
  labour theory of value, 21, 52
rights, individual, 71, 94, 216, 219, 223
  positive, 219, 220
risk, 116–19, 134, 138
  economic models of, 120
  globalisation of, 120
  management of, 64, 134
risk society, 120, 197
Robbins, Lionel, 22, 53
Robinson, Joan, 75
Romer, Paul, 54
Russia
  glasnost, 123
  market 'shock therapy' in, 123–4
  perestroika, 123
  revolution, 79, 99, 100

Sabel, Charles, 172, 174
sales effort, 182
Salleh, Ariel, 212
Saro-Wiwa, Ken, 158
Sassen, Sasskia, 87
satisficing, 31
Scandinavia, 107, 196
scarcity, 22, 53
Schon, Juliet, 182
Schumpeter, Joseph, 55, 150
science, 7
Scott, A. J., 178
self-determination, 82, 86
self-interest, 22, 28
service sector, 178
  and the care economy, 195–7
  global care chains, 197
  industrialisation of, 173
  international market in, 197
settler economies, 7
Shell, 158
Shiva, Vandava, 198
Simons, Herbert, 31
Situationist International, 224
Smart, B, 182
Smith, Adam, 8, 217
  class, 76
  colonialism, 85
  division of labour, 48, 167
  freedom, 217
  human welfare, 45
  international trade, 48
  'invisible hand', 96, 114, 148
  labour theory of value, 52

Smith, Adam (*cont.*)
  liberalism, 95, 96–7
  value, 21
Smith, Thomas, 216
social capital, 231–2
  types of, 232
social democracy, 101, 107, 196
  and environmental degradation, 209
social ecology, 212
social inclusion, 235
social liberalism, 219
social life, commodification and
    decommodification of, 106
social mobility, 75
social movement theory, 226–7
social movements, 212, 225–30
  factors in their development, 227
  and framing, 227
  and hierarchy, 229–30
  and market society, 229
  and society, 228–30
  structure of, 229–30
social networks, 231
social norms, 170
social services
  outsourcing of, 136–7
  privatisation of, 39
society, and the economy, 2
sociological economics, 12, 28–31, 180, 231
  consumption, 180
  social capital, 231
sociology
  economic sociology, 12, 28–31, 180, 231
  influence of Marx in, 10
  Weberian, 10
Soja, EW, 178
solidarity, 105, 166
Solow, Robert, 54
Sombatt, Werner, 180
Soskice, David, 109
South Korea,
sovereignty, 94
specialisation, 5, 48, 165–6
  flexible, 172, 174
Sraffa, Piero, 75
stagflation, 58, 122
state
  development of the capitalist state, 94–7
  development state, 109
  diversity of, 108–9
  as a force for cohesion, 99
  institutional and cultural histories of, 108
  legitimacy of, 93–4, 95, 97–101
  market logic in, 135–6
  marketising of, 133
  night watchman state, 97
  reduction of its role, 110–14

  role of, 37, 38, 93–105, 110–14, 115, 133–5
  sovereignty, 94
  welfare state, 101
  *see also* welfare state
status, consumption and, 183
stereotypes, 84
Stern Review, 95, 201
Strange, Susan, 120
structural functionalism, 166
supply and demand, 22, 23, 25, 119
surplus, 50–7, 58, 77
sustainability, 189–213
  and the market society, 205–12
Sweezy, Paul, 149–50, 182
Sydney Gay and Lesbian Mardi Gras, 183
systems theory, 205–6

Taiwan, 110
Tarrow, Sidney, 226
Taylor, Frederick, 169
technology, development of new, 173, 198
Thatcher, Margaret, 39, 111
think tanks, 111
Third Way governments, 136, 177, 221, 234, 235
Thompson, EP, 4, 41
Thompson, G, 157
Thrift, Nigel, 180
Tilly, Charles, 227
Titmuss, Richard, 171
trade, 8, 125, 130–3
  free trade agreements, 131
  global, 178
  liberalisation of, 120, 130
  between nations, 48
  protectionist measures, 132
  regulation of, 130
  theories of, 48–9
trade and labour unions, 79, 134, 153–4, 181, 234
  coercive tactics against, 154
  eight-hour day, 181
  and political parties, 79
tragedy of the commons, 202–3
transaction costs, 3, 11, 109, 151–2
transfer payments, 70
Treaty of Detroit, 154
triple bottom line accounting, 159
trust, 61, 124–9
  *see also* confidence
Tullock, Gordon, 112

uncertainty, 118, 135, 204
  and crises, 59–61
  and the precautionary principle, 205–6
  and probability, 119

underemployment, 176
unemployment, 58, 59, 62, 102, 122, 131
   and economic growth, 45
   effects of, 45
United Auto Workers, 154
United Nations
   Human Development Index, 47
   World Commission on Environment and Development, 63, 205
urbanisation, 72, 168, 215
US Farm Bills, 132
US, *Personal Responsibilitiy and Work Opportunity Reconciliation Act*, 177
US railroads, 143
US sub-prime mortgage crisis, 128, 130, 147
utility, diminishing marginal, 23, 24

value, 19–42
   contingent valuation, 204
   and inequality, 74–5
   and labour, 8
   labour theory of, 9, 21–2, 52, 62, 74
   marginalism, 23–5
   of nature, 208
   preference theory of, 21
   in the sphere of production, 21
   subjective view of, 53
   use value and exchange value, 20–5
values, 80, 177, 222
Veblen, Thorstein, 148
   consumption, 29, 184, 217
'visible hand', 148
Vogel, Steven, 113

Wachtel, H, 125
wage labour relationship, 5, 36, 118
wages, 59–60
   decentralised bargaining, 134
   efficiency wages hypothesis, 62
   family wage, 83
   gender gap in, 195
   minimum wage legislation, 60, 153
   regulation of, 60
Wallerstein, Immanuel, 87
Walras, Leon, 24
Waring, M, 191
Warren, Elizabeth, 130, 185
Washington Consensus, 122
wealth, 68, 70, 72
Weber, Max, 10, 29
   capitalism and the family, 193
   class, 78–9
   instrumental rationality, 223
   interpretive sociology, 10, 166–7
   legitimacy, 64

   opportunity hoarding approach, 78
   social interaction, 10
   the state, 94, 97
   status, 79
   work ethic, 29, 166, 170, 193
welfare, 93–115
welfare, occupational, 171
welfare economics, 27
welfare state, 39, 80, 117
   'automatic stabilisers' of, 104
   and civil society, 234–6
   compliance requirements, 176
   corporatist model of, 107
   devolution of state functions, 234, 235–6
   influence of religion, 107
   liberal model of, 106
   perceptions of the poor, 107
   political economy of, 101
   regimes, 105–8
   social democratic model of, 107
   social insurance, 105
   types of, 106–8
wellbeing, 45
Wheelwright, EL, 150
WikiLeaks, 224–5, 230
Williamson, OE, 152
willingness to pay, 22, 204
Wollstonecraft, Mary, 82
women
   and employment, 171
   exploitation of, 207
   and inequality, 82–6
   participation in paid work, 82, 83
   and property rights, 81
   right to vote, 82–3
work, 165–88
   and autonomy, 168, 173
   and a balanced life, 181, 186–7
   capacity to work, 38
   deskilling of, 168, 174
   and enforcement of social norms, 170
   fragmentation of, 175
   and identity, 167
   importance of, 165–7
   McDonaldisation of, 174–5
   organisation of, 14
   outside the household, 20
   and society, 165–75
   sweatshop conditions, 33–4
   and welfare assistance, 176
work ethic, 29, 166, 170, 193
work society, 167–8, 171
worker movements, 78, 98–101
workers' right to take strike action, 99
workfare, 176–7
working poor, 176

workplaces
   conflict, cooperation and control in, 152–3
   corporations and, 152–5
   hegemonic regimes of regulation of, 153
World Bank, 70, 86, 103
   social capital, 232
World Commission on Environment and Development, 63, 205

World Economic Forum, 157
World Social Forum, 212, 230
World Systems Theory, 49
World Trade Organisation, 131
   protest movement against, 156
   Trade-Related Intellectual Property Rights, 37

Yeltsin, Boris, 123